MW00653694

The Untold Story of Women of Color in the League of Women Voters

The Untold Story of Women of Color in the League of Women Voters

Carolyn Jefferson-Jenkins

Foreword by Gracia Hillman

 PRAEGER®

An Imprint of ABC-CLIO, LLC

Santa Barbara, California • Denver, Colorado

Library of Congress Cataloging-in-Publication Data

Names: Jefferson-Jenkins, Carolyn, author.
Title: The untold story of women of color in the League of Women Voters /
  Carolyn Jefferson-Jenkins ; foreword by Gracia Hillman.
Description: Santa Barbara, California : Praeger, 2020. | Includes
  bibliographical references and index.
Identifiers: LCCN 2019052451 (print) | LCCN 2019052452 (ebook) | ISBN
  9781440874499 (hardcover) | ISBN 9781440874505 (ebook)
Subjects: LCSH: League of Women Voters (U.S.)—History. | Minority
  women—Political activity—United States. | Women—Suffrage—United
  States.
Classification: LCC JK1881 .J44 2020 (print) | LCC JK1881 (ebook) | DDC
  324.6082/0973—dc23
LC record available at https://lccn.loc.gov/2019052451
LC ebook record available at https://lccn.loc.gov/2019052452

ISBN: 978-1-4408-7449-9 (print)
         978-1-4408-7450-5 (ebook)

24 23 22 21 20   2 3 4 5

This book is also available as an eBook.

Praeger
An Imprint of ABC-CLIO, LLC

ABC-CLIO, LLC
147 Castilian Drive
Santa Barbara, California 93117
www.abc-clio.com

This book is printed on acid-free paper ∞

Manufactured in the United States of America

Some of the materials in this book are used by permission of the League of Women Voters of the United States.

This book is dedicated to the thousands of women in the "fight" whose names will never be known, but whose contributions have made progress possible. To those individuals who supported, encouraged, and facilitated the participation of women of color in the League of Women Voters of the United States. Especially to my grandmothers, Barbara Ester Dean Williams and Ellen Zimmerman, and my mother Lillian Zimmerman Jefferson.

Contents

Foreword

The Untold Story of Women of Color in the League of Women Voters contributes a wealth of information to the historical context of the League of Women Voters. It is a story that needs to be told as the league prepares to celebrate its centennial. Dr. Jefferson-Jenkins's enduring dedication to the league and her unique perspective on the organization are buoyed by her commitment to inform about the many women of color who were then, and are today, equally committed to the organization. In a broader context, these heroic women made enormous contributions to the struggle for the voting rights of all women, even as their right was simultaneously denied.

Earlier in her career, Dr. Jefferson-Jenkins was the principal author of *One Man, One Vote: The History of the African-American Vote in the United States*, a book published by the League of Women Voters of Cleveland (Ohio) Educational Fund. That was my first introduction to Dr. Jefferson-Jenkins. Among the book's accolades was recognition that it was important to tell the story of how America had struggled to overcome the injustices of denying the right to vote to African Americans. The Cleveland League was congratulated by elected and public officials and academics for publishing the story. The year was 1991, and I had just been appointed as the first African American executive director of the League of Women Voters of the United States and its Education Fund. I remember thinking at that time that the Cleveland League had sent a strong signal to its sister leagues and indeed the country about the value of publishing the story and the long list of impressive African American political achievements. It was my honor to serve as executive director, and the Cleveland League's signal gave me a sense of comfort in my new role. Fast forward to today, it is of no surprise that Dr. Jefferson-Jenkins had the foresight and determination to tell the stories of the remarkable women of color who are unveiled in this book so that they will be recognized during the centennial commemorations of the Nineteenth Amendment and the league.

I dedicated most of my career to protecting voting rights in America and waging voter education campaigns to increase voter registration and turnout. I invested heavily over the years to achieve progress and positive outcomes for unfettered modern-day voting rights, including equal access to the ballot and full participation in electoral processes, as well as for opportunities to achieve elected office. It started with my community organizing efforts in the early 1970s to get a recalcitrant city clerk in Massachusetts to agree to bring the voter registration books out of city hall and into public housing community centers—not a simple thing to achieve at that time. Of no surprise, the diverse task force that worked on this effort was comprised of about ten strong-willed women. We were white, African American, and Puerto Rican and spanned an age range from twenty to sixty. There was a local league in that city, but it chose not to participate. Our endeavor was successful, and for the first time in that city, a barrier to voter registration had been lifted for dozens of citizens.

It was not until my voting rights-focused career segued into the national nonprofit sector in Washington, D.C., that I was exposed to the racial tensions within the women's movement, created by presumptive leadership, lack of transparency, and limited inclusion. Regrettably, in the 1970s and '80s, many of the white women who led advocacy organizations took umbrage at attempts to discuss what could and should be done to ease, if not eliminate, the racial tensions internal to the women's movement. Nor did they want to examine and discuss exactly what about the history of their respective organizations contributed to the long-standing disquietude. That was then. This is now. Racial tensions persist. Let's tell the story and have the conversations.

The struggle to overcome political racial injustices rendered on African Americans, Latinos, and Native Americans by the hindrance of their right to vote and fully participate in electoral matters continues today. For the most part, the hindrances are politically ill-willed efforts to abridge the right to vote of certain Americans, but it is the "struggle" to render, brand, and accept these efforts as political injustices that prevents the eradication of the abridgement. For numerous reasons, leadership in America seems to have a difficult time wrapping its mind, conscience, and heart around the notion that forward progress is best achieved in a full historical context. In July 2018, Brent Staples of *The New York Times* editorial board wrote an opinion titled "How the Suffrage Movement Betrayed Black Women." He highlighted findings from the research of others that exposed biting racism within the women's suffrage movement. It was an eye-opening zinger that laid down a marker for those organizations and public officials that were preparing to commemorate the centennial of the Nineteenth Amendment. The league took heed from Mr. Staples's article and vowed to America that it "will do better." To Dr. Jefferson-Jenkins's credit, she began researching and writing this book a few years before Mr. Staples's op-ed because she knew there was a story in the league's history that needed to be told. America will be well served if all who organize Nineteenth Amendment commemorative events, and especially the league, include the living women and families of those no longer alive who are mentioned in this book and of others they discover from their own research.

Topics of race, gender, inclusion, and presumptive leadership are discussed but remain difficult conversations. Long-standing organizations, such as the League of Women Voters, have an opportune time right now to be forthright thought leaders for these difficult conversations. Such conversations are opportunities to listen and learn, and while there may be moments of discomfort and robust debate, they do not have to be unpleasant or divisive. Even a cursory examination of the histories of these organizations reveals that they have firsthand experience from which to create the platforms for these conversations.

The Untold Story should be required reading for historians and political scientists who seek to inform about the historical struggles for universal voting rights in America. It should be required contextual reading for thought leaders and practitioners who are engaged in electoral processes and have opportunities to archive complete, inclusive, and factual information about everyone who was similarly engaged in protecting democracy. And perhaps most importantly, it should be required reading for all girls, so that they will come to know the names of unrecognized and forgotten women of color who toiled in the political vineyards to create the pathway for women to be full participants in today's electoral processes. I say this knowing that the protection of democracy and universal suffrage requires a never-ending commitment to justice and inclusivity.

Gracia Hillman,
Former Executive Director, LWVUS and LWVEF
Commissioner, U.S. Election Assistance Commission
Senior Coordinator for International Women's Issues,
U.S. Department of State

Acknowledgments

I want to acknowledge all who made this adventure possible. To those I know and those I may never know who supported and encouraged me. You have all sown a seed into my life so that I can do the same for the next generation.

To my Washington, D.C.–based support team, Dr. Marilyn Sephocle, Melanie Campbell, Irene Natividad, Carla Bundy, Gracia Hillman, Wade Henderson, and Ellen Buchman, who provided cover, comfort, and counsel.

To Dr. Dorothy Height, Marian Wright-Edelman, and C. Delores Tucker, who provided words of wisdom. To Dr. Josie R. Johnson for taking the time to share her experiences as the first black national board member in the league with me. Patricia Sweet, former executive director of the League of Women Voters of California Education Fund who facilitated my first publication *One Man, One Vote: The History of the African-American Vote in the United States.* To Mildred Madison and the Honorable Jean Murrell Capers, who served as my Cleveland League mentors and supporters.

To the historians whose books introduced me to black women's history and taught me about the influence of history on the present and future—particularly, the scholarly studies of Dr. Evelyn Brooks Higginbotham and Dr. Rosalyn Terborg-Penn.

I am deeply indebted to the many historians and researchers at the Smithsonian National Museum of African American History and Culture and the National Archives, as well as to the scores of librarians and archivists at the Library of Congress Manuscript Division who accommodated my endless requests for information in such a professional manner.

A particular thanks to all of the local and state leagues who hosted me during my tenure as president and allowed me to share my vision of the league.

Special thanks to the League of Women Voters of Greater Cleveland, Ohio, who gave me my league roots; to the Leagues of Colorado, who gave me my league wings and supported and encouraged me through challenging times; to my new league family in North Carolina who is giving me my league landing and helping me to make new league memories.

To Western College for Women, Oxford, Ohio, for providing a solid foundation for my achievements, and to the alumnae, who have been my biggest cheerleaders—especially Jacky Johnson, the Western College archivist who facilitated the housing of my papers at the Western College/Miami University Library.

To Cathy Somer and Donna Kelly for lending their editorial expertise.

And last, but not least, my deepest gratitude is reserved for members of my family and friends who have been with me through every step of this journey.

Introduction: More Than a Footnote

History enthusiasts know that the most important part of history is the story. They also know that any organization that endures for a hundred years certainly has a story to tell. This is especially true of a grassroots membership organization such as the League of Women Voters of the United States. From its twentieth-century characterization as a "mighty political experiment" designed to help twenty million women carry out their new responsibilities as voters, to its twenty-first-century mission of "Making Democracy Work®," the league remains one of the nation's most important citizen advocacy and education groups at the local, state, and national levels since its founding in 1920. It is a force to be reckoned with because of the efforts of *all* who have contributed to its success.

Why this story? Why now? If women have received almost no mention in most history books, women of color have received even less or are virtually invisible, their story relegated to the footnotes. The same is true of the published histories of the League of Women Voters. At each historic milestone, another portrayal of the league is written. February 14, 2020, marks the centennial of the founding of the League of Women Voters and the next major opportunity to recount a more inclusive and comprehensive history of the organization. To celebrate the league's endurance is to celebrate its unabridged story. The unabridged version must tell of the contributions of women of color who affiliated or attempted to affiliate with the league so that it becomes part of the mainstream narrative.

Given the league's rich heritage and the complexity of the organization, it is clear that no one book or historical account can comprehensively convey the organization's successes, failures, and limitations in its relationship with women of color. But what is also clear is that in its hundred-year history, countless women of color made noteworthy contributions to the women's suffrage movement and its legacy organization, the league. Their story deserves to be told. Their contributions to the organization should be elevated to the main narrative, not just gleaned from the content of the footnotes that accompany it.

The Untold Story of Women of Color in the League of Women Voters goes beyond being a revisionist history and moves readers closer to the goal of a complete history of the league. The story it tells helps us understand the dynamics of the league as it struggled at the intersection of gender and race. It complements existing league histories and represents this rarely exposed internal organizational struggle. *The Untold Story* is an account of how the evolution of the league's principles, policies, and practices affected the women of color who chose membership in the organization as well as the leaguers who supported them. It is a story of individual and organizational resistance, resilience, and renewal that began with the original suffragists and whose relevance continues today.

Winning the vote for women required seventy-two years of advocacy, but for most women of color, it required an additional forty-five years with the passage of the Voting Rights Act of 1965. This need for additional advocacy parallels the internal struggles of the league in addressing integration and full participation of women of color in its membership. It would take seventy-eight years from the league's founding to elect a woman of color as national president, ushering in what was to be a new chapter for the organization in 1998. At its hundred-year anniversary in 2020, women of color in national leadership will still be regretfully underrepresented.

The Untold Story is not intended to criticize the league but to honor those women who tried to hold the organization true to its principles yet who are virtually invisible in its mainstream historical accounts. Because its emphasis is on actions or inactions occurring at the national level, this story is intended to motivate local and state leagues to conduct their own research and enhance this account with their own histories.

In compiling this story, I had no idea how little I knew about the complicated involvement of women of color in the league's history and how their influence formed the foundation for my election as the first and only woman of color to have served as national league president in the organization's hundred-year history. My examination of existing histories left me wondering if the entire story of the league was being told. As I attempted to better understand the relationship between the women upon whose shoulders I stand and the league, I was struck by the omission of any discussion of the internal organizational struggles with race and the external influence of race on decision-making, as well as the minimal mention of the important influence of these women in the main narrative. By focusing on the footnotes of these histories, however, I learned of the resilience of women of color in the struggle for full inclusion and acceptance of the value that they brought to the organization. Their story reveals the tension between their desires to be fully recognized members of the league and advocate for the issues unique to navigating both gender and race and the league's practices that precluded such inclusion.

Telling the story of women of color in what history considers a "white women's" organization allows for an analysis of the organizational dynamics in the context of changes in the broader society that reinforced the inclusion or exclusion of these women at different chapters in league history. Their story exposes the strategic choices the league made between principle and practicality and the choices women of color made to unite with and influence change from within the organization. By calling attention to this history, I hope to move the conversation from the practical, why the league initially encouraged the participation of women of color in activities in "their" communities while excluding them from full membership and participation in the organization, to principle, the need to prioritize their inclusion as an integral part of the future.

The League of Women Voters is more than the sum of its parts. Celebrating the accomplishments of *all* members and supporters in recounting league history is important. Embracing the hard and often painful aspects of the organization as it struggled with its relationship with its members of color, however, provides a more comprehensive accounting. Although *The Untold Story* emphasizes action taken at the national level of the league, as a federated membership organization, local and state leagues were impacted by these decisions. In practice, however, individual local and state leagues often took action on membership issues for women of color when the national league did not. Much of that rich history still resides in the archives of state and local leagues.

Every story, every woman of color discussed in this book is exceptional and representative of the hundreds of women who, over the past one hundred years, have contributed to the league's enduring legacy at the local, state, and national levels. These women have often been marginalized, placed in the footnotes of league history. This failure of historians to acknowledge the contributions of people of color to society shaped my perceptions for years. I recognize that whatever I accomplished in the League of Women Voters was because of the efforts of those women who came before me, both black and white, who challenged the league to be true to its principles. I have been the beneficiary of so much that I feel I have a responsibility to push the league's thinking and ignite further action to preserve and celebrate the totality of the league's heritage. Now, as a former national president, I have a platform to ensure that for future generations, this oversight does not persist in League of Women Voters' history. Otherwise, the story of the league is incomplete.

League History: Another Perspective

The history of the League of Women Voters is a paradox. It is a story of controversy, compromise, and collaboration. It is a story of strategic choices and recurrent themes, with organizational decisions based on the facts as leaders understood them at the time. Those choices, which reflected how the organization addressed issues of diversity, equity, and inclusion, continue to define the organization today. The relationship of the league with its members of color has been an interesting study in contrasts between principle and practicality. *The Untold Story* presents a snapshot of this organizational dynamic at specific moments in the league story.

Current histories of the league devote minimal attention to the nexus between the contributions of women of color to the organization and their fight *within* the league for equal status. The courage that it often took for these women, both black and white, to fight for the league to be true to its principles is central to any narration of the league story. Women of color who chose to participate in the League of Women Voters did so for a variety of reasons. Like other leaguers, they represented a wide range of views on issues. Women of color rejected all attempts to have their membership defined solely by race. These courageous women, whose stories are as complex as the organization itself, just wanted to be league members, to advocate for and educate on the issues they were passionate about. They understood both the power of the league to shape the political conversations in the nation and the importance of their contributions as members to strengthen the organization.

The league's history has seldom been fully researched. Current league histories focus primarily on program issues and organizational impact in influencing legislation. Minimal research has been compiled on specific women who have been associated with the league, particularly women of color. When the main narrative of these histories is viewed through "rose-colored" glasses, touting only triumphs, it obscures the fact that league members of color often had a different experience in the organization—a parallel experience that needs to be examined.

The primary histories of the League of Women Voters, *In the Public Interest: The League of Women Voters, 1920–1970; For the Public Record: A Documentary History of the League of Women Voters*; and *The League of Women Voters Through the Decades*, contain only cursory discussions of the dynamics of gender and race, with most explanations appearing in the footnotes.

In preparation for the league's fiftieth anniversary in 1970, an April 1968 press release promoted a history of the league written by Dr. Louise Young, a league member, researcher, and historian. Prior to that point there was no general history of the League of Women Voters of the United States. Dr. Young's version provides a foundation for the inclusion of the contributions of all women in any subsequent history of the league.

> Dr. Young proposes to portray the league as a microcosm of the politically responsible and responsive women in American society, claiming that by "learning to politicize their social role, league members have set an example for all."
>
> Dr. Young also hopes to make clear that "living, breathing individuals accomplished the recorded deeds"—not the league as an institution—and to stress that the history of an organization is primarily the essence of innumerable biographies.[1]

In preparation for the league's seventy-fifth anniversary in 1995, Nancy Neuman, league president (1986–1990) wrote in *The League of Women Voters in Perspective: 1920–1995,* published by the LWVEF, that recounting league history and accomplishments "gives us many reasons to be proud of our past and yet challenges us to create our own future."[2] President Neuman's combined national-level league experience and academic expertise provided a unique perspective of the organization, representing the organizational dynamics using a broader social history context. She stated in her introduction:

> This publication is a tribute to the thousands of women whose contributions made the LWV a powerful American institution and to contemporary league leaders for enriching that heritage.[3]

Consistent with other league histories, however, it does not mention the struggles of women of color *within* the organization or the organization's struggle with the tension between gender and race.

Other works that trace the organization's history include *Forty Years of a Great Idea* (1960), a pamphlet published by the League of Women Voters, and Marguerite Wells's "A Portrait of the League of Women Voters at the Age of Eighteen" (1938). In her general introduction to *Papers of the League of Women Voters 1918–1974,* Susan Ware states: "The League of Women Voters offers a rich and complex institutional history, with each decade bringing new challenges as well as continuing responsibilities."[4] Using these works as the basis for viewing league history, it becomes evident that there is much more to be learned about the league through a review of its documents, convention minutes, presidents' speeches, national publications, information from local and state leagues, and the still-to-be-told stories of its members.

Each attempt to tell the league's story brings forth little-known facts and less-recognized power players. Each interpretation adds a different perspective. As early as 1938, Marguerite Wells, national league president (1934–1944) affirmed the need for the league to take a more objective view of its history.

> The truest portraits may be those done by sympathetic artists. But the candid camera also has its uses. Poses from which the most may be learned are those which catch the subject at unbecoming angles. Let us turn, therefore, from the composite portrait done by League admirers to snapshots of the League taken by its own members, officers, program chairmen, members and ex-members of boards. . . . Faithful are the wounds of the candid camera.[5]

League Principles and Race

From its inception, the league's principles were often at odds with its action and/or inaction in addressing the issue of race in society and in the organization. In 1912, W. E. B. Du Bois, president of the National Association for the Advancement of Colored People (NAACP), publicly challenged the reluctance of the National American Woman Suffrage Association (NAWSA), the league's predecessor, to accept black women. In an attempt at appeasement, the NAWSA invited him to speak at its next convention and published his speech as a pamphlet. Despite these gestures, NAWSA continued to minimize the role of black suffragists. History records that it accepted some black women as members and some black societies as auxiliaries, but its general practice was to ignore or reject such requests. This was partly because attitudes of racial superiority were the norm among white Americans of that era and partly because NAWSA believed it had little hope of achieving a national amendment without at least some support from Southern states that practiced racial segregation.[6]

Carrie Chapman Catt's pronouncement, as president of NAWSA, at its fiftieth convention in St. Louis, Missouri, in March of 1919, did nothing to change the philosophy toward the acceptance of women of color into the newly formed League of Women Voters: "I propose the creation of a league of women voters to finish the fight and aid in the reconstruction of the nation." The philosophy to "finish the fight" did not make a distinction between the Nineteenth Amendment—white women's rights—and the fact that black women faced an additional challenge, that of racial segregation. A series of actions and public statements by national league leaders illuminate this disparity.

In her book *The Ladies Have Spoken: Recurring Tensions in the Discourse of the Presidents of the League of Women Voters: A Thesis*, Eleanor Ray Osborn reviewed league presidents' speeches through 1994. She found that "tracing these value tensions determines if an organization has maintained, altered, or discarded its founding values and, as a result, changed its mission." Osborn's research reveals that although the league was subject to external influences and many social changes as well as internal operational adjustments, the organization had adhered to its founders' values.

In 1923, Maud Wood Park, the first president of the League of Women Voters, described the league as an "everywoman's organization," despite the fact that organizational documents reveal that the league made a strategic choice to shrewdly discourage the inclusion of women of color in its ranks. Understanding the structure of the league adds valuable insight into its functioning. The league's stated mission, values, and principles do not distinguish between white women and women of color, but in practice, the acceptance of women of color was not universally applied.

The principles are "concepts of government" to which the league subscribes. According to the LWVUS bylaws, the principles serve two functions: 1) authorization for adoption of national, state, and local program (Article XII); and 2) a basis for taking action at the national, state, and local levels (Article XII). The League of Women Voters is organized to parallel the three levels of government: local, state, and national. Bylaws are the fundamental rules by which the league governs itself. They include

---

LEAGUE OF WOMEN VOTERS MISSION

The League of Women Voters is a nonpartisan political organization that encourages informed and active participation in government, works to increase understanding of major public policy issues, and influences public policy through education and advocacy.[1]

1. League of Women Voters. http://lwv.org.

rules that the organization considers so important that they cannot be changed without prior notice to members and the vote of a specified majority.

The first three articles of the national league bylaws state the league's name, present the league's policy and purpose, and define membership in the league. Individual leagues may decide what to include in the remaining articles of their bylaws, provided those laws reflect democratic procedures. The federated structure of the organization provided the opportunity for national leaders to allow flexibility to state and local leagues to deal with the issue of race and membership. Although the bylaws did not exclude women of color as members, what happened in practice in local and state leagues was quite different.

While there is some evidence that conversations about diversity, equity, and inclusion occurred each decade, the most robust conversations about race, from a national leadership perspective, took place during three periods of league history: the 1920s–1930s, when the reality that black women were still prohibited from the benefit of women's suffrage required local and state leagues to ask for guidance from the national leadership; the 1950s–1960s, when integration and other civil rights issues became a priority national conversation that the league could not ignore; and the 1990s–2000, as major demographics shifts began to impact the nation.

Convention 1946 was a monumental turning point for the league: changing its name from the National League of Women Voters to the League of Women Voters of the United States (LWVUS) and changing its focus from national leadership to its grassroots membership. The new emphasis on the league as a membership organization, however, did not address the internal challenges of women of color for equal membership status. League documents indicate that discussions about the need for greater diversity of membership were occurring behind the scenes in each of the three periods where there was the most activity around the issue taking place, often with the national leadership referring issues back to the state and local leagues as required by the 1946 change in organizational structure. The parallels between league changes regarding integration and societal changes regarding integration are mentioned in the league's recorded history only as they have an impact on changes in league programs.

Unfortunately, simply espousing diversity does not change the culture of an organization. In the case of the league, cultural change occurs only when an issue becomes an organizational priority. Convention speeches and other correspondence indicate that Percy Maxim Lee (1950–1958), league president during the second most pivotal time for change in the league, was not shy about discussing issues of race, within a certain context. Lee was also concerned about making the league leaner and more efficient.[7]

> Racial tensions ran high throughout this period as integration became a mandated way of life in many parts of the country. Lee acknowledged the extent of such feelings in 1958 when she said that "racial conflicts are as old as man [sic] . . . [because] man is his own worst enemy." She was undaunted by the scale of this problem preferring to look upon the "growth and changing patterns of life" as common to everyone and offering "the League unparalleled opportunities of service and creative leadership.[8]

As the league continued through the subsequent civil rights era of the 1960s and into the twenty-first century, every decade saw the league wrestle with when, where, and how to address the issue of race both in society and in the organization itself. Until Convention 2016, women and men (since 1974) who were citizens and at least eighteen years old could join the league as voting members. Associate (nonvoting) membership was available for younger people and noncitizens. At Convention 2016, the minimum age for membership was changed to age sixteen. The delegates to that convention felt the need to change the league's membership requirements to promote diversity and inclusion and reflect the current demographics of the nation. League membership should reflect the society in which we live. With the surge in league membership that occurred in 2018, it is my hope that the league's new focus on diversity, equity, and inclusion will again make this a league priority, one that will fundamentally and forever alter the core of the organization.

Focus and Structure of the Book

According to historians of the women's movement, little research has been done on the League of Women Voters independent of its impact on the women's suffrage movement. The research that does exist has been completed in the fields of political science, business, and women's studies. Most of it focuses on the formation of the league and how women traditionally used the organization as preparation for entering politics. *The Untold Story* adds a different dimension to league history by focusing on the story of the evolving relationship between the League of Women Voters and its members of color, as well as of the strategic choices the organization's national leaders made to engage in, ignore, or remain silent on issues surrounding the unique position of these women to navigate gender and race. To provide context, this book analyzes convention records, speeches, newspaper articles, correspondence, photographs, drawings, and first-person accounts from the rich collection of LWVUS papers housed in the League of Women Voters office in Washington, D.C., and the Manuscript Division of the Library of Congress.

The Untold Story is structured around organizing themes that show the progression of the ideological relationship between the League of Women Voters and its members of color, emphasizing its policies and practices, symbols, and messages. Chapter titles are chosen to disclose the philosophical shifts in attitude at each stage of the organization's evolution. It should be noted that this book represents my interpretations of league dynamics at the national level through twenty-first-century eyes. The content within each chapter is chronological, but the book itself is not. Each chapter is self-reliant and can be read independently of the others.

Chapter 1, "Lest We Forget," reminds us that the league must not forget its past as a prelude to its future. This chapter synthesizes the existing histories of the league, identifying themes and providing context for subsequent chapters. It discusses the history of the tension between suffragists and abolitionists and its lasting effect. It cites some of the omissions in existing histories of the league. It focuses on the need for a comprehensive history, one that highlights the strategic choices the organization made and how those choices shaped the league. This chapter reveals that women—and men—of color have always been a part of the suffrage movement. It affirms that we—women of color—were there too! Our story must be told.

Chapter 2, "To 'Finish the Fight,'" focuses on the league's founding and the dissonance between its principles and practice related to integration in society and in the organization. It examines league culture, membership, and opinion on issues of the day and the resultant strategic choices league leaders made regarding membership for women of color. It analyzes the long-term impact of these decisions on the organization. To "finish the fight" and embrace the league as an "everywoman's organization" appeared to be more rhetoric than reality for women of color. It describes the establishment, development, and impact of the Special Committee on Negro Problems and what happened at the national level of the organization that set the tone and policy for local and state affiliates. It highlights the exchanges of the women who participated in this league initiative.

Chapter 3, "For the Sake of the Cause," examines why women of color sought membership in the league despite often being discouraged from joining. It examines the paradox of the organization's attempt to reconcile changes in society and changes in the league. It investigates the league's restructuring in 1946 and the tension that arose from the changes being advocated. It notes the absence of a national presence of women of color in the league, when there was no such absence in other national grass-roots organizations. It discusses the dual involvement of black leaguers in other organizations, such as "colored women's clubs," which had the same mission, vision, and purpose as the league. It frames the league's choices in the environment of national civil rights legislation that prohibited seg-regation. It highlights the sense of hope that women of color had that through their participation, the league would be true to its principles.

Chapter 4, "The Lessons of the Hour," relies on correspondence received by the national leadership and reports of the Special Committee on Inter-Racial Problems to illustrate how the action and/or inaction of the league served to continue the controversy between league principles and practice. This controversy, collaboration, and compromise allowed the league to operate on parallel tracks with its members of color.

Chapter 5, "Through Amber-Colored Glasses," is a tale of two realities and addresses the fragile balance women of color had to maintain in order to participate in the organization, resulting in a parallel experience. It focuses on the realities as these women navigated the nexus of race and gender in the organization and in society. It cites turning points in league history on issues of race and addresses the resilience of women of color in making sure that they were not invisible. It concentrates on equal rights versus equal opportunities and black women's understanding that they could not view the league through rose-colored glasses because they were being viewed through a color lens themselves.

Chapter 6, "The League Way," reflects an organizational identity crisis and covers how the league's organizational focus changed, particularly during the 1960s. This decade presented the biggest challenge to "the league way," as more women of color saw the benefit of belonging to the organization and as changes in society illuminated league inconsistencies in principle and practice. This chapter reviews the league in transition at its fiftieth anniversary and its seventy-fifth anniversary. It communicates the league's move toward a global agenda and its numerous diversity cam-paigns. It cites turning points in league history and explains that leaguers of color knew all was not perfect with the organization but hoped that their inclusion would bring about needed change.

Chapter 7, "The Weight of History," focuses on the pressures inherent in breaking racial barriers and affecting change in an entrenched organiz-ational culture. It explores external societal challenges the organization faced entering the twenty-first century and the impact those challenges had on the internal operations of the league, leading to my election and reelection as the first—and by the hundredth anniversary, still the only woman of color to serve as national president in league history. It discusses how the league chose to address the perception of the organization, as identified in its numerous self-studies, as a middle-aged, well-educated, middle- to upper-income white women's organization. It tackles the debate of whether my election as president reflected an evolution or revolution for the organization. The section "A Matter of Principle" emphasizes the renewed discussions on the fidelity of league organizational values and principles in a changing national demographic landscape and contemplates membership belief in the league and its ability to remain relevant. Additionally, it features excerpts from my major addresses to league membership on the possibilities for the organization to be both inclusive and impactful.

The epilogue, "Moving Forward—The Unfinished Fight," brings the story full circle. It summarizes the hundred-year evolution of the League of Women Voters and its relationship with its members of color, both failures and successes. It honors the contributions of these women to the organization. It explores the hopes, dreams, and possibilities of the organization as it moves forward in the twenty-first century. It considers what is next for the organization as it reinvents itself to remain relevant and continue to have purpose. It concludes that in order to remain relevant and find its purpose, the league must continue to prioritize diversity in its membership. It emboldens the organization to "finish the fight."

As a grassroots membership organization, the league has a history that is enriched by the stories of its members. Unfortunately, the majority of the league's papers remain uncatalogued, and pertinent historical documents that *are* catalogued are often incomplete and housed in multiple locations. Furthermore, the availability and accessibility of historical information about the league are dependent on the filing systems of its leaders and staff or on who was charged with recording the league's actions on various issues at the time. Experiences differ in leagues by geographic region, membership size, and history of outreach. Each state and local league has its own history of how it addressed issues of race and when and how women of color participated. Local and state leagues have enormous resources in their state archives and university historical societies. Many of the materials produced by its national office, as well as by its state and local chapters throughout the United States, pertain to the league's positions on issues rather than on how the league relates to the larger membership. Therefore, we may never know if a given study or action ever led to the league's taking a position on a related matter, and if so, what position and when.

Throughout the book, references to women of color reflect the language of the times. Thus, the terms *colored, Negro, Afro-American, African American, black,* and *women of color* appear in accordance with accepted usage at the time.

Conclusion

The capacity to tell stories is what keeps history alive. All stories have settings, characters, plots, and endings. But, for the League of Women Voters of the United States, there is an opportunity for a new beginning. As I thought about the approaching centennial of the founding of the League of Women Voters, I wondered what I could do to help ensure that this organization with which I share pride in accomplishments lives up to its principles, changes with the times, and remains the voice for citizens and force for change it envisions itself to be. And so, I decided to write this book, realizing that we, league members and leaders, can better understand and appreciate ourselves if we know the story of *all* the women who made significant contributions to the history of the league.

> The current feminist movement still has a lot of work to do in terms of white women recognizing the very layered (intersectional) experiences of women of color, especially black women.[9]

The hundredth anniversary is the perfect opportunity to bring to life the untold story of the contributions of women of color, to move their story from the footnotes and into the mainstream narrative.

When the league is at its best, it is a powerful membership organization; when it is anything less, it is less. Adding the stories of the unique challenges of league members of color does not take away from anyone else's story, but adds to the might of the league story. I hope that *The Untold Story* evokes deep emotion: sadness, wonder, joy. I hope it helps the next generation see the value of belonging to organizations that may not initially appear inviting. I have had a great experience in the league, and by telling its unabridged story, I want to honor the organization to which I choose to devote my time and energy.

The League of Women Voters of the United States was born from the struggle for the right to vote. We—women of color—were there, too! From the beginning! Our voices as women of color must be heard in recounting this history, and our story must be told. By so doing, we will forever and fundamentally alter the core of the league.

We are more than a footnote!

Notes

1. Young, 1989.
2. Neuman, 1992, 6.
3. Neuman, 1994, 2.
4. Ware, 1985, v.
5. Wells, 1962, 9–10.
6. Du Bois, 1928.
7. Osborn, 1994, 91.
8. Ibid., 122.
9. hooks, 2015, 122.

CHAPTER ONE

Lest We Forget

The history of the past is but one long struggle upward to equality.
—Elizabeth Cady Stanton

While Stanton's quote referenced equality for women, in a broader sense, the prolonged struggle for equality for women of color has plagued the League of Women Voters of the United States throughout its hundred-year history. It was seventy-two years from the 1848 meeting at Seneca Falls to the 1920 passage of the Nineteenth Amendment. During that seventy-two-year struggle, the Thirteenth Amendment, Fourteenth Amendment, Fifteenth Amendment, Sixteenth Amendment, Seventeenth Amendment, and Eighteenth Amendment to the U.S. Constitution were ratified. After the passage of the Nineteenth Amendment and the founding of the League of Women Voters, it took another seventy-eight years (1998) before a woman of color would be elected to the national presidency of the organization.[1] "Lest we forget," the tension between gender and race was not resolved with that first victory for women. Women of color had to soldier on to achieve equality in the nation and in mainstream organizations such as the League of Women Voters. Analyzing the history of that continued struggle and its impact on the future provides context and is necessary to help the organization remain relevant.

The hundreds of letters, diaries, court testimonies, newspaper articles, manuscripts, journals, organizational proceedings, biographies, autobiographies, and oral histories make it clear that each period of league history exposes a remarkable set of revelations about the organization's response to one of its most enduring dilemmas. In the foreword to *In the Public Interest*, Percy Maxim Lee, league president (1950–1958), stated:

> It is sad to reflect that succeeding generations know less and less about the struggle for woman suffrage and the people who worked so tirelessly and unselfishly to achieve it . . . When I was president of the League of Women Voters I was acutely aware of how little members knew about their past. They were too busy building the future to examine the lessons of earlier times.[2]

The league's centennial should be a catalyst for current and future historians to challenge visions of its past in which women of color fail to appear as significant actors either intentionally or unintentionally. Lorraine Gates Schuyler's research in *The Weight of Their Votes* exposes the racism and class biases of white women suffragists. Her findings indicate a deliberate effort to win southern white support, by disassociating their cause from black voting rights issues.[3]

This chapter reminds us that we must not forget our past and its influences on our future. It synthesizes the existing histories of the league, identifying themes, and providing context for subsequent chapters. It discusses the history of the tension between suffragists and abolitionists and the lasting effect of that strain. "Lest we forget" reveals some of the omissions in existing league histories. The chapter unmasks the need for a more comprehensive history of the organization, one that highlights the strategic choices made and how those choices shaped the league's future.

We Were There Too!

Women—and men—of color have always been a part of the suffrage movement and its successor organizations. Historians acknowledge that while women and African Americans have often had common political interests, the alliance of their movements has not always been easy. The prioritizing of competing goals, racism within the women's movement, and the pressures exerted by Southern women to block colored women's participation all produced many moments of friction and estrangement from 1848 to 1920.[4] Tensions between Negro leaders and the women's suffrage leadership intensified after the Civil War, when the Fifteenth Amendment enfranchised black males but did not extend the vote to women. Frederick Douglass, noted reformer, abolitionist, and statesman, debated the women's rights advocates at the proceedings of the American Equal Rights Association Convention in New York in 1869, arguing that the race issue was the more urgent of the two causes.

The conversation about prioritizing race or gender continued as the suffrage movement evolved. In 1892, Anna Julia Cooper, activist and educator, wrote the first book, *A Voice from the South by a Black Woman from the South*, analyzing the conditions of blacks and women from a feminist perspective. The book indicated her awareness that being black and being female required a dual focus.

Rosalyn Terborg-Penn states in her research,

> African American women contributed significantly to the passage of the Nineteenth Amendment, which enfranchised all American women in 1920. As a result, the history of the movement was shaped by Black Suffrage activism and by white racism.[5]

Many of the activities of colored women participants were not recorded in official histories of the movement. After the National American Woman Suffrage Association (NAWSA) transitioned to the League of Women Voters, the pattern of excluding the contributions of women of color persisted.

Because of the opposition to race equity, women suffragists of color chose to maximize their leverage. Colored women's clubs were established parallel to those of white women, not only because white women's clubs (with the exception of those in New England) did not allow black women to be members, but also because black women could focus on somewhat different priorities within these organizations.

In 1894, Josephine St. Pierre Ruffin organized the Woman's Era Club, one of the first Negro women's civic associations. Ruffin stated:

> It is the women of America—black and white—who are to solve this race problem, and we do not ignore the duty of black women in the matter. They must arouse, educate

Anna Julia Cooper (1858–1964). (Library of Congress)

Rhode Island Executive Board. (Library of Congress)

and advance themselves. The white woman has a duty in the matter also. She must no longer consent to be passive. We call upon her to take her stand.[6]

In 1896, the National Association of Colored Women (NACW) formed, bringing together more than 1,000 black women's clubs under the leadership of Josephine St. Pierre Ruffin, Mary Church Terrell, and Anna Julia Cooper. Mary Church Terrell, whose autobiography documents her attendance at nearly every NAWSA meeting in Washington, D.C., encouraged black women and men to support women's suffrage out of a sense of justice.

A range of views existed within the Negro community on the subject of women's suffrage, but the historic relationship between women's issues and the question of color in American society was strengthened in the years leading up to the achievement of suffrage. At the 1899 convention of the NAWSA in Grand Rapids, Michigan, Susan B. Anthony, in response to a request from a Negro participant, Mrs. Lottie Wilson Jackson, put the NAWSA on record as regarding the two causes (Negro suffrage and women's suffrage) as completely separate. The Michigan suffrage clubs drew no color lines. So, Mrs. Jackson's issue that colored women should not be compelled to ride in smoking cars seemed appropriate. That convention members did not view this as an issue they wanted to take up illustrates the prevailing thought about boldly addressing the issue of racial segregation.[7]

A significant step in the direction of a new attitude of Northern suffragists toward the South and the Negro had been taken by Mrs. Carrie Chapman Catt in her presidential address to the 1901 NAWSA convention. She mentioned the following as one of the three obstacles that loomed largest as impediments to women's enfranchisement:

> [T]he inertia in the growth of Democracy which has come as a reaction following the aggressive movements that, with possibly ill-advised haste, enfranchised the foreigner, the negro and the Indian. Perilous conditions, seeming to follow from the introduction into the body politic of vast numbers of responsible citizens, have made the nation timid.[8]

The 1903 NAWSA convention continued the theme of dissension. According to historians,

> if the 1899 convention of the NAWSA shattered the old alliance between Negro freedom and woman suffrage, the 1903 convention sealed the new pact between woman suffrage and white supremacy. The convention took place in New Orleans in March just after a newspaper of that city attacked the organization for its supposedly unacceptable attitude on the race question. The officers replied in a letter to the editor explaining that as a nationwide body, the NAWSA included individuals of all sections who held the views customary in their respective areas; that the association as such held no view at all on race; that the association recognized the doctrine of states' rights as governing the relation of local clubs to the National; that the NAWSA deplored attempts by antisuffragists to arouse sectional feeling against the Association; and that the race question was irrelevant to the purpose of the NAWSA.[9]

The letter that appeared in the March 19 issue of the *Times Democrat* was signed by Susan B. Anthony, Carrie Chapman Catt, Alice Stone Blackwell, Laura Clay, Kate M. Gordon, Harriet Taylor Upton, and Anna Howard Shaw. The primary source was "The Race Question at New Orleans," published in the *Woman's Journal*, NAWSA's magazine, on March 28, 1903.

Belle Kearney, temperance reformer, suffragist, teacher, admitted white supremacist, and the first woman elected to the Mississippi State Senate, addressed the 1903 NAWSA convention, raising the specter of black male political power to argue for the enfranchisement of white women.

BELLE KEARNEY, "THE SOUTH AND WOMAN SUFFRAGE," NAWSA CONVENTION, NEW ORLEANS, LOUISIANA, MARCH 15–25, 1903

The enfranchisement of women would insure immediate and durable white supremacy, honestly attained, for upon unquestioned authority it is stated that in every southern State but one there are more educated women than all the illiterate voters, white and black, native and foreign combined. As you probably know, of all the women in the South who can read and write, ten out of every eleven are white. When it comes to the proportion of property between the races that of the white outweighs that of the black immeasurably. The South is slow to grasp the great fact that the enfranchisement of women would settle the race question in politics. The civilization of the North is threatened by the influx of foreigners with their imported customs; by the greed of monopolistic wealth and the unrest among the working classes; by the strength of the liquor traffic and encroachments upon religious belief. Some day the North will be compelled to look to the South for redemption from those evils on account of the purity of its Anglo-Saxon blood, the simplicity of its social and economic structure, the great advance in prohibitory law and the maintenance of the sanctity of its faith, which has been kept inviolate. Just as surely as the North will be forced to turn to the South for the nation's salvation, just so surely will the South be compelled to look to its Anglo-Saxon women as the medium through which to retain the supremacy of the white race over African.[1]

1. League of Women Voters. http://lwv.org.

Miss Kearney's speech was enthusiastically received, and at its end Mrs. Catt said she had been getting many letters from persons hesitating to join the association "lest it should admit clubs of colored people."

"We recognize States' rights, she said and Louisiana has the right to regulate the membership of its own association, but it has not the right to regulate that of Massachusetts or vice versa" and she continued: "We are all of us apt to be arrogant on the score of our Anglo-Saxon blood but we must remember that ages ago the ancestors of the Anglo-Saxons were regarded as so low and embruted [sic] that the Romans refused to have them for slaves. The Anglo-Saxon is the dominant race today but things may change. The race that will be dominant through the ages will be the one that proves itself the most worthy . . . Miss Kearney is right in saying that the race problem is the problem of the whole country and not that of the South alone. The responsibility for it is partly ours but if the North shipped slaves to the South and sold them, remember that the North has sent some money since then into the South to help undo part of the wrong that it did to you and to them. Let us try to get nearer together and understand each other's ideas on the race question and solve it together."[10]

William Lloyd Garrison Jr., for one, assailed the convention and all its works. In a letter to the *Woman's Journal*, on May 21, 1903, he insisted that there was a logical connection between Northern suffragists' approval of Negro disenfranchisement in the South and their silence in New Orleans.

> One looks in vain among the speeches for a clear statement of the principles upon which suffrage rests, or any protest against their unblushing violation in Louisiana and the other ex-slaveholding states. Under the circumstances, to borrow Whittier's words, "silence is crime." To purchase woman suffrage at the expense of the negro's rights is to pay a shameful price.[11]

The Negro question had, before the Civil War, been inseparably linked with the cause of women's equality; now it was merely one of a number of issues that had essentially nothing to do with their enfranchisement. Harriet Taylor Upton of Ohio, after having been asked how suffragists ought to approach the Negro question, complained:

> It does make me so cross to think they are always quoting the darkey to us. The colored question is no more the question of the suffragists than it is the man who already has the right to vote. It isn't half as much.[12]

Mrs. Upton's response was echoed by many in the suffrage movement. In response to why such sentiment provided grounds for skepticism of the movement's intent by Negro, foreign-born and Native American, W. E. B. Du Bois, suffragist, educator and author of a pamphlet published by the NAWSA, responded in the April 1915 issue of *The Crisis* when he said that "the reactionary attitude of most white women toward our problems" had caused many Negroes to oppose women's suffrage.[13]

NAWSA POSITION ON THE RACE QUESTION, LETTER TO THE NEW ORLEANS
***TIMES-DEMOCRAT* DURING MARCH 1903 CONVENTION**

A discordant note in the harmony was struck by the *Times-Democrat*, which, in a long editorial, Woman Suffrage and the South, assailed the association because of its attitude on the race question. The board of officers immediately prepared a signed statement which said in part:

The association as such has no view on this subject. Like every other national association it is made up of persons of all shades of opinion on the race question and on all other questions except those relating to its particular object. The northern and western members hold the views on the race question that are customary in their sections; the southern members hold the views that are customary in the South. The doctrine of States' rights is recognized in the national body and each auxiliary State association arranges its own affairs in accordance with its own ideas and in harmony with the customs of its own section. Individual members in addresses made outside of the National Association are of course free of [*sic*] express their views on all sorts of extraneous questions but they speak for themselves as individuals and not for the association. . . .

The National American Woman Suffrage Association is seeking to do away with the requirement of a sex qualification for suffrage. What other qualifications shall be asked for it leaves to each State. The southern women most active in it have always in their own State emphasized the fact that granting suffrage to women who can read and write and who pay taxes would insure white supremacy without resorting to any methods of doubtful constitutionality. The Louisiana association asks for the ballot for educated and taxpaying women only and its officers believe that in this lies "the only permanent and honorable solution of the race question." . . .

The suffrage associations of the northern and western States were for the ballot for all women, though Maine and several other States have lately asked for it with an educational and tax qualification. To advise southern women to beware of lending "sympathy or support" to the National Association because its auxiliary societies in the northern States hold the usual views of northerners on the color question is as irrelevant as to advise them to beware of the National Woman's Christian Temperance Union because in the northern and western States it draws no color line; or to beware of the General Federation of Women's Clubs because the State Federation of the North and West do not draw it; or to beware of Christianity because the churches in the North and West do not draw it.[1]

1. League of Women Voters. http://lwv.org.

The Negro's Hour

From the outset of the new women's movement, suffragists depended on existing antislavery societies to be their publicists and collaborators in seeking freedoms and rights denied both African Americans and women. That unity of purpose disintegrated in the aftermath of the Civil War with the enactment of the Fourteenth and Fifteenth Amendments to the U.S. Constitution. Section 2 of the Fourteenth Amendment introduced the word *male* into the Constitution for the first time. The Fifteenth Amendment omitted the word *sex* but did include "race, color, or previous condition of servitude" as reasons not to deny voting.

Elizabeth Cady Stanton and her friend and colleague Susan B. Anthony were mad as wet hens over the exclusion of women from the two amendments and did not accept the proposition that this was the "Negro's hour."

Consequently, in 1869 they organized the National Woman Suffrage Association, and, in the same year, Lucy Stone and her husband, Henry Blackwell, formed the American Woman Suffrage Association. It was the first time that American women had organized on behalf of their own interest.[14]

In 1850, both Frederick Douglass and Sojourner Truth, well-known abolitionist and women's rights activist, were present at the first National Woman's Rights Convention in Worcester, Massachusetts. At virtually every women's rights convention thereafter during the decade, Douglass was a featured speaker. In 1851, at one of these meetings in Akron, Ohio, Truth, a former slave, delivered her "Ain't' I a Woman" speech. Other black women, such as Frances E. W. Harper and Sarah Remond, also actively participated actively in the women's rights movement activities.

Then came civil war over the slavery issue, and the promised triumph was snatched away. With the war's close, women's rights became hopelessly enmeshed in the politics of the Fourteenth and Fifteenth Amendments. Protests by Susan Anthony and Elizabeth Cady Stanton over the insertion of the term "male" into the former—a clear betrayal by their abolitionists allies—initiated a rift in the women's movement; New England feminists clustered around Lucy Stone were willing to delay their demands for the ballot until the freed slaves had secured full citizenship, while others, led by Stanton and Anthony, rejected any compromise.[15]

The divergence between abolitionists and suffragists began prior to the passage of the Nineteenth Amendment, when tensions between black leaders and the women's suffrage leadership arose after the Civil War, when the Fifteenth Amendment enfranchised black males but did not extend the vote to women. In May 1865, Wendell Phillips, as the new head of the American Anti-Slavery Society, turned the society's sights on ensuring black Americans' civil and political rights, especially suffrage. The old-line anti-slavery agitators understood that trying to extend suffrage to black males would require a huge political battle. Trying to extend suffrage to women, too, at the same time would be impossible for the nation to accept. Frederick Douglass, William Lloyd Garrison and Phillips, agreed that while women should have the vote, the black man's life depended upon his ability to protect himself through it.

> The terrible War Between the States had not, after all been waged for women's right to vote. This was "the Negro's Hour;" "the Woman's Hour" would come eventually, but its time had not arrived.[16]

Douglass debated the women's rights advocates at the proceedings of the American Equal Rights Association Convention in New York City on May 12, 1869, arguing that the race issue was the more urgent of the two causes.[17] He made the following remarks:

> I must say that I do not see how any one can pretend that there is the same urgency in giving the ballot to women as to the negro. With us, the matter is a question of life and death . . . When women, because they are women, are hunted down through the cities of New York and New Orleans; when they are dragged from their houses and hung upon lamp-posts; when their children are torn from their arms, and their brains dashed out upon the pavement; when they are objects of insult and outrage at every turn; when they are in danger of having their homes burnt down over their heads; when their children are not allowed to enter schools; then they will have an urgency to obtain the ballot equal to our own.[18]

Shortly after that convention, Elizabeth Cady Stanton precipitated a split in the women's movement that lasted decades, rather than support passage of the Fifteenth Amendment, which gave black men the vote without enfranchising women. Her stance fueled the argument over who should have the vote first. Susan B. Anthony defended Stanton's position and suggested that as downtrodden as blacks were, Douglass would not switch places with a woman.[19] This split caused the formation of the National Woman Suffrage Association (NWSA) led by Stanton and Anthony. The American Woman Suffrage Association (AWSA), led by Lucy Stone, backed the Fifteenth Amendment.

Opposition to the Nineteenth Amendment was greatest in the South, where few women had emerged to join the suffrage movement. White

Southerners feared that expanding the black voting population would upset the social order. Southerners had largely nullified the black male vote through the use of poll taxes, tests for registrants, intimidation, and violence. While the prevailing sentiment among many in the movement remained that this was the "Negro's hour," in many testimonies before legislators, records indicate that Southern suffragists repeatedly expressed that women's suffrage would not jeopardize "white supremacy." Legislators, however, remained unconvinced.

Many women's rights activists felt that their cause had been betrayed by their former friends in reform; they believed that the cause of blacks and women had not just been separated out of "temporary necessity" and that the cause of women had been set back. For one suffragist faction to alienate its former abolitionist allies and to refuse compromise might not have been the wisest course. The argument was made that if blacks and Chinese immigrants could vote, why not women? In February 1890, the organizations reunified and held their first convention as the NAWSA.

A Delicate Balance between Race and Gender

The delicate balance between race and gender emerged on two fronts—in the dissension between suffragists and abolitionists and in that between white women and women of color in the organizations identified with the movement. Despite the fact that the majority of the photos prominently displayed to promote the cause were of whites only, the abolitionists' movement included hundreds of free black women. Women such as the Fortens whose daily challenge to navigate between gender and race is reflected in a poem by Sarah L. Forten:

> We are thy sisters . . .
> Our skins may differ, but from thee we claim
> A sister's privilege and a sister's name.[20]

The Fortens were one of the most prominent black families in Philadelphia. Wealthy sailmaker James Forten and his wife, Charlotte Vandine Forten, headed the family; their three daughters were Margaretta (1815–1875), Harriet (1810–1875), and Sarah (1814–1883). The Fortens were active abolitionists who took part in founding and financing at least six abolitionists' organizations. Sarah was a writer whose poems were widely published.

Due to the exclusion of women from already established American antislavery societies, in 1833, Margaretta Forten, with her mother,

Charlotte Forten Grimke (1837–1914)
(Moorland-Spingarn Research Center,
Howard University)

Charlotte, and sisters, Sarah and Harriet, cofounded the Philadelphia Female Anti-Slavery Society with ten other women. The goal of this new society was to include women in the activism being done for the abolition of slavery and "to elevate the people of color from their present degraded situation to the full enjoyment of their rights and to increased usefulness in society."[21] Forten often served as recording secretary or treasurer of the society, and she helped draw up its organizational charter and served on its educational committee. She offered the society's last resolution, which praised the post-Civil War amendments as a success for the antislavery cause. The society distinguished itself at the time as the first of its kind in the United States to be interracial. Although the society was predominantly white, historian Janice Sumler-Lewis claims the efforts of the Forten women in its key offices enabled it to reflect a black abolitionist perspective that oftentimes was more radical.

Women of color were never depicted as a critical mass in accounts of the suffrage movement because of policy, practice, custom, or culture, not because they did not contribute. While treated as outsiders, they pledged to not be invisible.

> By the second decade of the 20th century, hundreds of thousands of American women, representing different social classes, races and ethnic origins had joined the movement for woman suffrage, a struggle that had been going on since 1848.[22]

Colored women's support for women's suffrage often paralleled that of white suffragists, especially as the movement progressed. Although strategies to achieve the vote were similar, the experiences of the two racial groups differed dramatically. Black women, in their struggle for the right to vote, fought racism and sexism simultaneously. They consistently navigated the indignities and inconveniences that segregation demanded with passion and a sense of purpose.

Leadership of colored women was manifested in local and regional women's suffrage activities, primarily through Colored Women's Clubs or at the invitation of white suffragist leaders. The national presence of colored women leaders was often overshadowed or dismissed by white suffragists and the white press and other publications, which served as the major source of suffragist information. Because time and financial resources were required to maintain a high level of involvement, class was another factor that influenced women's participation in the organized women's suffrage movement.

The majority of colored women suffragists enjoyed higher social status than the masses of women of their race. Despite their perceived privilege, they recognized that their notion of womanhood was modeled on the experiences and problems of a small percentage of females who, like them, were almost exclusively white, middle class, and relatively well educated. However, the assumption that middle-class white women's experiences represented all women's experiences was not only made by early suffragists; it continued to shape the ideal of womanhood well into the second wave of the American feminist movement and beyond.[23]

A Cycle of Achievement and Setbacks

White women's suffrage leaders made strategic choices to use racist ideology to their own advantage within the context of a racist society, which put intense political pressure upon women of color in the movement. While colored suffragists, such as Mary Church Terrell (National Association of Colored Women), Ida B. Wells-Barnett (Alpha Suffrage Club), Frederick Douglass, and W. E. B. Du Bois were there from the beginning, by the turn of the century, they doubted that any suffrage victory would include them. Colored women's presence in the movement undermined the physical separation of the races that segregation demanded and therefore presented a distraction that white women suffragists were unwilling to address.

In an editorial in the June 1912 issue of *The Crisis*, a journal published by the NAACP and considered one of the leading forces in the New Negro Movement and the Harlem Renaissance, Du Bois, a leading black intellectual of the day and editor of *The Crisis*, pointed to a failure on the part of the NAWSA to address the disenfranchisement of Negroes in law and in practice. In response to Du Bois's editorial, President Anna Shaw wrote, "The woman suffragists are wincing a bit under the plain speaking of *The Crisis*."

> There is not in the National Association any discrimination against colored people. If they do not belong to us it is merely because they have not organized and have not made application for membership. Many times we have had colored women on our program and as delegates, and, I personally, would be only too glad to welcome them as long as I am president of the National Association.
>
> At the State convention in Ithaca a few days ago, when I was conducting the question box, I was asked what I did in Louisville in regard to admitting women of Negro blood to the convention and my reply was: "I did nothing in regard to admitting women of Negro blood to the convention. Our association does not recognize either Negro blood or white blood; what we stand for is the demand for equal political rights for women and men, and we know no distinction of race." Our whole contention is for justice to women, white and colored, and I do not think it will be possible ever to change the platform of the National Association in this respect.[24]

There was a reported rumor in Ohio which indicated that at the Louisville, Kentucky, meeting, a resolution condemning disenfranchisement of colored people in the South was "snowed under." The NAWSA disputed this account:

> All this is pleasant and encouraging, but does it present facts in the case exactly? Early in August Miss Martha Gruening sought a chance to have a colored delegate introduce the following resolution at the Louisville Convention and speak on the floor:
>
> "Resolved, that the women who are trying to lift themselves out of the class of the disenfranchised, the class of the insane and criminal, express their sympathy with the black men and women who are fighting the same battle and recognize that it is as undemocratic to disfranchise human beings on the ground of color as on the ground of sex."[25]

It was reported that President Shaw refused absolutely to invite the colored lady suggested and that she said over her signature several weeks before the convention:

> I must oppose the presentation of that resolution at our national convention. I do not feel that we should go into a Southern State to hold our national convention and then introduce any subject which we know

beforehand will do nothing but create discord and inharmony [*sic*] in convention. The resolution which you proposed to introduce would do more to harm the success of our convention in Louisville than all the other things that we do would do good. I am in favor of colored people voting, but white women have no enemy in the world who does more to defeat our amendments, when submitted, than colored men and until women are recognized and permitted to vote, I am opposed to introducing into our women suffrage convention a resolution in behalf of men who, if our resolution were carried, would go straight to the polls and defeat us every time.[26]

Despite the primacy of race issues, many women of color were activists for women's rights. Writer and lecturer Frances Ellen Watkins Harper, one of the first black women to support the AWSA, said that "when it was a question of race, she let the lesser question of sex go."[27]

Because women in Illinois, New York, and Texas had the right to vote before the Nineteenth Amendment was ratified, some black women had experienced certain benefits of suffrage.

The league's history exposes a cycle of achievements and setbacks in circumnavigating its responses to the conversations on gender and race in both society and the organization. From the internal organizational struggle of the NAWSA to the "let the Negro have his moment" attitude that existed in the suffrage movement in response to black men getting the vote before women, it's clear that the League of Women Voters was constantly challenging assumptions about its role. Each decade in the league's history brought distinct periods of attempts to address or ignore issues of race, equity, and inclusion. Some efforts were more

Frances Ellen Watkins Harper (1825–1911). (Science History Images/Alamy Stock Photo)

intense than others, with few making any systemic change in the organizational culture. Most notably, the 1920s, 1960s, 1970s, and 1990s served as catalysts for attempted changes in organizational policy and practice.

Throughout league history, formal data was not collected on race. The response to the lack of specific membership data collection by race was that to collect such data was anathema to the league's philosophy of being open to all. But informally, there were inquiries made to the national president from local and state leagues asking how they should handle requests from women of color to join the organization. These requests led to the unofficial establishment of "colored leagues," first recorded at the 1920 convention and not supported in league bylaws. The existence of these leagues will be discussed throughout the subsequent chapters.

In the 1970s, at the insistence of two black national board members, an attempt was made to collect data on the racial composition of the membership. That data collection lasted for two years and then disappeared as a priority. The only recorded data about race was anecdotal and came from observations of individual local leagues. Studies commissioned by the league to assess its organizational challenges also provided insight into the racial makeup. These studies include the 1956–1958 University of Michigan Survey of the League of Women Voters; the 1968–1970 study *Structures and Procedures Committee*, which examined ways to streamline the league's gathering of grassroots suggestions at regional meetings; the 1972–1980 studies conducted by the league; the 1972–1974 study that was the league's first in twenty years; and the most recent 2016–2018 league self-study, *Transformation Journey*. These studies all reveal that the composition of league membership has not changed over the years.[28] Controversy, compromise, and collaboration have occurred in relation to the issue of race, yet for six years in the twenty-first century, 2010–2016, by choice or oversight, there was no racial/ethnic diversity on the national board of directors.

The strength of the league has always been its membership as reflected in its bylaws, principles, history, and rhetoric. League members of color, however, often get lost or are invisible in its images and attitudes. The two most widely read histories of the league, *In the Public Interest* and *For the Public Record*, focus primarily on issues and impact and only cursorily the role women of color played and the impact of their contributions on the organization and organizational dynamics.

Barbara Stuhler, national board member (1958–1964) and benefactor of the Barbara Stuhler Library, in the preface to *For the Public Record: A Documentary History of the League of Women Voters*, recognized that the voices of women of color offer a unique perspective and an account of the history of the league not through "rose-colored" glasses, but through "amber-colored" ones—amber being the lens of race. Viewing through that lens underscores a different experience, often with a much different outcome. Stuhler stated:

> In recent years even though the League has embarked on a course of action that has succeeded in diversifying its membership in terms of age . . . its gender, and its ethnic and racial composition, the membership has remained in large part, white, middle class, middle-aged and female. One significant sign of that success was the election in June 1998 of Carolyn Jefferson-Jenkins of Colorado, the first African-American to serve as president of the LWVUS.[29]

Conclusion

History is messy, uncomfortable, and sometimes unbelievable, but unpleasant truths allow for valuable lessons to be learned. The league has not forgotten Carrie Chapman Catt's suggestion that the anniversary of its birth should be celebrated decennially, to review past achievements and mark future goals, but a comprehensive history demands more. The irony inherent in Catt's suggestion is not lost upon those who continue to study the league, as her own racist remarks are scrutinized as prohibiting the league from an ideology of full inclusion. The hundredth anniversary celebration provides the opportunity to move beyond this legacy and rectify the omissions of the contributions of women of color in the league.

Most written histories of the national league do just as Catt suggested—they feature achievements and the impact on issues emphasized by the national leadership of the time. Because that leadership has always been predominantly white, analysis of the influence of race on membership and the organization as a whole has been scant, contingent upon the priority placed upon it by those in charge. Several dissertations, written in the last few years, take a more critical look at the organizational dynamics and the often-admitted dissonance between principle and practice. While these researchers' efforts have been hampered by the inconsistent availability of records and methods of recordkeeping, their conclusions help form a more comprehensive accounting of the league's historic evolution. Several prominent black women from the colored women's clubs are routinely mentioned, but that does not reflect the hundreds of other black women who attempted to leverage their influence through league channels.

Records of league conventions and councils, along with other correspondence between state and national leadership, accepted by the Library of Congress beginning in the 1960s, provide a clear picture of the discussions of the inclusion or exclusion of women of color and the strategic decisions that codified this philosophy. There is as much to be learned from what is present in the records as what is absent. As a result of her efforts to persuade the Library of Congress to accept league documents as a historical collection, Dr. Louise Young was inspired to write what was to be one of the first comprehensive histories of the league: *In the Public Interest*.

The book was published to celebrate the league's fiftieth anniversary. The book was an effort to present the "league's modern characteristics as part of the legacy and point out the continuity of its program and purpose since its earliest days."[30] Dr. Young's historical account portrayed the league as a "microcosm of the politically responsible and responsive women in American society." She emphasized that "living, breathing individuals accomplished the recorded "deeds"—not the league as an institution." She stressed that "the history of an organization is primarily the essence of innumerable biographies."[31]

Because of the thoroughness, diligence, and objectivity of her research, I relied heavily on Dr. Young's work as the foundation of my study. While *In the Public Interest* provides a methodical and unique insight into the evolution of the organization, it does not mention the role and contributions of black women in the main narrative, nor was that its intended focus. Nowhere in the index is there mention of the role of black women or mention of the premier black women's groups. Fortunately, Dr. Young captured many of the decisions surrounding the league's struggle with the issue of race, with clarifying details in the footnotes. Why is this important? Because a complete history is important if the league is to move forward with integrity in the spirit and vision of its founding. It is profoundly evident that no one book should bear the responsibility of accomplishing that monumental task.

Additionally, I relied heavily on Barbara Stuhler's *For the Public Record: A Documentary History of the League of Women Voters*, which uses primary source documents to tell the story of the league. Though it mentions the plight of women of color, most of that information is relegated to the footnotes. Because league leaders, at some level, recognized the importance of the contributions of women of color, they had a consistent relationship with the National Council of Negro Women. Despite the fact that the history of black women's clubs intersects with that of the league, there is no elaboration of the ongoing connection with the National Council of Negro

Women.[32] None of the notable black women leaders who worked tire-lessly on the periphery of the league were listed in the index. From a broader perspective, Ann Gordon questions whether this omission was intentional or simply an oversight.[33]

> Feminist theorists have addressed the relationship of race and feminism in at least two different ways. One approach is to view race as integral to gen-der and explore the ways in which gender identity is constructed in rela-tion to race, and how racial identity is equally constructed in relation to gender. The other follows a method whereby the voices of women of color are added to the conventional curriculum in a sort of separate but equal manner. This latter approach has been called the "additive approach." Because it simply adds the voices of those historically excluded from the mainstream feminist canon, but does not examine the constitution of these voices within the context of power that have given rise to them, it carries the risk of essentializing gender and race, or assuming these cat-egories to be fixed and timeless.[34]

The league's evolution was impacted by what was happening in society, but societal changes in matters of race did not serve as a catalyst for the organization to make racial equity and inclusion a program priority. The league saw itself as the voice of the "public interest" but was unresponsive to those internal policies and practices that marginalized women of color in its ranks. Tension between being a league member and being a league member of color rivaled the legacy of the tensions between suffragists and abolitionists.

In her history of the women's rights movement, *Women in Action: Rebels and Reformers*, published by the League of Women Voters Education Fund for the league's seventy-fifth anniversary celebration, Elisabeth Israels Perry acknowledged:

> The most prominent women's organization for a long time consisted pri-marily of native-born, middle to upper class women of European Amer-ican origins. Women representing these mainstream groups therefore dominate the story of women's political activism in the modern era. As historians uncover more of the activities of women of various income lev-els and ethnic and racial backgrounds, American women's political history will continue to be rewritten.[35]

Most recently, the 2018 League of Women Voters of the United States (LWVUS) self-study concluded that unless the organization makes stra-tegic choices to adapt to the changing demographics of the United States,

> In the end, we will remember not the words of our enemies, but the silence of our friends.
>
> —Dr. Martin Luther King Jr.

it will most assuredly revert to a time when the demographic was white, middle-aged, middle to upper income. As we move toward a more inclusive history of the league and make sense of its complexity, we must remember that history is messy. There are competing interests, goals, and motivations. There are lessons to be learned about how all women learn to work together without the residue of race.

After one hundred years, the league must make peace with its history and use the lessons learned to shape its future. The women whose stories will be told are not in any existing history of the league as more than a footnote. Their contributions to the league have been often overlooked or suppressed. Theirs is a story of passion, purpose, and persistence, where race and gender are inextricably linked and the lines between the two sometimes blurred. As the league approaches its hundredth year of existence and the celebrations begin, we need to make sure that the voices of the women of color who served in various capacities are heard.

We should live in a time where the contributions of women of color to the League of Women Voters are given the recognition that they deserve in comprehensive historical accounts—in the main narrative. Until that time, it remains necessary to supplement history as in *The Untold Story*, "lest we forget."

Notes

1. At the hundredth year of the League of Women Voters, there will have been only one African American president.

2. Young, 1989, ix–x.

3. Schuyler, 2006, 135.

4. McGoldrick, 1995, 270–273.

5. Terborg-Penn, 1998, 1.

6. Waisman and Tietjen, 2008, 67.

7. Kraditor, 1981, 170.

8. Ibid., 197.

9. Ibid., 200.

10. League of Women Voters Papers.

11. Kraditor, 1981, 203.

12. Ibid., 173. Harriet Taylor Upton to Laura Clay, August 31, 1906, Clay Papers, UK.

13. Ibid., 198.

14. Stuhler, 2000, 9.

15. Young, 1989, 11.

16. Weiss, 2018, 133.

17. The women's rights movement split in 1869 into two groups: the American Woman Suffrage Association (AWSA), led by Lucy Stone, which backed the Fifteenth Amendment giving black males the vote, and the National Woman Suffrage Association (NWSA), led by Susan B. Anthony and Elizabeth Cady Stanton.

18. Dodson, 2017.

19. Ibid., 188–189.

20. Sarah L. Forten, 1837; Pendleton, 1912, 126.

21. Historical Society of Pennsylvania, Collection no. 490; Stanton et al., 2018.

22. Perry, 1995, 1.

23. *Internet Encyclopedia of Philosophy*, 2015.

24. League of Women Voters Papers.

25. Ibid.

26. DuBois, 1978.

27. Sterling, 1984, x.

28. League of Women Voters Papers, "Transformation Journey Executive Summary Update April 2018," common challenges identified include: membership that is not reflective of our communities.

29. Stuhler, 2000, xii–xiv.

30. League of Women Voters Papers, April 1968, Press Release.

31. Ibid.

32. Stuhler, 2000, 63.

33. Gordon et al., 1997, 63.

34. *Internet Encyclopedia of Philosophy*, 2015.

35. Perry, 1995, 7.

To "Finish the Fight"

The imperative is to define what is right and do it.

—Barbara Jordan

During the seventy-two-year struggle for women's suffrage, beginning with the women's rights convention at Seneca Falls, New York, in 1848 and ending with the passage of the Nineteenth Amendment, passed by Congress June 4, 1919, and ratified August 18, 1920, the world was changing on a number of fronts. Six constitutional amendments had passed,[1] all moving toward what would be recognized as a seminal event for women's suffrage. And not without note, the United States had engaged in World War I (1914–1918), "the war to end all wars."

One and a half years in advance of the ratification of the Nineteenth Amendment, the League of Women Voters emerged in 1919 as an auxiliary of the National American Woman Suffrage Association (NAWSA). Carrie Chapman Catt proposed the organization of the League of Women Voters "to finish the fight." Catt and others realized that the winning of suffrage would not be an ending, but rather a beginning—the beginning of full citizenship for American women.

> I propose a League of Women Voters, nonpartisan and non-sectarian, to finish the fight and to aid in the reconstruction of the nation. What should be done can be done; what can be done let us do.[2]
>
> Carrie Chapman Catt

Unfortunately, this sentiment would not carry over to the treatment of women of color in the new organization or the nation.

Six months before the Nineteenth Amendment's final ratification, NAWSA's leaders were seeking to hold intact the immense suffrage army of two million women activists.

As NAWSA's Jubilee Convention opened in St. Louis on March 24, 1919, Carrie Chapman Catt challenged the nearly victorious women to stay on the battlefield as an army of women citizens "to finish the fight" for the changes in "custom, laws and education" so imperatively needed. In a charged atmosphere, the convention voted to launch an auxiliary organization in the enfranchised states, and to dissolve the NAWSA when its task was completed.[3]

Delegates to the Victory Convention at Chicago's LaSalle Hotel in February 1920, formally agreed to reconstitute NAWSA as The National League of Women Voters, affirming its independent existence and adopting a constitution and bylaws. These actions provided for a Washington, D.C., headquarters and a four-member executive board. League records do not indicate whether women of color were allowed to stay at the hotel or participate in the convention that made these decisions. The policy of the LaSalle Hotel at the time regarding Negroes would have determined whether black delegates could attend and under what circumstances. It is noted from previous actions, however, that the Illinois NAWSA and subsequent league members supported integration.

As the National American Woman Suffrage Association disbanded and the League of Women Voters emerged, the legacy of the tension between the abolitionists and the suffragists lingered. The culture of excluding women of color from full membership status continued into this new organization. Early leaders struggled over both intentions and responsibilities, as well as over the structure, purpose, and financing of the new organization. The strategic choices the new league leaders made regarding their relationship with women of color formed the foundation for a long-term impact on future organizational decisions. The League of Women Voters' founding reflected the dissonance between its principles of touting the passage of the Nineteenth Amendment as a victory for all women and its practices of segregation in league culture, membership, and opinion on issues of the day.

The call to "finish the fight" and the subsequent characterization of the league as an "everywoman's organization" appeared to be more rhetoric than reality for women of color. The lack of overt attempts to integrate league membership was evident in the decisions of the national leadership. The establishment, development, and impact of the Special Committee on the Study of Negro Problems set the tone and provided policy guidance for local and state affiliates. That issues of race were referred to as a "problem" speaks to the sentiment of the women who led this experimental organization.[4]

While the passage of the Nineteenth Amendment brought women the constitutional guarantee of full voting rights in 1920, most women of color would not be a part of the victory, even though enfranchisement was due in part to their efforts. The levers of power related to race did not change hands.

An "Everywoman's" Organization

As the history of the organization's evolution reflects, the league struggled with a perennial question as it examined how it operated: Are all women the same?[5]

> Viewing themselves as representative of organized women, League leaders sought to transform the enthusiasm for a common goal into collective commitment to more limited, but specific goals. Internal differences arose, which if hastening the development of procedures for reconciling conflicts, exacted an emotional toll. . . . More difficult to absorb was the reaction of the older suffrage leaders whose millennial hopes were not immediately realized.[6]

Despite its inability to reconcile its internal organizational issues of race and gender and its legacy of separatism from the NAWSA, the league continued to position itself as an "everywoman's" organization—even while its own ideology reflected segregated membership, not in its bylaws, but in its operation.

In the Public Interest, one of the most comprehensive histories of the league, prominently displays a photo of the November 1917 Suffrage Parade in New York but does not mention that blacks were relegated to the back of the parade.[7] Black women leaders, while forming their own separate organizations, encountered racism from the same elected officials for whom they campaigned. Yet, black women's discontent and frustration with white women's organizations in the 1920s translated not into an abandonment of politics, but into the emergence of new leaders, alliances, and strategies.

In 1920, all but two states (Louisiana and Wyoming) belonged to the newly established League of Women Voters. State delegates elected the national board and adopted programs at conventions. Local leagues had no vote at conventions, and any communication from a local league to the national league was required to go through the state league.[8]

The league's Pan-American Conference, April 20–23, 1922, disclosed that LWVUS leaders found international outreach easier than forging an authentic relationship domestically with women of color and overtly addressing the multidimensional and complicated internal U.S. politics regarding race. Delegates from twenty Latin American countries and Canada attended. More consideration was given to delegates from the Pan-American Union than to the black members in the United States. The national league leadership made no attempt to organize among black women, and Southern black women, who were frequently denied their voting rights under the Nineteenth Amendment, found little sympathy among their white counterparts.[9]

As indicated in the following statement, the league frequently focused on its programs over its internal struggle with people:

> State leagues had been even more successful. In a swiftly gathered harvest of seeds sown over the two preceding decades, some 420 "needed" laws had been won, and 64 undesirable laws successfully opposed. The largest number had been in the fields of child welfare, where 45 states had enacted a total of 130 laws. But important incremental gains were also recorded in enhancing women's legal disabilities and the striking down of discriminatory statutes.[10]

While these legislative achievements could be seen as successes for the league, in many instances they did not apply to black women. Behind the scenes, the league questioned its purpose as an "everywoman's" organization but hesitated to take any action toward its own discriminatory practices or those of the nation. Why? Historians imply that league members of the time believed that all black women could benefit if white women gained, hence their reluctance to aggressively pursue issues of race.

The "everywoman's" organization was the moniker given the league by President Maud Park in April 1923 at the convention in Des Moines, Iowa. That convention placed emphasis on many issues both internal and external—Sheppard-Towner Act (1921), child labor, women candidates, voter participation, the Cable Act (1922), and the Civil Service Reclassification Act (1921)—but none publicly on race.

By 1924, the league was organized in 346 of 433 congressional districts, the District of Columbia, and Hawaii. The Committee on the Realignment of the Program was established in 1933, but restructuring took another decade to accomplish. The league was not ready to change. Like many other organizations, the league barely survived the Depression. In 1942, the league had become ingrown and rigid, with the state board standing in the way of communication between the national board and local members. The 1944 convention marked the birth of the modern league as a federated membership organization. Convention 1946 adopted a new structure for the league, changed the name and purpose, and adopted a new policy statement. What was known from 1920 to 1946 as the National League of Women Voters in 1946 became League of Women Voters of the United States.

Between Principle and Practicality

Transitions for the newly formed organization would become a binary choice, transactional versus transformational. On the issue of membership integration, the league often replaced principle with practicality. The national level's lack of advocacy on behalf of women of color contradicted the adopted league values. Women of color were allowed to engage when the league needed them to serve as liaisons to "their" community in a transactional manner but not as an integral part of the organization, which would have been transformational. This dynamic was not lost on women of color, who endured the legacy of the suffragists' exclusion.

> Those African-American women who had the opportunity to become suffragists moved in two directions, identifying with the mainstream, white woman suffrage organizations on the one hand, and developing their own agendas in Black woman suffrage organizations on the other.[11]

At the 1921 Cleveland Convention, delegates encountered a public challenge by Walter White, Mary Ovington, W. E. B. Du Bois, and James Weldon Johnson, influential black leaders, to respond to the needs of black women for rights and justice. Minnie Fisher Cunningham, who served as the League of Women Voters' first executive secretary and default historian, retained thorough and insightful documents of league leadership meetings that, when later published, revealed the contentious conversations about the issue of race and the league.

> The LWV first confronted the racial dilemma at its 1921 convention, when Addie Hunton, a prominent African-American clubwoman and field secretary for the NAACP led a delegation to ask the LWV's assistance in protesting voting discrimination. The black women were granted time to speak, but some southern delegates protested, and the incident pointed up the difficulty of mending the continuing racial split that had divided the suffrage movement. The board of directors meeting at the close of Convention then grappled with the "Negro question."
>
> Several prominent northern women offered a resolution to form an Interracial Committee to study ways of promoting racial harmony; it was turned down in favor of one drafted by southern women to create a Special

Committee on the Study of Negro Problems. Eulalie Salley of South Carolina, Director of the Third region presented this.

The board at Salley's request, created the Committee by its own authority, without bringing it to convention. It offered the chairmanship to Julia Lathrop of Illinois. Addie Hunton was notified of the action by letter.[12]

Addie Waites Hunton (1866–1943). (History and Art Collection/Alamy Stock Photo)

League bylaws did not distinguish membership by race, but in practice, the developing Southern leagues found the idea of accepting members of color extremely controversial in the early years, given the entrenched Southern culture and custom of segregation. The Southern leagues represented only 15 percent of the total national membership and were not as strongly rooted as those in some other regions of the country. Their colored membership was negligible.

Only six of the eleven state leagues represented at the Atlanta Conference of Southern Presidents reported having any black participation, and black membership appeared to have been less than a hundred for the entire region, with many drawn from black colleges. While there were individual leagues who were willing to confront the issue, none of the Southern leagues as organizations desired to challenge the pervasive racial attitudes in their communities. Some leagues reacted constructively by accelerating voter-service activities and providing channels for moderate elements to temper extreme expression of opinions, but all sought to avoid internal disruption by maintaining an official position of neutrality on the integration issues.[13]

Tensions over the race issue were not new. They had, indeed, divided the suffrage movement in the Southern states and continued to divide the league. According to the minutes of the Meeting of the Presidents of the Southern States in Atlanta, Georgia, the work of the Special Committee on the Study of Negro Problems was hampered by the difficulty encountered by Southern leagues in securing representatives.[14] Those states reporting information were Alabama, Arkansas, Florida, Georgia, Louisiana, Mississippi, North Carolina, South Carolina, Tennessee, Texas, and Virginia.

Minnie Fisher Cunningham ceased to be the league's executive secretary in 1923. She later returned to the board as vice president and led the work of the Special Committee on Negro Problems. The committee had no budget, and the LWV insisted that its activities not be publicized. The other league subcommittees—child welfare, education, the legal status of women, women in industry, social hygiene, and living costs—were fully supported, funded, and publicized by the national leadership of the organization. Each standing committee was made up of a national chair and the head of the relevant committee in each state league. The strategic decision to treat this subcommittee differently placed what was perceived as the practicality of the times over the principles of the league.[15]

At Convention 1924, in Buffalo, NY, Cunningham, several officers—Maud Park, Julia Lathrop, Belle Sherwin—and several other white members again met with a group of black delegates led by Irene Goins, president of Chicago's Douglass league, and Carrie Horton of the Chicago Federation of Colored Women's Clubs, along with Beatrice Grady of Missouri, Sue M. Brown of Iowa, and Alice Webb of Chicago. The black women, astutely stressing the need to prevent "exploitation by unscrupulous politicians," asked that the league cooperate with colored women's clubs and black colleges in citizenship education work. In an attempt to stimulate the activity of the Special Committee on Negro Problems as a way of responding to this request, the league leadership appointed Minnie Fisher Cunningham as chair of the committee.[16]

Belle Sherwin, throughout her presidency (1924–1934), "persistently" explored the character and function of the league and how these were related to its stated aims and policies. Her guiding question was always, "At what point did knowledge meet life and become politically effective?"[17] Under her leadership, the Committee of Nine was appointed by the board to study all aspects of participation in the political process, including the status of women in the parties, as well as voting patterns, literacy and registration requirements, incidence of poll tax, provisions for absentee voting, and the frequency of elections. The poll tax and registration issues show that the league was aware of race as an issue but not that they did anything about it. At the 1926 convention, the Committee of Nine appointed the previous year to examine women's electoral participation reported to the convention on the results of its investigations. It had found that voting statistics were in key respects "empirically crude."[18]

To the question "To what extent do white women and colored women work together politically?," the same negative reply about not publicizing the Special Committee's activities was received.[19] The issue of "colored leagues," however, was ever present. In the minutes from the Conference of the Department of Organization, Highland Park, Illinois, December 14, 1927, Wednesday Morning Session, leadership reported that although no official statistics were available on the number of women of color who were members or the number of "colored leagues," to their knowledge, there were three colored leagues in California, one in Chicago, one in St. Louis, and one in Tacoma, Washington.[20]

The number of colored leagues and members of color was anecdotal information derived from reports by states given at annual meetings. League bylaws did not authorize segregated leagues, yet they existed, despite being incongruous with the league mission. National leadership reported that there had been four requests from St. Louis. The response to these requests was that

> It is not desirable to encourage the organization of colored leagues, but that the educational goal which is desired can better be promoted by classes in other work among colored women, without formal organization.[21]

So while separate leagues were not encouraged, there was no further conversation about inclusion of women of color as "full" members of the league. This decision begs the question, were colored leagues considered second-class? Were they a part of the bigger conversation? Nothing in league documents indicates that colored leagues were afforded the same status as other leagues; at the time, they were more practically viewed as "units."

Internal and external publicity reports from 1923 to 1928 dealing primarily with the external perception of the organization did not address how the league's program choices incorporated the overarching issue of race. The first league program priorities included protecting women factory workers, promoting pay based on occupation not gender, maternal health, and equal property rights for married women.

In the 1929 organization meeting, there was no mention of race or diversity in membership, however, socioeconomic distinctions were used as the basis for discussion about exclusion in membership. Comments were made about the amount of time a woman might have to devote to the league; working women of low socioeconomic status (farmers, for example) have less time. The conversation of the national leadership did not focus on color because no one of color was at the

Mary Church Terrell (1863–July 1854). (Library of Congress)

table, despite the fact that at every league convention, representatives from the National Council of Negro Women (NCNW) were invited as speakers and guests.

True to her presidential agenda, Belle Sherwin set up a Committee on the Realignment of the Program in 1933. This was also an opportunity to address issues of integrated membership, but that was not a priority. The actual restructuring took another decade to accomplish. The league was not ready to change. At the 1934 convention, Marguerite Wells, president from 1934 to 1944, warned that league's purpose was larger than its departments and single issues, and in that same year, the league launched its first major public relations effort.

Anna Lord Strauss (1944–1950), who ran from the floor in 1944 and became president on a platform of change, led the league into Convention 1946, during which the organization adopted new structure. This new structure identified three kinds of members: voting members, at-large members, and associate members. Voting members were eligible women voters in recognized leagues. Associate members were all other members of recognized local or college leagues. At-large members lived outside a local league area. "Anyone who subscribed to the league's purpose and policy could join."[22] The league's purpose was "to promote political responsibility through informed and active participation of citizens in government and to take action on governmental measures and policies in the public interest."[23] Using these criteria, women of color should have been recruited and retained just as any other member. The existence of colored leagues or groups of women of color relegated to colored units was anathema to this principle. Additionally, because only one league would be recognized in a community, designated "colored leagues" had no standing under existing bylaws, policy, or practice.

World War II (1939–1945) produced a new kind of league meeting. By 1948, the league had reorganized, except for Allegheny County, Pennsylvania, league, which refused to adopt the new bylaws or change its name. Also in 1948, the "unit" meeting was institutionalized by the league. This new structure would have an impact on the growing conversation about segregated leagues by rebranding them as units.

The league's reluctance to confront its own issues with race continued into the next decade. The organization focused on global injustice in the late 1940s. It was never perceived as being a group that shied away from difficult issues. While the league celebrated its participation in the March 4, 1948, International Conference on Human Rights held at the U.S. Department of State, according to Carole Stanford Bucy's research, the league was unwilling to assert any national advocacy in the area of civil rights other than through its already adopted programs, which were broader in scope.

> In 1948 the League founded at the culmination of a movement to end one form of inequality, was silent on the continued segregation of African-Americans. The League was not addressing anti-lynching because the majority of its members were not interested in the subject.[24]

The national league leadership did not take a more aggressive or substantial role in changing discrimination in society until it was acceptable to do so, a distinct contradiction between principle and practicality. In the 1950s, racial equality challenged the liberal identity and the culture of all women's organizations. It was during this decade, the league reached its organizational maturity. As a grassroots, federated organization, state and local leagues, within the framework and principles of the league developed their own programs for issues arising within their communities. It was at the state and local levels that the organization was the strongest and where the most significant action occurred.

Recognizing the variability in local communities, particularly with the movement of middle-class groups to the suburbs, the national leadership, under the auspices of the Carrie Chapman Catt Memorial Fund, initiated a study of those impacted leagues in large industrial centers. With Mrs. Errol Horner as director, a study was undertaken in several cities to observe how voluntary associations, including the league, were coping with the depletion of civic effort in the inner cities and an increase in urban problems unique in their complexity.

In addition to the published report, in April 1953, Horner presented the national board with a constructively critical memorandum directly applicable to the league's own role. The lack of activity resulting from the findings was accredited to the fact that local leagues at the time were preoccupied with other concerns. Only the Cook County (Chicago) league responded actively to the memorandum's proposals.[25]

As it was the league's practice to provide guidance to state and local leagues, the national league leadership published materials to explain league priorities. In 1951, the *National Voter*, the league's primary membership communication instrument, was created. Its symbols and visual recruitment tools reflected a "white women's" organization. Women of color were excluded in league images, their efforts intentionally concealed. The league's internal struggle with race mirrored the tension in society. It was not until the 1960s that some diversity in organizational images appeared. Most publications were still not fully representative. The choice of images was intentional and was primarily dependent on the league leadership at the time.

On August 11, 1953, the national league distributed to all state and local leagues the publication *How to Get and Keep Members*. This publication made no mention of strategies for outreach to diverse groups, nor did it mention race as a factor in recruitment, allowing local and state leagues to make decisions about inclusion that were acceptable in their respective communities. "The League's voice on a given issue had to be rooted in an organizational consensus, procedurally crafted to ensure that it represented a preponderance of membership opinion."[26]

The cover of the membership publication was that of white women deliberating issues. Since there had been, by this time, numerous conversations about the role of women of color in the organization, and since the publication was released one year prior to the *Brown v. Board of Education* (1954) decision, which the league clearly knew would impact the debate on integration, this intentional representation of the league was a missed opportunity to become more inclusive. League membership segregation, then, in the words of *Brown*, was defacto, not dejure.

The national league leadership found cover from pursuing the issue of membership integration by focusing its conversation on the issue of school desegregation posed by the *Brown* decision. Percy Maxim Lee, president (1950–1958), was first to address the beginning of school desegregation. Her reported comments to leagues pointed to the tension between an internal focus versus an external focus. On the subject of school desegregation, the league was silent. Because of the controversies related to both race and religion that were tied to educational issues, the league was not able to develop a comprehensive national position on education.[27]

A characteristic of the Lee administration was a readiness to assume that innovation and change were necessarily aspects of organizational growth.

> But an organization of long standing might find that the original methods of implementing its founding goals no longer applied. It was essential then to reexamine these goals as well as its bylaws and structure. As the price of survival it had to refit itself to the time and occasion.[28]

Once the broader issue of civil rights surged to the forefront of the national agenda with the unanimous Supreme Court decision in May 1954 striking down school segregation in *Brown v. Board of Education of Topeka*, President Lee quickly convened a gathering of the presidents of eleven Southern state leagues in Atlanta in July. In her opening address, Lee sharply stated the dilemma: fidelity to principle versus organizational well-being.

> Every effort must be exerted to protect the integrity of the League and its usefulness and at the same time promote the principles in which it believes. The league must find a way to exert calm, unemotional and wise leadership in search for solutions.[29]

In 1955, the "Report on League Interest in Integration" brought the issue of race front and center. In 1958, it was reported that at one of Lee's meetings, the consensus was that "it is impossible to ignore the problem of integration; it would be disastrous . . . to become involved in it."[30]

In her last presidential address in 1958, President Lee felt compelled to elaborate on national league policy concerning school integration. She defended the neutral policy of the Southern leagues as "the only tenable course" where the pressures were greatest. League history offered substantial evidence that "under certain circumstances an indirect approach in seeking solutions may be more effective than a direct attack." She concluded "that activity . . . would handicap, possibly destroy the league's ability to help toward a constructive solution."[31]

By the early 1960s, it was apparent that civil rights was a national, not a Southern, issue and that a more active league commitment was imperative. A conference of urban leagues, which had been held in 1960 after several Northern industrial cities had appealed to the national board for help, led to an initial proposal for a project aimed at identifying and training "natural leaders" from inner-city areas to establish a two-way communication between the urban core and the suburban rim.

Ruth Phillips, a president (1958–1964) with a lengthy experience in the Illinois league and a long-standing interest in inner-city problems, presented the proposal to the national board in March 1961. Board opinion, though, was divided, and nothing happened until the summer of 1963, when the issue of civil rights could no longer be ignored, leading the way for the league to reconsider its priorities.[32]

In 1963 President Phillips sent a memorandum to local presidents, urging initiation of local efforts. "We have no Current Agenda item, we have no national consensus, but we need not sit with folded hands. . . . The crisis is national; the problem is local . . . In every League some sort of action is need."[33] This memorandum was already prepared when President John F. Kennedy, on July 9, 1963, summoned three hundred women representing ninety-three organizations to the White House to rally support for the comprehensive civil rights legislation just submitted to Congress. President Phillips and other league representatives attended the gathering. Even most Southern leagues responded favorably, reflecting a change in social climate induced by the mounting sense of urgency. By that time, many local leagues throughout the country were already deeply involved in local antidiscrimination measures in such fields as housing.[34]

It was not until 1964 that the league adopted a study of civil rights as part of its national agenda.

> With the 1964 elections in prospect, Ruth Phillips sought to revive earlier initiatives by proposing a program of political education for minority groups. The League's Education Fund drafted an imaginative project for civic leadership training in urban ghettos—its maiden effort in the inner cities—which received funding support from the Sears, Roebuck Foundation.[35]

The civil rights issue in the 1960s became intertwined with the question of social welfare. The 1964 convention authorized a study of equal access to education and employment, in collective realization that it was a "glaring omission," as one league put it, that a domestic issue of such moment was not already on the league's national program, especially since it was already on many state and local programs. Leagues had already been involved in *Baker v. Carr* (1962) and *Reynolds v. Sims* (1964).

> The reawakened preoccupation with social groups who had failed to share in the overall prosperity of the fifties and sixties, many of them minorities

locked into ghettoes in the large northern cities, emerged against a background shaped by the civil rights struggle, the widespread urban riots in
the sixties, the War on Poverty launched by President Lyndon Johnson.
Yet, as with most of its program choices, the League's shift of emphasis
represented convergence of forces from both inside and outside the League
that had been at work for several years.[36]

Despite evolving thinking, the league found itself without a position
on which to base national legislative action on behalf of the Voting Rights
Act of 1965. "Pressed by events and stung by its powerlessness to take
action on any significant issue," a league document records, the 1970 convention adopted a bylaws amendment that enabled the league to act "to
protect the right to vote of every citizen" without the formality of adopting voting rights in its national program.[37]

Conclusion

The event that brought the league into existence, the ratification of the
Nineteenth Amendment, forever politicized women's relationships. The
laudable concept to "finish the fight" often found the league at odds with
itself in a complex society and complicated organization. The organization's ideological journey progressed from dealing with the legacy of contention that arose in acquiescing to the passage of the Fifteenth
Amendment in what was termed "the Negro's Hour" to the aspirational
goal of becoming an "everywoman's" organization while not overtly
addressing the issue of race in society. In both instances, the league operated between principle and practicality, often choosing practicality over
principle. Despite the strategic choices league leaders at the national, state
and local levels made to discourage women of color from advocacy for full
membership status, these women continued to affiliate with the
organization.

It is important to distinguish between what some hoped—and others
feared—would happen and what transpired. The legacy of separatism
apparent in the NAWSA and transferred to the League of Women Voters
permeated the organizational culture and can be seen in the controversy
in 1996 surrounding the ceremony to honor Carrie Chapman Catt at her
alma mater. In a *New York Times* editorial, "Suffragette's Racial Remark
Haunts College," a spokesperson for Iowa State University stated, "Mrs.
Catt made one controversial statement in a losing effort to win ratification
in two Southern states of the 19th Amendment, which gave women the

right to vote. 'White supremacy,' she said, 'will be strengthened, not weakened, by women's suffrage.'"[38]

As the League of Women Voters of the United States approaches its centennial, the "fight" is still not finished. The dichotomy of Catt's thinking is reflected in one of her more enlightened comments: "If we learn from the experience, there is no failure, only delayed victory."[39] Within the context of a changing society with changing demographics, the league's relationship with its members of color must be more than transactional, using black women for access to black communities; it must be transformational, whereby league membership is such an integral part of the organization and is fully reflected in ideology, images, and operations. While local and state leagues ultimately make the choice, it is the leaders at the national level who hold them accountable.

As Dr. Young concluded in her research of the league,

> Each generation is part of an ongoing cycle that carries forward a measurable deposit of social change as mutations find expression in action . . .
> The experience of their predecessors holds instructive lessons for this new feminist generation, though the transmittal of a revolutionary experience is always difficult.[40]

To "finish the fight" is just the beginning. Historians argue that faced with an either-or proposition of race versus gender, black women invariably choose race as the more pressing issue. Why, then, did women of color choose the League of Women Voters, a "white woman's" organization, to align with? The reasons that surface are as complex as the decisions they had to make. What becomes clear is that they endured the challenges of league membership *for the sake of the cause.*

Notes

1. The Thirteenth Amendment (passed by Congress January 31, 1865, and ratified December 6, 1865) eliminated slavery and involuntary servitude, except as a punishment for crime in the United States. The Fourteenth Amendment (passed by Congress June 13, 1866, and ratified July 9, 1868) prohibited states from making or enforcing any law that would abridge the privileges or immunities of citizens of the United States or deprive any person of life, liberty, or property without due process of law or equal protections of the law. The Fifteenth Amendment (passed by Congress February 26, 1869, and ratified February 3, 1870) stated that the rights of citizens of the United States to vote shall not be denied or abridged by the United States or any state on account of race, color, or previous condition of servitude. The Sixteenth Amendment (passed by Congress

July 2, 1909, and ratified February 3, 1913) gave Congress the power to lay and collect taxes on incomes. The Seventeenth Amendment (passed by Congress May 13, 1912, and ratified April 8, 1913) enumerated the number of senators from each state. The Eighteenth Amendment (passed by Congress December 18, 1917, and ratified January 16, 1919; repealed by amendment 21) prohibited the manufacture, sale, or transportation of intoxicating liquors within the United States and all territories.

2. League of Women Voters Papers, Carrie Chapman Catt.

3. Young, 1989, 33.

4. The name of the Special Committee on the Study of Negro Problems is also referred to in correspondence as the Special Committee on Negro Problems and beginning in 1924 as the Special Committee on Inter-Racial Problems.

5. *Internet Encyclopedia of Philosophy*, 2015, http://www.iep.utm.edu/fem-race/#H3.

6. Young, 1989, 2.

7. Ibid., 8.

8. Ibid., 51–52.

9. Ibid., 63; McArthur and Smith, 2003, 102.

10. Ibid., 75.

11. Terborg-Penn, 1998, 9.

12. McArthur and Smith, 2003, 102–103.

13. Young, 1989, 172.

14. League of Women Voters Atlanta, 1921.

15. Because of the Special Committee's stated charge and inability to gain traction in its varying iterations over the decades, it will be more thoroughly discussed in chapter 3 through various league correspondence and executive documents.

16. McArthur and Smith, 2003, 107.

17. Young, 1989, 82.

18. Ibid., 93.

19. League of Women Voters Papers, Wright to Sherwin, 1927, April 25.

20. League of Women Voters Papers, Library of Congress, 20.

21. League of Women Voters Papers, Library of Congress, minutes Conference of Organization, Highland Park, Illinois, Wednesday morning session, 1927, December 14, 20.

22. Neuman, 1994, 25.

23. Ibid.

24. Bucy, 2002, 170.

25. League of Women Voters, *Report of the Metropolitan Project Committee*, 1953.

26. Young, 1989, 153.

27. Bucy, 2002, 226.

28. League of Women Voters Papers, Library of Congress, Lee, 1950.

29. Young, 1989, 172.
30. Ibid., 173.
31. Ibid., 173.
32. Ibid., 174.
33. Ibid., 173.
34. Ibid., 173.
35. Ibid., footnote 48.
36. Ibid.
37. League of Women Voters Papers, Convention Folder, 1970, 4–5.
38. *New York Times*, 1996, May 5.
39. League of Women Voters Papers, Carrie Chapman Catt.
40. League of Women Voters Papers, Convention Folder, 1970, 4–5.

CHAPTER THREE

For the Sake of the Cause

One ever feels his twoness—an American, a Negro; two souls, two thoughts, two unreconciled strivings; two warring ideals in one dark body, whose dogged strength alone keeps it from being torn asunder.

—W. E. B. Du Bois

"For the Sake of the Cause" examines the various dimensions of the paradox between principle and practicality in identifying the "cause" for which women of color sought membership in the League of Women Voters. It discusses the dual involvement of black leaguers in other organizations that had the same mission, vision, and purpose of the league. This chapter frames the strategic choices that the national league leadership made in the environment of the nation's civil rights legislation that legally prohibited—but often customarily and institutionally allowed—segregation. It notes the absence of women of color in national league leadership, despite their visibility and effective leadership in other national organizations. "For the Sake of the Cause" highlights the sense of hope that women of color retained that through their participation, the league would choose to be a revolutionary organization rather than a reformist one, using the same aggressiveness on issues of racial equality as it had used on suffrage.

Historic context requires that since the League of Women Voters is the legacy organization of the NAWSA that, any discussion of why women of color associated with the league must begin with the suffragist position on the value of their contribution. The expression *for the sake of the cause* had a dual meaning: for white suffragists, it was a phrase used to discourage the advocacy of racial equality in the attempt to pass the Nineteenth Amendment; for colored suffragists, it was the rallying cry that kept them in the fight. Suffragists' historians note that despite racism in the movement, of the women of color who responded to the women's suffrage arguments and activities, the vast majority supported "the cause" of full suffrage. This tension between which "cause" would take precedence would exist throughout the movement and carry into the organizational dynamics of the League of Women Voters.

Fanny Jackson Coppin, suffragist, educator, missionary, and lifelong advocate for female higher education, said, "During my entire life I have suffered from two disadvantages. First, that I am a woman, second that I am a Negro."[1] This order would be reversed as the inclusion of women of color began being considered a hindrance to the effectiveness of the movement. Colored clubwomen were angered by NAWSA assumptions that they would terminate their activities "for the sake of the cause" to ensure passage of the Nineteenth Amendment. Colored clubwomen understood what white clubwomen did not: they were seeking more than NAWSA membership; they were seeking NAWSA support for the enfranchisement of all.

Racial equality took precedence for these black women activists, but the struggle for women's rights was a close second. When the women's rights movement split in 1869 and two separate suffragists' organizations were formed, most black spokeswomen supported the National Woman Suffrage Association, headed by Susan B. Anthony and Elizabeth Cady Stanton, which was the more radical (albeit sometimes racist) of the two groups. Black women continued to work with white feminists until

Fanny Jackson Coppin (1837–1913). (Science History Images/Alamy Stock Photo)

the end of the century, when suffragist leaders, courting support from the South, made them feel unwelcome.

The most notable active black feminists included Margaretta Forten; Harriet and Hattie Purvis; Maritcha Lyons; Louisa, Katherine, and Charlotte Rollin; Josephine Ruffin; Anna J. Cooper; Dr. Susan McKinney Steward; Dr. Rebecca Cole; Ida B. Wells; Mary Church Terrell; and Ellen Crum daughter of Ellen Craft. Harriet Tubman was a familiar face at suffrage meetings. She spoke at a convention in Rochester that was chaired by Susan B. Anthony in the 1880s. Sojourner Truth began her participation in the women's movement in the 1850s, when she spoke at a convention in Worcester, Massachusetts. Her last appearance at a women's rights meeting was as a delegate to the National Woman Suffrage Association's convention in Rochester in 1878.[2]

Deeply divided by race, class, religion, ethnicity, and region, women do not always identify with one another, and as a result, women's collective identity—their sense of solidarity as women—has waxed and waned. The reasons for these women of color to join the organization were as varied as any women of the time but adhered to the two categories current-day researchers have identified. People who join civic associations consider the act either in their personal interest, however defined, or in line with the values they hold. In that sense, these members looked at membership as an investment.[3]

After the passage of the Nineteenth Amendment and the transition of the NAWSA into the League of Women Voters, women of color continued to seek membership in this outwardly mainstream organization. Despite often being discouraged from joining, these women were committed to the ideological "cause" of full suffrage and social equality, and this motivated their quest for inclusion. It was an investment in a "white" organization, but one that was not devoid of competing issues of gender and race. Being a member of the League of Women Voters was a choice between invisibility in the organization, assimilation, or something in between.[4]

Although individual blacks held membership in some of the predominantly white state leagues, separate black leagues operated in Oakland, San Francisco, Los Angeles, Chicago, and St. Louis. Delegates from the Oakland, Chicago, and St. Louis groups were represented at the league's national conferences in the 1920s. Women of color were also represented on the state boards of the California and Illinois leagues. Leaders of the black leagues were, at the same time, leaders of their state federated clubs, the constituent members of the National Association of Colored Women's Clubs (NACW).[5] Records indicate that because of this overlap and the recognized need to have access, when needed, to the black community, lines of communication remained open between the NACW and the black units of the league.

Both Customary and Institutional

The politics of race divided the woman suffrage movement. Conservative suffragists advocated alienating black women and black men, claiming they were threats to the success of the passage of the Nineteenth Amendment.

> At an 1869 gathering of the Equal Rights Association Stanton and Anthony urged delegates to repudiate the Fifteenth Amendment because it opened the way for black male suffrage while ignoring women's claims. Because of the situation in the South where black men's votes were vital for survival, most abolitionists, including Frederick Douglass, believed that suffrage for black men should take priority. During the heated debate, angry feminists spoke of "Sambo," the ignorant black man whose rights came before those of "women of wealth, education and refinement." At one point in the debate The President, Mrs. Stanton, argued that not another man should be enfranchised until enough women are admitted to the polls to outweigh those already there. [Applause] She did not believe in allowing ignorant Negroes and foreigners to make laws for her to obey [applause].[6]

Colored women in the pre-suffrage era sometimes challenged their treatment by white leaders but ultimately decided that the segregationist norms of the time that encouraged and provided the environment for such treatment would be their next frontier.[7] Before women's suffrage, colored women had built a strong community tradition among urban blacks, setting up mutual aid societies, self-improvement clubs, temperance societies, churches, schools, and orphanages.[8]

Frances Ellen Harper was the only leading black woman who supported the American Woman Suffrage Association headed by Lucy Stone and Julia Ward Howe (until the two groups merged in 1892). Frederick Douglass's and Frances Harper's words of 1869 were still valid fifty years later. Douglass said that in America, a black woman is victimized "not because she is a woman, but because she is black." Harper felt that for white women, the priorities in the struggle for human rights were "for sex, letting race occupy a minor position."[9]

Elizabeth C. Carter, president of the Northeastern Federation of Women's Clubs (colored), admonished Ida Husted Harper for her arrogance and patronizing testimony, which presumed that black women were not politically sophisticated enough to use NAWSA membership as a strategy to gain the vote. There was dissension among the ranks, as not all black women agreed.

The NAWSA accepted black members but discouraged them from attending the organization's conventions in the South. Adella Hunt Logan, an educator at Tuskegee Institute, attended some anyway, possibly passing for white when she did so. Her biography indicates that she was the daughter of a white planter and mixed-race mother. In the 1890s, educators Anna Julia Cooper (1858–1964), Mary Church Terrell (1863–1954), Mary Murray Washington (1865–1925), and journalist Ida B. Wells (1862–1931) founded women's clubs that helped Negro families migrating to Northern cities. While their focus was helping Negroes specifically, by helping them, they were helping society as a whole. Women of color initiated efforts to advocate for and act on issues that were being ignored by mainstream organizations.

In an attempt to leverage the significance of including women of color, Mary Church Terrell, in her address to the NAWSA, pointed to the accomplishments of colored women and their value to the movement.

The Progress of Colored Women
By
Mary Church Terrell,
President National Association of Colored Women
An Address delivered before the National American Women's Suffrage
Association at the Columbia Theater, Washington, D.C.,
February 18, 1898, on the occasion of its
Fiftieth Anniversary

I hope, that the progress they [colored women] have made and the work they have accomplished, will bear a favorable comparison at least with that of their more fortunate sisters, from the opportunity of acquiring knowledge and the means of self-culture have never been entirely withheld. For, not only are colored women with ambition and aspiration handicapped on account of their sex, but they are everywhere baffled and mocked on account of their race. Desperately and continuously they are forced to fight that opposition, born of a cruel, unreasonable prejudice, which neither their merit nor their necessity seems able to subdue. Not only because they are women, but because they are colored women, are discouragement and disappointment meeting them at every turn.

And so, lifting as we climb, onward and upward we go, struggling and striving, and hoping that the buds and blossoms of our desires will burst into glorious fruition ere long. With courage, born of success achieved in the past, with a keen sense of the responsibility which we shall continue to assume, we look forward to a future large with promise and hope. Seeking no favors because of our color, nor patronage because of our needs, we knock at the bar of justice, asking an equal chance.[10]

The two most notable suffragists thought the opposite. Elizabeth Cady Stanton's language was volatile in her speeches. She often stated that "blacks will take over if you give them the right to vote." Her contemporary Susan B. Anthony, at a NAWSA conference in 1898, used a similar argument that there was an "inconsistency of conferring the right to vote . . . upon the newly emancipated slaves and denying it to the cultivated white women."[11]

In response, Charlotte Forten Grimke wrote a letter to the editor published in the *Washington Post*:

> These expressions [at suffrage meetings] have for years prevented many of us from attending the conventions held in this city. They have disgusted us. I do not hesitate to say that they can only be characterized as contemptable; for their direct effect is to strengthen a most unjust and cruel prejudice; to increase the burdens which already weigh so heavily on a deeply wronged people.[12]

Despite the appeal of women of color to combine efforts, the

> The National American Woman Suffrage Association, having adopted a states' rights policy toward its member organizations in 1903, paved the way for its southern wing to argue the expediency of woman's suffrage in nullifying the intent of the Fifteenth Amendment and buttressing the cause of white supremacy in general.[13]

The 1903 NAWSA Convention Proceedings on the principle of "states' rights" affirms the philosophy of the suffrage movement leadership.

> That this Association, as a national body, recognizes the principle of States rights, and leaves to each State Association to determine the qualification for membership in the Association, and the terms upon which the extension of suffrage to women shall be requested of the respective State Legislatures.[14]

Technically, this meant that state affiliates would have the autonomy to determine qualifications for membership in their clubs and to use whatever arguments they saw fit for suffrage within their territories. In practice, "states' rights" also meant freedom for Southern members to express racist views from NAWSA convention platforms and freedom for

Northern members to announce that the Southerners possessed the right to do so without being controverted.

In *Disfranchisement* by W. E. B. Du Bois, published by the National American Woman Suffrage Association Headquarters in the section on "The Problem of Democracy," Du Bois states:

> There are, however, people who insist on regarding the franchise not as a necessity for the many but as the privilege of the few. They say of persons and classes, "They do not need the ballot." This is often said of women. It is argued that everything that women might do for themselves with the ballot can be done for them; that they have influence and friends "at court," and that their enfranchisement would simply double the number of ballots. So, too, we are told that Negroes can have done for them by others all that they could possibly do for themselves with the ballot, and much more because the whites are more intelligent.[15]

The national leaders of the movement were willing to sacrifice black support to pacify Southerners in an attempt to secure their support.

> With the best will and knowledge no man can know women's wants as well as women themselves. . . . So too with American Negroes: The South continually insists that a benevolent guardianship of whites over blacks is the ideal thing. They assume that white people not only know better what Negroes need than Negroes themselves, but are anxious to supply those needs.[16]

In the early years following suffrage, ideals of racial cooperation and equality were not widely accepted. Few organizations dominated by white women made racial equality a priority, and the League of Women Voters was no exception. Efforts to protect the status quo in Southern customs and institutions presented struggles in the league that paralleled society. Carrie Chapman Catt, Alice Paul, Ida Husted Harper, and other icons of the women's movement added insult to injury by expressing their racist positions in correspondence, segregated marches, and various public statements.

In 1919, the Northeastern Federation of Women's Clubs, a Negro organization, applied for cooperative membership in the NAWSA. Although admitting the federation was eligible for membership, the association begged it to postpone its application temporarily, until the Nineteenth Amendment had been passed and ratified. Writing on behalf of Mrs. Catt, Ida Husted Harper explained to the federation's president:

> Such is the situation. Many of the Southern members are now willing to surrender their beloved doctrine of States' rights, and their only obstacle is

fear of "the colored woman's vote" in the States where it is likely to equal or exceed the white woman's vote . . . The opponents [of the amendment] are not leaving a stone unturned to defeat it and if the news is flashed through-out the Southern states at this most critical moment that the National American Association had just admitted an organization of 6000 colored women, the enemies can cease from further effort—the defeat of the amendment will be assured.[17]

Ida B. Wells-Barnett and Susan B. Anthony clashed over Anthony's will-ingness to indulge the prejudices of white Southern women for the sake of expediency.

Not to be discouraged by the actions of the NAWSA leadership, Mary McLeod Bethune (1875–1955), Charlotte Hawkins Brown (1883–1961), Jane Edna Harris Hunter (1882–1959), and Nannie H. Burroughs (1879–1961), all daughters of former slaves or sharecroppers, led educational and welfare movements to aid black youth. The YMCA supported their efforts by the founding of separate "colored" branches of the organization to develop character-building programs for colored girls. While the move-ment remained overwhelmingly middle-class, white, and native-born, some state organizations, such as those in New Jersey and New York, recognized the need to cross racial, ethnic, and class barriers and actively recruited Negro and immigrant members after 1915.

Catt used the race question frequently. At the Jubilee Convention of the NAWSA in March 1919 in St. Louis, which Catt entitled "The Nation Calls," delegates discussed the question of race and black leaders directed their displeasure toward Southern suffragists like Laura Clay of Kentucky. Convention delegates supported the Nineteenth Amendment, but some agreed that changes should be made in wording to allow the South to determine its own position on the black female electorate. The substantial opposition to the adoption of the Nineteenth Amendment throughout the South was due to the perception of many whites that black women were eager to win the right to vote in the entire region.

Five months before ratification, white supremacists had circulated pro-black woman suffrage articles from black periodicals such as the *New York Age* and *The Crisis* in order to show whites how effective the women's suffrage amendment would be in strengthening the black electorate. As for the women's suffrage leadership, it appears that white women outside of the South used Southern white women's overt prejudice as an excuse for the NAWSA's discriminatory policies while hiding their own similar feelings about black women.[18]

On the eve of the passage of the Nineteenth Amendment, black women had been virtually abandoned by most white female suffragists. Calls for interracial cooperation to assist black women win the vote from leaders such as Josephine St. Pierre Ruffin, Mrs. A. W. Blackwell, Mary Church Terrell, and S. Willie Layton were unheeded.

> The Nineteenth Amendment victory was a shallow one for Black women, an anticlimax especially for those in the South who had dared to believe that winning the vote could enable them to participate in the electoral process.[19]

The transition from the NAWSA to the League of Women Voters was similarly disappointing to women of color. Information about the league's activities encouraged politically minded black women to seek membership in either separate or integrated units; however, they were usually discouraged from joining at all. While there is a growing body of research on the suffragists' activities among black women leaders, very little is known about their political participation in the decade after the ratification of the Nineteenth Amendment. The full meaning of the Nineteenth Amendment would be denied to black women.[20]

> While the ratification of the 19th Amendment immediately and permanently altered the ways in which male politicians responded to the demands of white clubwomen, disenfranchisement ensured that most black women would remain unable to approach their representatives as constituents . . . For the most part, however, organized African-American women had no ballots to leverage. Nevertheless, they did not merely acquiesce to their disenfranchisement. They turned to the Republican Party, the courts and the federal government to demand their rights as citizens.[21]

The National Association of Colored Women's Clubs (NACW) and the National League of Republican Colored Women contributed to the success of the amendment's passage without having their contributions fully acknowledged. Black leaguers had to choose whether to fight for acceptance in the League of Women Voters or use their energy to register and educate voters and improve the lives of people of color through other organizations.

The Nineteenth Amendment blurred the lines of gender and race that were so central to the order of the Jim Crow South. To continue the alliance with women of color and not appear to challenge the culture of segregation, the lines of communication remained open between the NACW and black units of the League of Women Voters. Curiously, league bylaws did not codify the existence of separate leagues for women of color, yet the organization took no stand to clarify its position on this matter. League leaders believed it to be part of a much larger societal conversation.

On a visit to the White House in her capacity as National League of Republican Colored Women president, Nannie Helen Burroughs diplomatically exhibited her disdain for such treatment of women of color as she received greetings from President Calvin Coolidge and Mrs. Coolidge. "I am glad to be able to give a touch of color to this meeting . . . No political party in America is 100 percent American without a touch of color."[22]

Hettie Tilghman, a leader among black California women in the league, referred to the overlap in membership for the NACW and her state's two black leagues, the Alameda County League of Colored Women Voters and the San Francisco Colored League.

While the national leadership of the league was hesitant to take action, some local and state leagues moved to include women of color as equal members. On October 6, 1920, the St. Louis League of Women Voters organized a Colored Committee to bring before the larger body racial concerns related to education, health, child welfare, and citizenship. In an editorial in the *St. Louis American*, Mrs. B. F. (Carrie) Bowles, another black league member and member of the NACW, praised the St. Louis league for being "one of the very few leagues in the U.S. in which colored members enjoy every privilege of the organization on terms of absolute equality."[23] Mrs. Bowles's assessment was correct—very few leagues allowed colored members or treated those who chose to join with the same privilege as white members. The irony is not lost that the league was founded in

Nannie Helen Burroughs (1879–1961). (Library of Congress)

St. Louis and St. Louis had the largest number of Negro

members in its league. St. Louis routinely sent a black delegate to the eight annual conferences of the league.

Mrs. Bowles, who headed the Colored Committee, which functioned as an important liaison between the league and the large black female population in St. Louis, would present a report to the state and national leadership. Under Bowles's direction, the committee assumed a number of projects: providing scholarships to black students, entertaining national league officers at gatherings in the black community, forming junior leagues among

Hettie Blonde Tilghman (1871–1933). (History and Art Collection/Alamy Stock Photo)

black girls, and contributing financially to the budget of the St. Louis league.[24]

On June 18, 1924, Florence Harrison of the national league met with the black members to discuss their plans for the development of citizenship schools. Attached to Harrison's report were the black women's plans for the national Get Out the Vote Campaign. In their appeals to the National Woman's Party and the National League of Women Voters, women of color highlighted the disenfranchisement of women of both races in Southern states.

In 1926, the Illinois State League of Women Voters elected a black woman, Margaret Gainer, to membership on its board of directors. The Douglass League of Women Voters, the black unit of the league in Chicago, was headed by Irene Goins.

On October 11, 1929, Ruth Siemer, executive secretary of the St. Louis league, sent a letter and copy of the report to Miss Gladys Harrison, executive secretary of the National League of Women Voters. She noted that:

The object of the committee in compiling this report was primarily for use as a reminder to delinquents, and former members who had left the league, of the privileges and benefits of membership in the League. It is more in the nature of an appeal than a record of their activities.[25]

Mrs. Bowles presented their report in October 1929. The committee praised the principles of the league but conceded that "of all the many branches of this organization to be found in all parts of the United States, only a few extend the privileges of membership to colored women on terms of absolute equality." Mrs. Bowles recognized the League of Women Voters of St. Louis for being an example of what the league could and should be for women of color. The St. Louis league was notable for having been the first to send a colored delegate to the national convention.

The report of the Colored Committee clearly stated that since its organization on October 6, 1920, the group considered its principle functions to be presenting the city leagues' perspective on racial problems related to education, health care, child welfare, citizenship, or any other issue included in the league program and acting as an intermediary between the organization and the great body of colored women of the city, in order to promote mutual understanding. Mrs. Bowles conveyed that the St. Louis league had "given all possible consideration and assistance with every problem presented."

She noted as accomplishments the schools for citizenship, the lectures on legislative questions of the day, the scholarship given to Miss Virginia Rowan to attend the University of Illinois, hosting national officers, and contributing to the budget of the St. Louis league. At the conclusion of the report, Mrs. Bowles and Mrs. E. C. Grady, who had both attended national conventions, made an appeal to league leadership:

> Surely, this type of work deserves the consideration and assistance of every intelligent colored woman in the city. At one time we were proud to record 300 colored members in the St. Louis League.[26]

From the moment they were enfranchised Southern women, white and black, worked to expand the electorate, seemingly along parallel paths.

> As African American women in the region considered the first ten years of woman suffrage, the power of the ballot was as clear as it was unattainable . . . Thus the effects of the Nineteenth Amendment for southern black women differed not only from southern white women but also from black women elsewhere in the country.[27]

Marguerite Wells, national league president (1934–1944), in reflecting on the first eighteen years, wrote as a subtitle in *A Portrait of the League:* "Acting Together vs. Working Together."

It would be a strange failure on the part of the League of Women Voters if, at the point where political action begins, it were unsuccessful in its relations with people . . . To join with people in action is therefore the final test of political effectiveness. In the area of action people meet: arriving from various directions, they meet, they mingle, and they function—sometimes in opposition, sometimes in accord . . . For those who are working for the same given objective, relationships of course are closer and perhaps more delicate and exacting. . . . Among the League's virtues apparently is that of knowing how to work with people.[28]

Strategic Decisions

Strategic decisions were made "for the sake of the cause" by both black and white suffragists. In the years following the Civil War and the attempt by many to retain the cultural status quo, many white women declared their rights deserved a priority over the issues of race. In her pursuit of equal rights for women, Alice Paul defined Negro women's push for voting rights as a "race"—not a "woman's"—issue.

To attract support in the South, the NAWSA's strategy involved distancing itself from black supporters to avoid offending Southern beliefs while openly suggesting that women's suffrage, especially educated suffrage involving some literacy test, was a way to maintain white supremacy. Since blacks were not allowed by law to read under slavery and the segregated schools provided after emancipation were generally inferior, the ability to pass a literacy test for the majority of them was negligible.

Susan B. Anthony personally did not favor educated suffrage, held liberal views, and treated blacks with dignity and respect. She entertained blacks in her home and often had friendly exchanges about issues related to race and women's rights. When Anthony turned down a request from black women to form their own chapter of NAWSA, Wells-Barnett criticized her, saying, "She might have made gains for suffrage, but she confirmed white women in their attitude of segregation."[29]

Similar snubs arose throughout the history of the NAWSA and well into the evolution of the League of Women Voters. Other organizations discriminated against black clubwomen as well. Although colored leaders expressed concern about the motives of white suffragists, they encouraged others to support the ideas of the women's suffrage argument. In recognizing that women of color needed a political voice in order to bring about change, some encouraged blacks to put aside their fears about the racism apparent among many white woman suffragists and to support the movement for the good of the black race.[30]

Frederick Douglass's profound statement, made in 1866 and again in 1868, when large-scale violence against Negroes gave their enfranchisement an urgency it could not have had for white women, exposed the severity of the tension of the time between race and gender. He declared: "To you, the vote is desirable; to us it is vital."[31]

Henry B. Blackwell, Massachusetts abolitionist and husband of Lucy Stone, published an essay in 1867, "What the South Can Do," containing statistics that showed that there were more white women in the South than there were Negro men and women combined. Hence, the enfranchisement of women would greatly increase the white majority in the electorate and thus ensure white supremacy. This in time became the single most important argument used in the South.[32] Despite the documented accomplishments of black elected officials in the Reconstruction South, anti-Negro suffrage advocates argued that Negro suffrage had proved a failure because of the lack of preparedness of the freedman for political power.

This attitude, while more overt in the South, was also perceptible in activities in the Northern states. The famous suffrage parade in front of the White House, cosponsored in 1913 by the NAWSA and the Congressional Union for Woman Suffrage (National Woman's Party) of Washington, D.C., serves as an example. When Adella Hunt Logan read in the NAWSA newspaper, *The Woman's Journal*, that white women said they could not march in the parade if any black women participated, she immediately went into action to subvert the exclusionary plan. Black leaders of the time believed that white suffragists were racists.[33]

Logan wrote to Mary Church Terrell and other black women suffragists in D.C. encouraging them to march. Logan, Terrell, and other black women took part in the parade, even though they knew it would be segregated. The participants that day included members of the Delta Sigma Theta Sorority, then newly formed at Howard University, just weeks after having dissolved its affiliation with the Alpha Kappa Alpha sorority.

As projected, black suffragists were to be segregated at the back of the parade with one exception. Illinois sent an integrated delegation to the march, but its leader, Grace Trout, acquiesced to the national leaders' insistence that blacks march together in the rear of the parade. Ida B. Wells-Barnett, president of the Alpha Suffrage Club of Chicago, refused to be segregated. Two white women, Belle Squire and Virginia Brooks, supported her but lost the battle. Wells-Barnett left the delegation but stepped out of the crowd of onlookers to rejoin them when the delegation passed in front of her. The *Chicago Tribune* printed a picture of her marching triumphantly between Brooks and Squire.

Spectacular suffrage parade in Washington on the day before President Wilson's inauguration. Before the parade, NAWSA leaders had asked Mrs. Ida B. Wells-Barnett, eminent Chicagoan and president of a suffrage club of Negro women, not to march with the Chicago delegation, since unnamed Southern women had said they would not march in a parade with racially mixed contingents. The request was made publicly during the rehearsal of the Illinois contingent, and while Mrs. Barnett glanced about the room, looking for support, the ladies debated the question of principle versus expediency, most of them evidently feeling that they must not prejudice Southerners against suffrage. Eventually Mrs. Barnett was banished to the Negro women's contingent. She replied that she would march with Illinois or not at all. When the parade began she was nowhere to be seen, but later she quietly stepped out of the crowd of spectators and joined the Illinois ranks. Two white Illinois women then took their places on either side of her, and the rank of the three women finished the parade without incident.[34]

NAWSA was perfectly content to secure the vote without enfranchising any Negroes. The organization had no problem with disenfranchising Negroes if it "proved necessary or feasible."[35] A more succinct analysis of the majority of suffragists' attitude toward this question, states' rights versus Negro suffrage, appeared in a private letter from Walter F. White, NAACP, to Mary Church Terrell on March 4, 1919:

> Just as you say, all of them are mortally afraid of the South and if they could get the Suffrage Amendment through without enfranchising colored women, they would do it in a moment.[36]

The inability of Congress and the NAACP to protect the rights of black

Ida B. Wells-Barnett (1862–1931). (Alpha Historical/Alamy Stock Photo)

women voters led the women to seek help from national white women's suffrage leaders. Not surprisingly, these attempts also failed.

> The racist policies of the National American Women Suffrage Association continued in the 1920s with its successor organization, the League of Women Voters, to discourage black participation. Black women leaders, while organizing their own separate organizations, encountered racism from the very elected officials for whom they campaigned. Yet black women's discontent and frustration with white women's organizations, with the Republican Party, and with a racist society in general during the 1920s translated not into an abandonment of politics but into the emergence of new leaders, alliances, and strategies.[37]

Despite their widespread and concerted efforts to seize the opportunities offered by the Nineteenth Amendment, black women were largely unsuccessful in obtaining access to Southern polls.

> The experiences of black women in the South thus stood as an important counterpoint to the experiences of white women in the region. Despite tentative efforts, organized Southern white women did not use their ballots to demand a sweeping amelioration of conditions for black men or women.[38]

To prevent replication of Southern strategies, political activities varied among black women in other regions of the nation. In the North and the West, black women organized to vote, campaigned for candidates, and ran for public office.

The League of Women Voters turned its focus to welfare and political reforms. No organizations of Southern white women, given this focus, called for an end to Jim Crow in the 1920s. In Atlanta, the League of Women Voters appointed a committee to consult with black leaders about citizenship education for the city's black residents. Annie Blackwell's prediction from North Carolina concluded that white women reformers, once enfranchised, would use their ballots to further white supremacy. As she put it,

> if women of the dominant race had a broader and clearer vision of the Fatherhood of God and the Brotherhood of man, they would exert that influence now in the legislative halls and criminal courts.[39]

Racism and classism in the early twentieth century were evident in all facets of society and were particularly overt in the South. Even as they challenged many aspects of the political status quo, Southern white women embraced elements of the hierarchical social order that benefitted them. "When black women challenged discrimination at the polls, their own representatives, far from treating them like constituents, referred to them as 'nigger' in the Congressional Record."[40]

By seeking their endorsements and inviting them to address state legislative bodies, leading Southern Democrats recognized the voting potential of white women's organizations.

The league was seen as the most influential "white" women's organization of the time.

> The compass guiding the League was the public interest. Of course, this notion is susceptible of differing interpretation, and on most major issues there was a spectrum of opinion among the membership as to the precise policy direction in which public interest pointed. But the very process of consensus formation yielded results that could be claimed as a fair approximation of public interest at any given juncture.[41]

State and local leagues worked within the confines of existing laws in their communities. Southern leagues offered no resistance to the "white primary," and the "poll tax" was not an issue the national organization chose to address.

> For most white women, to be sure, the desire to expand the electorate did clearly end at the color line. League membership throughout the region was restricted to whites only, and newspapers undoubtedly would have taken note if white women's organizations had worked consistently to register black women.[42]

Though met with more courtesy by national leaders of the League of Women Voters, women of color found this organization no more willing to assist black women voters in their legislative causes. Throughout the region, leagues challenged disenfranchisement in the most innocuous manner by opening citizenship schools run by mostly white clubwomen with time to spare. When Mary McLeod Bethune, National Council of Negro Women, started an interracial coalition of women's organizations— the Coordinating Committee for Building Better Race Relations—in the 1930s, the league did not join. Eleanor Roosevelt, an active league member and a later league president from New York, was an individual exception.

Also in the 1930s, many queries were made about the league's work on "Negro problems" and working with Negro women. On March 18, 1930, the league received a list of Negro colleges and universities from the registrar at Howard University that it had previously requested. William M. Cooper, director of the Office of Extension Services at The Hampton Normal and Agricultural Institute, reached out to Belle Sherwin, league president, in April of 1930 offering to assist the league in quantifying these matters.

> Hampton Institute through its extension department stands ready to do whatever it can to promote such programs for Negroes. Your committee may feel free to call for our services whenever the opportunity comes.[43]

He was referring to programs in "vocational efficiency and advancement, methods of saving, wise use of leisure, personal health." There is no indication in league records that the league acted upon this opportunity to collaborate.

Despite the league's inaction, progress for women of color was being made in some political circles. Alice Callis Hunter, who later became the first woman of color to be elected president of a local League of Women Voters in the District of Columbia (1963–1965), won appointment to the Consumer Advisory Committee of the Council of Economic Advisors in the New Deal.

According to the National Association of Colored Women's Clubs, local Leagues of Women Voters sponsored citizenship classes for black women in all Southern states where black women could vote. Tennessee and Virginia were singled out as having successful working relationships. The Tennessee League of Women Voters appointed two prominent Negro clubwomen, Dr. Mattie E. Coleman, "state negro organizer," and J. Frankie Pierce, "secretary of colored suffrage work," to serve as liaisons. Coleman and Pierce were invited to address meetings of white women voters. Their continuous message was, "We are asking only one thing—a square deal."

> League leaders in South Carolina decided not to publish their citizenship course materials "on account of the negro women" fearful that African-Americans would make use of the voter education information to register and vote.[44]

This attitude established the tone for the future of the league's philosophy and its benign reaction to the urgency of acting on issues of race.

Reformists Rather Than Revolutionaries

The conduct of the primarily elite and middle-class women of the NAWSA and later the Congressional Union and the National Woman's

Party signaled the insensitivity toward the plight of women of color. The NWP journal, *The Suffragist*, featured no photographs of women of color from 1914 to 1919, although we know that professional black women like Mary Church Terrell and S. Willie Layton were members. In addition, during the entire six-year period of its publication, there were only two news items referring to positive accomplishments of Negroes in relationship to the woman suffrage movement. There were, however, numerous negative references to "Negroes," such as the cover of a 1917 issue with a cartoon drawn by Congressman John M. Blair.[45]

The practice of making women of color invisible in print and photography reflected the mores, attitudes, and political views of middle-class and elite Americans of the time.

> Black women were either invisible or expendable because they, even more than poor white women, represented a lesser class, which created problems for many of the white women in the women suffrage network.[46]

Many white suffragists believed it was advantageous for the cause to ignore women of color. Black women were feared because whites, especially in the South, believed that black women would vote if given the opportunity. To many suffragists, black women were not worthy of the right to vote. Carrie Chapman Catt believed in conciliation by any means, including urging Southern white women not to attend the 1916 national convention in Chicago because the Chicago delegates would be mostly black.

In 1918, attempting to convince Southern members of Congress to support the Nineteenth Amendment, Catt wrote Representative Edwin Y. Webb from North Carolina:

> The women of New York are now the political equals of the men of New York, but the white women of the South are the political inferiors of the negroes [sic] who can qualify to vote. Upon theory that every voter is a sovereign, the present condition in the South makes sovereigns of some negro [sic] men, while all white women are their subjects.[47]

The question remains, why did the majority of white women in the woman suffrage movement abandon or discriminate against women of color? Perhaps they lacked the multi-consciousness of working class and poor women, who were oppressed because of class, or of women of all classes who were oppressed because of race, if not class.[48]

News of league activities encouraged politically minded black women to seek membership in either separate or integrated units. Contrary to perception, the Southern states were not the only ones dealing with the issues of separate leagues for women of color.

Ohio black women opposed racial separation in league work. Members of the Ohio Federation of Colored Women's Clubs had hoped to integrate various local leagues after Sybil Burton, president of the state league, addressed their meeting and solicited their cooperation in mobilizing the vote. Burton admitted that the Ohio league found it unnecessary to execute educational classes for black women in the state because J. Estelle Barnett, a league member and black woman editor of the newspaper *In the Queen's Garden*, had used her paper to disseminate information on ballot marking and the necessity for voting.[49]

Delilah Beasley of Oakland expressed frustration during her efforts to establish a black league in Los Angeles. She encountered prejudice throughout the state and especially in Los Angeles itself. Beasley, a pioneering reporter and historian on the activities of Negroes for the *Oakland Tribune*, was in constant communication with the league leadership in California and at the national level.

> Although California has not been, as yet, included among the States represented on this special committee, inter-racial work of a very interesting kind has been reported from that State. Mrs. Beazley [sic], a colored delegate to the 1925 convention from Oakland, California has sent several interesting reports of league work among women of her race in California. The Alameda County League operates, apparently, as a distinct unit of colored women members, with official representation on the general board. Mrs. Beasley reports on her efforts to organize the colored women in Los Angeles, and strongly recommends that the negro women be organized as separate units with Board representation, but not as auxiliary members to a white league.[50]

Mrs. Beasley's efforts demonstrated the apprehension of women of color about choosing to use their influence in separate "colored" leagues or continuing to exercise their preference to access membership in the local league. Her conclusion was to urge the formation of "full colored leagues" as auxiliaries to the white leagues in order to get things done. She stressed the need for black women to develop their own leadership separate from whites so that "they *do not antagonize the members of the white league by their presence.*"[51] She communicated frequently with the national leadership about prejudice and the acceptance or lack thereof of Negro members as "full" members.

In excerpts from a letter from Mrs. Beasley to Mrs. Warren W. Wheaton, press secretary of the National League of Women Voters, on March

23, 1926, Mrs. Beasley expressed her frustrations and offered some guidance for consideration by the national leadership to attend to the issue of
race in membership. This letter was placed in the file on the Inter-Racial
Problems Committee, where it had been summarized as "Excerpt from
Letter of Mrs. Delilah Beasley (colored)." Interestingly, it was deemed
necessary to identify her by race.

> The state president of the California League has through my assistance
> and that of my friends finally suceeded [sic] in organizing in Los Angeles a
> Colored Unite [sic] of League of Women Voters. The president Mrs. Char-
> lotte S. Bass, the Editor of the California Eagle is a very dear friend of
> mine. I have written her and said; I would write you and ask you to write
> her welcoming her into the League (at my request) and that I would ask
> you if you would not include her on your mailing list and send her at least
> one of the priciple [sic] addresses delivered at the Press dinner.
>
> I have had a terrible time getting this league going. You see there is a
> great deal of prejudice in this state toward my race. And especially in Los
> Angles [sic]. I have discovered that in cities where there are full Colored
> Leagues and not auxilleries [sic] the colored women develop Leadership.
> They do not antagonize the members of the white league by their presence.
> In this way I hope the league will help solve the race problem. I of course
> expect the colored unite [sic] to have representation on the various boards
> the same as the Alameda County League of which I am a member. But I do
> wish you would suggest to the President Miss Sherwin, that if she will
> recommend [sic] the organizing of all Colored Leagues and no auxilleries
> [sic] I believe it will save future trouble. It will also train Negro Leadership
> among colored women to that extent that scheming politicians will no
> longer have a chance to exploit their vote.[52]

Mrs. Wheaton's response to Mrs. Beasley's letter indicated support for her
efforts and pledged advocacy with the appropriate members of the
national leadership. Wheaton also replied, "As for a list of colored auxiliaries or Leagues, I am not quite sure I can furnish you that, because we
have no record in this office. I will let you know further about it."[53]

The number and content of the communications forwarded to the
national leadership showed the need for increasing clarity and guidance.
Excerpts from an April 25, 1927 letter from Eva Nichols Wright from the
seventh district to President Belle Sherwin is representative of the correspondence. In preparation for the general council meeting that was to
occur from April 26 to April 30, Mrs. Wright outlined the results of a
questionnaire she had forwarded to "key women interested in the political welfare of colored women voters in a number of northern and western

Delilah Beasley. (Courtesy of the California Historical Society)

states having a large colored population." Her conclusions were that in response to the questions about the interest of colored women for membership in the League of Women Voters and the extent to which white and colored women worked together, the negative replies were discouraging.

In order, therefore, that the women of color in these United States may not encounter a similar fate of political exploitation which colored men have suffered for over a half century, it is very earnestly hoped that The League of Women Voters will actively cooperate with the educated forward looking women of color and grant them unintermittent [sic] recognition and full participation in their programs.[54]

She requested that this important matter be brought to the attention of the council "to the end that some definite action may be taken that will encourage and hearten many intelligent colored women who will prove an appreciable asset if afforded fair opportunity to work with the National League of Women Voters."[55] A response on behalf of President Sherwin was sent to Mrs. Wright on May 5, 1927. The response did not directly resolve her question about colored women joining the league. She was thanked for her input, and her letter was forwarded to the chairperson of the Inter-Racial Problems Committee for further response. One element of the response was of particular interest.

There is a committee of the Council of the League of Women Voters which has each year since 1921 met in conference with representatives of your people and which has prompted work toward the end which you so rightfully emphasize is needed. We most sincerely wish that we might have done more, but I assure you we never lost sight of that need as a part of the obligations of the League of Women Voters.[56]

There was no record of any additional follow-up.

In documents stored in the league files from the 1920s, several league organizational issues were discussed: college leagues, city leagues, state convention attendance, post-convention board meeting, and colored leagues. Excerpts from the minutes from the Conference of the Department of Organization on Colored Leagues, December 14, 1927, offer insight into the conversation on this issue.

Mrs. Anderson Chairman reported that since April of that year, there had been four requests in her league for the organization of new colored leagues. She acknowledged that at present there were known to exist three colored leagues in California, one in Chicago, and one in St. Louis, and there was one in Tacoma, Washington. "It was agreed that difficult situations are likely to arise from time to time because of such Leagues and that, should they increase in number, and the physical difficulties such as finding meeting places would constitute a serious question."

She reminded the leaders that at the previous council, it had been decided that it was not desirable to encourage the organization of colored leagues, "but that the educational goal which is desired can better be promoted by classes in other work among colored women, without formal organization."[57]

The decision to discourage colored leagues gave no real explanation for the league's condoning separate leagues through their silence, nor did it indicate that women of color were welcome to "full" league membership. Local and state leagues consistently asked for guidance from the national leadership. Their response was intentionally ambiguous.

The complication of the establishment and existence of colored leagues continued throughout the decade, as reflected in a 1928 letter to the national board from Ohio. Ohio black women opposed racial separatism in league work. With no uniform guidelines, Agnes Hilton, president of the state league, preferred to leave the decision of accepting blacks to the individual leagues, whose racial policies varied by community. Oberlin accepted blacks freely and equally. Zanesville received black members but made them unwelcome at their luncheons and other social gatherings. The Toledo league sought independent advice from the national league when black women desired membership. The general consensus of the Toledo league was against integration, but the league encouraged black women to form their own separate units. The Cincinnati league likewise contemplated the formation of an all-black unit. The reply from the national league tended to be discouraging in every way, while acknowledging that a few of the states had black leagues and a few others actually integrated individual black women into their ranks.

Mrs. Hilton expressed concerns about the lack of guidance being provided by the national board. She articulated the sentiments of the Ohio leadership.

> We are a little troubled as to what is the best thing to do in regard to the colored people, and therefore would like to have any information from you as to what the National league advises. I suppose conditions being so different in the different states you may prefer to have each state League work it out in the way it thinks wisest, and even different Leagues in one state may adopt different methods. If you have any suggestions to offer us, we will be very grateful to you for them.[58]

Ann Williams Wheaton, press secretary, responded to Hilton's query on behalf of the national board on August 17, 1928.

> You are right in believing that the situation in every state has governed the kind of affiliations colored women have made with the state organizations. There are a very few states that have colored Leagues and there are a very few which permit colored women to join as individual members.
>
> It is my understanding that those who have had experiences in this matter believe it is far better not to encourage organizations of colored Leagues. It has been found that the educational work of the League can be better promoted by classes and other work among colored women, than by formal organization.[59]

The contents of the verbatim minutes of the 1928 council meeting show the ideological discussions that were still being had about the league, its membership, and the issue of race among its ranks. It is recorded that a "Negro" attended the council meeting in 1928 and that she contributed "materially." This representation of the role of "Negro" women as contributing members to the league contradicted earlier assertions that women of color did not possess the intellectual acuity to be league members.

As required by the national board, the Special Committee on Inter-Racial Problems provided their annual progress report to council attendees. The topic of segregation was not undertaken, but rather how Negro women could make a difference with Negro institutions. The committee wanted to be sure that everyone knew it was a responsibility of all committees to fulfill the responsibilities of the committee charges. Detailed in the verbatim minutes of the general council meeting of 1928 was the report on the ability of the Inter-Racial Committee to gain traction. Miss Adele Clark, chairman, provided the report. In her introduction, she indicated the committee had been a committee of the council and not the convention since 1921 because leadership thought that "its most interesting subject matter is that which concerns us as a family, rather than the public as a whole." Miss Clark reported that the committee had gained actual membership, with nine states having appointed members. During the 1927 council meeting, a meeting of the special committee was attended by representatives from Alabama, Florida, Georgia, Louisiana, Mississippi, North Carolina, Tennessee, Virginia, Maryland, New York, Ohio, Illinois, and Missouri.

To assess the impact of its work, the committee sent a questionnaire to all participating states, inquiring about the value of the committee's program. Answers were received from a number of states, showing that cooperation between state and local leagues with other groups working along interracial lines was in effect in several sections, especially in the field of public welfare and legislation.

To affirm the committee's momentum and impact, Miss Clark reported that "The Committee endeavored this year, to hold a more formal conference, and on yesterday met for a conference, with women of both races appointed by the various State Leagues."[60] This marked a change from the committee's previous work, whose conferences were usually composed of people who happened to be present, as these were women of both races who had been appointed by the states leagues to attend. Missouri, Illinois, Virginia, North Carolina, and Tennessee were represented, and there were also representatives from several of the other states, eighteen persons being present in total. Miss Clark was pleased to note that for the first time a "negro woman from one of the southern states (Virginia) was present."[61] It should be noted that Miss Clark was President of the League of Women Voters of Virginia.

It was during this council meeting that the committee requested that the word *Problems* be officially changed to *Relations*. In justifying the request, Miss Clark stated, "It seems a small thing, but it has a good deal of significance to members of the negro race."[62] Another major request from the committee was that all other league committees become cognizant of their individual responsibility of interracial implications; the responsibility did not reside solely with the Committee on Inter-Racial Relations.[63]

After the report, Miss Clark moved that the name be changed from "Inter-Racial Problems" to "Inter-Racial Relations." The motion was seconded by Mrs. Williams of Tennessee. The motion was carried, reflecting recognition of the volatility of referring to race as a "problem." The committee recognized through its work, or lack thereof, over the years that *relations* was a better word.

Because of the league's reputation and recognition by other advocacy and education organizations of its Committee on Inter-Racial Relations, on December 7, 1928, President Sherwin received an invitation from Mary Van Kleeck, from the Russell Sage Foundation and chairman of the Executive Committee for the National Interracial Conference, which was to be held on December 17, 18, and 19 at Howard University. The National Interracial Conference was sponsored by sixteen organizations and attended by delegates from social welfare agencies, interracial organizations, and colleges and universities throughout the country. The theme of the conference was "Race Relations in the United States in the Light of Social Research."

> For a year, social studies and official statistics have been in process of analysis in order to present to the Conference a picture of contemporary Negro life as it affects both the white and colored races in the United States. The purpose is to increase the effectiveness of the work which is being done to improve these conditions and relationships.[64]

The presiding officers were Dr. R. R. Moon of Tuskegee Institute and President Mordecai W. Johnson of Howard University. Sponsoring organizations were the American Friends Service Committee, Interracial Section, American Social Hygiene Association, Committee on Interracial Cooperation, Council of Women for Home Missions, Federal Council of Churches, Commission on Race Relations, Fellowship of Reconciliation, The Inquiry, National Association for the Advancement of Colored People, National Catholic Welfare Conference, National Board YWCA, National Council for YMCA, National Federation of Settlements, National Urban League, Phelps-Stokes Fund, Protestant Episcopal Church, and Department of Christian Social Service.[65]

Despite engaging in opportunities to expand its presence and reputation as a concerned entity, by the end of the decade, the League of Women Voters had lost, largely by its own choice, the potential for being an important mobilizing force among black women.[66]

In 1938, the league abolished its system of regional directors, signaling a change toward a more centralized accountability. Marguerite Wells's

A Portrait of the League took what she called a "candid camera" look at the organization.

> The important question for the League to consider is not whether it is all that it is described as being, but whether and why it has failed, where and how has it succeeded, and is it willing to do those things that will halt failure and promote success.[67]

To confirm her remarks, Wells set out to solicit what others were saying about the league. She spoke with "random" observers rather than those sympathetic observers. She got comments from legislators, congressmen, political scientists, experts in civil administration, mayors, governors, civil service commissioners, businessmen, university directors, men, and women. Wells emphasized the importance of receiving feedback from a wide range of individuals and groups, not just those who had proved to be friends of the league. Throughout the treatise, there is no mention of the impact of race on the organization, its membership, or its operation, even though there was conversation about the league working in cooperation with other organizations.[68]

The National League of Women Voters had 556 local leagues in thirty-one affiliated state leagues as of April 1940. There were also twenty-nine college leagues. Standards for state organizations required adherence to league policies for certain fundamental methods of work, as well as a minimum number of members and the establishment of local leagues. There was no mention of "colored leagues" or the fact that there were any organizational policies or practices about separation by race.

Many black women chose to fight disenfranchisement through non-partisan, rather than partisan, organizations. Black women worked with the NAACP, for example, to establish citizenship schools. In Birmingham, the Colored Women Voters League was established. Across the region, Southern black women staged registration drives, provided citizenship information to would-be voters, and encouraged Negroes to make application at the polls without reference to partisan politics. All of these actions operated parallel to the league's efforts because colored leaguers were not considered full members and were therefore unable to leverage the complete resources of the league for their cause. Membership in the leagues throughout the South was restricted to whites only, and almost no league members were interested in helping Negro women obtain access to the ballot box.[69]

In 1944, the U.S. Navy started accepting black women into the WAVES. The league's philosophy on integration did not correspond. At the 1944 convention, the League of Women Voters underwent its first major reorganization since its founding. The name was changed from the National League to the League of Women Voters of the United States. It took effect in 1946. The organization recognized and stated emphatically that members were the league's most valuable asset, giving the organization clout, visibility, and credibility. This recognition, however, did not stress the inclusion of women of color. All public-facing documents intentionally flaunted only white women as representative of the organization.

An internal memorandum to the national board and staff from President Strauss (dated December 28, 1945) interpreting certain sections of the proposed bylaws, specifically at-large members, had a profound effect on the internal practice of the establishment and maintenance of "colored" leagues, which in fact did not exist, according to league bylaws. The "colored leagues" were, in fact, technically "units" of their local leagues and operated under their direct guidance.

> Only one local League in each community shall be recognized by the Board of Directors. The Board interprets this section to mean that there shall be not more than one local League in each unit of government in which the League can be active in more than one field of interest. Where possible this shall be the municipality. In other words the Board contemplates the existence of only one local League in a city or town but not in a county.[70]

Despite its attestations of the importance of members, when the league received a request from Ohio State University to conduct research on women's organizations and their information on women of color as members, the league's response was to minimize the importance of keeping data on members of color.

The 1950s witnessed an organization hesitant to take a national stand on race. While outside organizations recognized the power of the league to effect change in society, they were confused by the league's lack of interest in dealing with race both internally as an organization and in society. Percy Maxim Lee presided as president during the league's ambivalence toward racially integrating its internal operations in the 1950s. She rationalized avoidance of inviting blacks to join by noting:

> The League cannot be a law onto itself . . . It must not run too fast for its contemporaries of the American electorate to keep up. . . . It must in other words want the things that other "reasonable" American citizens want, edging a maximum diversity toward progressive goals.[71]

Through most of its history, the league made deliberate efforts to avoid alienating mainstream voters or, even worse, members to expand potential impact. Though difficult to assess positively by contemporary values, Lee's civil rights strategy was not unusual for the time, positioning the league in what she perceived to be the mainstream, perhaps in the hope that it could thereby progress the nation's attitudes gradually and with less opposition. She emphasized practicality over principle.

A letter was received in the national office on August 10, 1953, from John L. Clark, political analyst for *The Pittsburgh Courier*, one of the country's most widely circulated black newspapers, with a circulation of about 200,000. The *Courier* called for improvements in housing, health, and education in Pittsburgh and elsewhere in the nation, ideals the league espoused and should have supported. Mr. Clark indicated that in his travels in the eleven Deep Southern states over the past ten years, he had received conflicting information; he'd been told that there were local league units that accepted Negro women as members and that there were many instances in which Negro women never applied for membership. Upon asking for clarification, he was advised by Mrs. Albert Simons, president of the Charleston, South Carolina, league to seek clarification from the national leadership on national policy. He learned from Mrs. Simons that the Charleston league had between fifteen and twenty Negro women as members. He was working from the conclusions of his finding that disclosed that "Negro women in the south are not as active in government and politics as they are in northern cities and states."

> Knowing that the League of Women Voters supplies factual information that men and women should have, study and understand, I would like to have the official policy in regards to Negro women as members and permission to publish same.[72]

There was no record of the response to Mr. Clark's inquiry, but that does not mean that one was not provided. A handwritten note was attached to the letter, stating, "Hasn't this been answered?"

On August 11, 1953, the national leadership published a guide for state and local leagues entitled *How to Get and Keep Members*. This guide prompted many questions regarding the inclusion of women of color. The membership chairman of the Knoxville, Tennessee, league sent questions to the national office regarding Negro membership. The letter seems to indicate that they were genuinely interested in having black members, but the underlying assumptions—that Negro women who wished to join the league were uneducated and that they would need to be "taught"—are disturbing. Because of the customs and practices of segregation, even educated women of color were often relegated to domestic and unskilled work. The intent of the letter appears innocent but reinforces why the league was not viewed as an organization that welcomed black women for their value to the organization.

> The membership committee in Knoxville has made plans, in general adopted from the suggestions made in "How to Get and Keep Members," to expand the membership in Knoxville and Knox County. However, we have a problem on which we need some guidance . . . We have a large group of Negro women who do domestic work or other unskilled jobs. They are not formally educated but they do vote and are keenly interested in politics. One of their leaders is a league member. She wants to start a unit in her neighborhood. The problem, of course, is whether there is a place in the league for persons or a group of persons of no education. Our speakers at their meetings find that league language seems very complicated to such a group. We would like to believe that the league can do an educational job for such groups, but we are lacking in know how and in woman power. Do you have any material and have you had any experiences that can be useful to us? How do we find a spot for these women so that they can become effective league members as well as benefited by membership in it?[73]

The letter, stamped June 1, 1954, had a handwritten note stating, "Good question." The organizational secretary for the national league responded.

> Your letter poses an interesting question, one which we often ask ourselves. We say the League should be a cross-section organization, but can it really be? Our belief is that it can but it takes "working at it."[74]

This response, as was typical of the national office, did not address the issue but relied on its policy and practice to leave such matters to state and local affiliates.

The national leadership was keenly aware of the impact of the absence of their guidance on membership issues and women of color. Their attempts to justify their actions and/or inactions, per league policy and practice, needed to be supported with data. In a memo to state league presidents, Mrs. Lee outlined the premise of a survey of league membership to be conducted by the University of Michigan in 1955.

> For the past eighteen months the League has been cooperating with the Survey Research Center, Institute of Social Research, University of Michigan, in a study of the League. The study has been financed by the Schwartzhaupt Foundation. Its objective has been to learn more about the interests, backgrounds, and personalities of League members, and to learn more about the operation of individual leagues.[75]

Despite the collection of data that clearly identified the characteristics of league members, the national leadership continued to give ambiguous responses. In response to a query on the demographics of membership (dated December 10, 1958), the customary reply was given.

> According to the By-Laws of the League of Women Voters of the United States, any person who subscribes to the "purpose and policy" of the League is eligible for membership. Voting members are women citizens of voting age. Women who are not citizens, and men, can become associate members. We have no way at all of knowing how many Leagues in the South—or anywhere in the country—have Negro members. Since no records are kept that would indicate race, the only way one could know would be by personal knowledge. I know there are some Negro women in my own League—Virginia and I know there are some in the District of Columbia League.[76]

The 1960s and 1970s would find an organization still attempting to adhere to its principles and the leadership's dictates while struggling to determine the league's relationship with its members of color as a matter of practice. On rare occasions, such as during the early civil rights era, the national leadership exhibited conservative, hesitant tendencies in comparison to local league activists, who privately challenged national policies on matters like civil rights. Programs adopted by delegates at league conventions did not reflect issues of race, even though they enthusiastically took on controversial global issues. Some advocates termed the league as staid and conservative in relation to the national leadership's racial blinders prior to the 1960s.

> The commitment corollary to League membership suggested a profile for the typical participant that was confirmed by data collected in a League self-study just after its fiftieth birthday. She was a woman in her most active years: in 1972, 54 per cent were from thirty to forty-nine years old and another 21 percent were in their fifties. She was well educated: 68 percent had a college education, and nearly 40 percent had pursued some graduate training. She was married: 85 percent; only 2 percent were

divorced or separated, and 5 percent had never married. Her husband was generally a professional of some description. Only 25 per cent held a full time job.[77]

The changing sociological profile of American society as a whole had important implications for the league. The rapid entry of women into the labor market in the postwar years suggested a challenge in sustaining levels of membership and strength of activity. By failing to acknowledge the same characteristics in women of color, the league relegated them to a single monolithic stereotype in terms of membership.

Rather than being substantiated with data, the prevailing philosophy was entrenched in the organization's cultural assumptions of the past that there were no middle-class and upper-class educated blacks, that all blacks were poverty-stricken, and that only those with disposable income could be of value to a grassroots organization such as the league. The shifting composition of large city populations affected urban leagues, as large elements of the middle class migrated to the suburbs in the postwar period.

> The life circumstances of poverty-stricken women militated against League involvement. The disproportionate numbers of minority group women falling in this category made it difficult for League action to attract members from these sectors of society.[78]

Contrary to these assumptions, the league's own history supports that there were well-educated, middle- and upper-class Negroes whose sole exclusionary attribute to maximum participation or recognition by the organization was race.

Conclusion

Despite the obstacles black women and men endured during the struggle for women's suffrage within the NAWSA, they chose to persist in their pursuit of equality with its successor, the League of Women Voters. This relationship was more transactional than transformational for the organization and the members of color. During the period from 1920 to 1960, grassroots activism of women of color provided a staging ground for the explosive changes in the 1960s. Daily assaults on their civil rights hardened their resolve to effect change for the sake of the cause.[79]

Barbara Stuhler captured this organizational dynamic in her history of the league. Her lifelong membership and leadership in the organization allowed her a unique perspective of its operation. This perspective is illuminated in her summary of the league's lack of action on the issue of race and the factors that should have allowed it to be more proactive. She specifically called attention to American Indians and Negroes and the fact that the league was not interested in having either group as members, but instead in changing some governmental entity impacting the groups.

> The League attracted as members women who were well educated, middle class, and progressive in their thought. There were, of course, variations on the theme: some members were rich, some poor; some despite their station in life, became active in the League because of their frustrations with the way things were; a few became members as a means of expressing their new citizenship. The League was not—to use a contemporary term—multicultural. . . . The League was interested not in recruiting Indian women as members but to determine how best to improve the administration of Indian Affairs.
>
> In the same vein, the League formed a Committee on Negro Problems, later changed at the request of black members to the Committee on Interracial Problems. . . . The League appeared to be less interested in recruiting African-Americans as members than addressing issues that might improve their social and economic circumstances.
>
> In recent years even though the League has embarked on a course of action that has succeeded in diversifying its membership in terms of age . . . its gender, and its ethnic and racial composition, the membership has remained in large part, white, middle-class, middle-aged, female. One significant sign of that success was the election in June 1998 of Carolyn Jefferson-Jenkins of Colorado, the first African American president of the LWVUS.[80]

Cautious optimism reflected the tenacity of the women of color who continued to affiliate with the League of Women Voters. They hoped that the future of the organization would be guided by what leaders learned from the *lessons of the hour.*

Notes

1. Sterling, 1984, 411.
2. Ibid., 410–411.
3. Cashin, 2012, 4.
4. Higginbotham, 1997, 148–151.
5. Ibid.
6. Sterling, 1984, 414–415.
7. Dodson, 2017, 254.
8. Perry, 1995, 14.

9. Terborg-Penn, 1998, 132.

10. Hampson, 2004, 8, 15; Terrell, 1898, 8, 15.

11. Gordon et al., 1997, 5.

12. Ibid.

13. Schuyler, 2006, 136.

14. Kraditor, 1981, 59.

15. Du Bois, 1912, 9.

16. Ibid.

17. Kraditor, 1981, 214–215.

18. Terborg-Penn, 1998, 121.

19. Ibid., 12.

20. Schuyler, 2006, 135.

21. Ibid., 8–9.

22. Gordon et al., 1997, 146.

23. Ibid., 148.

24. Ibid., 148.

25. Ibid., 63.

26. Library of Congress Files, n.d., "League of Women Voters, Problems, Inter-Racial Committee 1928–1934."

27. Schuyler, 2006, 9.

28. Wells, 1962, 14.

29. Dodson, 2017, 253; Giddings, 2006, 253.

30. Terborg-Penn, 1998, 134.

31. Kraditor, 1981, 167. This paraphrase and its implications may be found in Benjamin Quarles's "Frederick Douglass and the Women's Rights Movement," *Journal of Negro History* 25, no. 1 (January 1940): 39–41.

32. Kraditor, 1981, 168.

33. Terborg-Penn, 1998, 121–122.

34. Kraditor, 1981, 213.

35. Kraditor, 1981, 216.

36. Ibid., footnote 96.

37. Higginbotham, 1997, 148–151.

38. Schuyler, 2006, 185.

39. Ibid., 186.

40. Ibid., 221.

41. Young, 1989, 178.

42. Schuyler, 2006, 133.

43. Library of Congress Files. From "*A Decade of League Work*," Tenth Annual Convention.

44. Ibid.

45. Terborg-Penn, 1998, 141–142.

46. Terborg-Penn, 1998, 134.

47. Ibid., 127; Catt letter to Webb.

48. Ibid., 132.

49. Gordon et al., 1997, 150.

50. Library of Congress. League of Women Voters, File Special Committee, Box II, 188.

51. Gordon et al., 1997, 149.

52. Library of Congress Box II, 188, received in League Office March 29, 1926, referred to A. W. The *Tribune* was founded February 21, 1874, by George Staniford and Benet A. Dewes. Mrs. Beasley had a weekly column on the Negro community and was its only black columnist at the time.

53. Library of Congress Inter-Racial Committee Box I, 293.

54. Ibid.

55. Ibid.

56. Ibid.

57. Library of Congress C3 Confidential, 20.

58. Library of Congress Special Committee Box I:50.

59. Ibid.

60. Ibid., Excerpt from the Verbatim Minutes of the General Council, 1928.

61. Ibid.

62. Ibid.

63. Library of Congress Special Committee on Inter-Racial Relations Box I, 293, 1–5.

64. Library of Congress Special Committee on Inter-Racial Problems Letter to Belle Sherwin, 1928, December 7.

65. LWV Papers, 1928.

66. Higginbotham, 1997, 150.

67. Wells, 1962, 6.

68. Ibid., 3.

69. Schuyler, 2006, 61.

70. League of Women Voters Papers.

71. Cashin, 2012, 85.

72. Library of Congress Special Committee Folder Box II:188; *The Pittsburgh Courier* was once the country's most widely circulated black newspaper, with a national circulation of about 200,000. It was established in 1907 by Edwin Harleston. From the beginning, *The Courier* called for improvements in housing, health, and education and protested the slum conditions in which black people were forced to live in Pittsburgh and elsewhere in the nation.

73. Library of Congress Special Committee Folder Box II, 188.

74. Library of Congress Integration Folder Box I, 293.

75. Library of Congress Special Committee Folder.

76. Ibid.

77. League of Women Voters Papers, The Report of the Findings of the League Self Study, 1975, 4–6.

78. Young, 1989, 157.

79. Perry, 1995, 24.

80. Stuhler, 2000, xiv.

CHAPTER FOUR

The Lessons of the Hour

If we learn from the experience, there is no failure, only delayed victory.

—Carrie Chapman Catt

The most robust files in the league archives are those that chronicle the history of the Special Committee on the Study of Negro Problems, ultimately named the Special Committee on Inter-Racial Relations, through its various iterations. While the cause of universal suffrage brought women of all races together in an attempt to sustain the efforts of achieving the vote, it did not strengthen that unity, particularly because of the league's ambivalence toward confronting organizational issues of race. There were lessons to be learned at each stage of the organization's evolution as it tackled the problem. The most aggressive activity was revealed in the discussions that took place between state and local leagues and the national leadership during the evolution of the special committee.

One of the most important lessons the league learned through the existence of the special committee was that as a grassroots membership organization, its dependence on members unmistakably impacted individuals as well as the organization. Leaguers' correspondence with the national leadership exposed a distinct divergence on issues of race. Insight into these conversations set the tone for what was to be in the future. Race was an emotional and personal issue. In an attempt to mitigate controversy, the league adhered to established processes to respond to any challenges. This chapter provides the opportunity to garner an authentic sense of the dialogue involved in the decision-making.

The controversy, compromise, and ultimate attempts at collaboration that manifest the league's position on its relationship with its members of color were initiated at the 1921 national convention held in Cleveland, Ohio, by black women who brought their complaints about disenfranchisement before the league. Although some white Southern suffrage leaders had refused to join the league, those Southern delegates at the 1921 convention threatened to walk out if the "Negro problem" was debated.[1]

Characteristic of league responses to what could be perceived as a challenge to internal accord, a compromise resulted wherein the colored women were allowed to speak before the body,

Three women at polling place. (Library of Congress)

but no formal action was taken by the organization. In executive action at the close of convention, the national leadership addressed the issue by establishing the Special Committee on the Study of Negro Problems.

Moved	By Mrs. Salley that the following resolution presented by her Region be adopted as amended by them:
	That a Special Committee shall be formed for the purpose of studying the problem in those States, having fifteen percent or over negro population. This Committee shall be composed of a Chairman appointed by the Board of the National League and a representative from each of the afore-said states, said representative to be chosen by the State Boards.
	It shall be the duty of this Committee to report to the National Board of the League of Women Voters before the next Convention.
Moved	That the Board be requested to authorize the aforesaid committee if possible without bringing the question to the

floor of the convention, and if they feel that the appointment of such committee is beyond their province that they
hand it to the resolutions committee.[2]

The board chose to appoint the committee without bringing it to the floor.
Its charge was amorphous, but the expectation was that the league would
"study" the issue. League studies generally took two years. By relying on its
process of "study," the national leadership could postpone addressing any
contention in the moment. There was a lack of clarity as to whether the committee was to address all Negro problems or the Negro problem in the league.
The fact that its title was "Negro problems" reinforced many of the prevailing
attitudes that anything related to Negroes was a problem. The term *problem*
has its own connotations, depending on the genesis of the conversation.

For the league to acquiesce to the conviction that problems of race
were separate and apart from other societal problems reflected the organization's broader thinking on segregation. The establishment of the Special
Committee served as an appeasement to Southern black women whose
suffrage rights were denied while acknowledging the requests of Southern white women to not prioritize the issue of race. Through such actions,
by the end of the decade, the League of Women Voters' commitment to
the cause of black women became doubtful.

Extensive correspondence between the national leadership and leaders
and members of the Special Committee on Negro Problems gives us
insight into the thinking of the league leadership on a critical issue for the
organization and exposes the difficulty the league had in contending with
how to move forward with this issue. To use the league's study process
only delayed the national league from actually formulating a position and
a course of action, while many local and state leagues were already
involved in their communities. Records indicate that there were no Negro
members appointed to the committee.

The lack of any sustainable progress is unmistakably detailed in the
decades of reports of the work of the Special Committee. A letter from
Adele Clark raised several interesting points for league leadership to consider in undertaking this study because of the perception it presented for
leagues not interested in integrating, especially Southern leagues. More
importantly, because of the ambiguity of the process of establishing the
committee, she asked for clarification on the committee's charge, the lim-
itation of the committee to those states that had 15 percent or more Negro
population, and the image of this study as being imposed from outsiders
or "Negroes themselves."

Virginia League of Women Voters
Miss Adele Clark, Chairman
Richmond, Virginia

May 21, 1921

Mrs. Maud Wood Park,
President, National League of Women Voters,
Munsey Building, Washington, D.C.

My dear Mrs. Park:

For some time I have wanted to write you with regard to the committee for the purpose of studying the race problem in our States having a large percentage of negro population. I feel that this was one of the most vital and far-reaching pieces of work accomplished at the convention, not only because it proved that women of the North and of the South can work together with sympathy and consideration of each other's view-point—however divergent—upon this vexed question, but because every phase of the work of the league, social or political, and every piece of work undertaken by the standing committees is affected in States of mixed population by the race problem. I believe that the serious study on the part of our women of the conditions and problems will go far toward finding some solution and adjustment.

Because of my intense interest in this particular development of our work, I am anxious for you to know how we feel in Virginia upon this matter; and because Virginia's view-point differs necessarily from South Carolina's upon many points involved, I wish without any disloyalty to Mrs. Salley, to say to you directly and confidentially just what is my position with regard to lowering the percentage, and with regard to announcing that the resolution asking for the appointment or formation of such committee originated in the 3rd or Southern region.

First: It was my idea, and that of Mrs. Dudley of Tennessee and Miss Morris of Louisiana, who helped compose the text of the resolution, that if possible it be so drawn as to admit States outside the South, Illinois, Indiana, New York, Missouri and Ohio being specifically mentioned in the discussion of the Third Region at the time that the above mentioned women and I were asked to put into writing the motion I had made that the National Board be asked to form such a committee. Personally, I was not familiar with the statistics as to percentage of population, and was under the impression that we were bringing several States outside of the South into this special study committee. I entertain the strong conviction that the wisest course for both North and South to pursue is to cease regarding the negro problem as a sectional one. It is in fact no longer so:

the main difference seems to be that in the North it is more of an urban problem, in the South more of a rural one.

For that reason it has occurred to me that we may be able to draw into the committee the Northern and middle Western States which it seems so desirable to include by so altering the text of the resolution under which the committee will work as to read: "those States having 15% or over of negro population, or containing cities having that percentage of negro population."—and I so wrote last night.

Under the 1910 census I am afraid this will not reach the desired results: and I am earnestly hoping that the 1920 census figures are by now available for our use. Personally I have no objection to lowering the percentage to 10%, or any reasonable figure.

I think that the work of the committee would not be so effectual if the percentage were very low—i.e. so low as to have a *majority* of the State[s] included outside of the South. The psychology of the case is so peculiar, there is such extreme sensitiveness on the part of the South upon anything that savors of outside interference, that the very purposes of frank and conscientious study might be thwarted if it were felt that the questions might be decided by States where the problem is not so acute.

The next point I wished to bring to your attention was that it seems to me that the most desirable method of bringing this committee to the attention of members of the League is to state that the resolution was adopted by the Board, or perhaps I should put it that the committee was created by the Board upon the request of the Third Region. I was a little disappointed to note that in the recent bulletin sent out from headquarters the fact that the Third or Southern Region desired this committee to be formed was not mentioned, but rather the impression was given that the committee was appointed more as a result of the request of the colored women than as an outcome of the desire of the Southern women to make a study and survey of the situation.

I am certain that the effect in the South of our initiating this move in our Region will be infinitely better for both white and colored than if it were to be thought that the impulse for its formation came from the outside or from negroes themselves. The psychology of the South is such that if we can arouse the feeling of "Noblesse oblige" toward the negro great good may be accomplished.

And the negroes themselves will, I think, be encouraged by our wishing to help, in fact they are very much gratified here when we call on them for conference.

We felt in the Regional discussions that the two most important items to the South were covered by this action—namely, that we were doing this ourselves, and not having anything "put over on us", and that due regard was being paid to the States as units by having the personnel of the committee selected by each State.

Cordially yours,
Adele Clark[3]

In a second letter of the same date, Mrs. Clark wrote to Mrs. Park in anticipation of a committee meeting that was to occur May 23 or 26, 1921, asking for an adjustment to the adopted resolution creating the Special Committee.

> As to the race problem committee, it occurs to me that it might be well, if the new census reports do not show a sufficient percentage of negroes in the State population to include Missouri, Illinois, New York, Ohio, or Indiana for instance, to so amend the resolution by which the committee was created as to read:
> Resolved: That a special committee shall be formed for the purpose of studying the problems in those States having 15% or over of Negro population, or containing cities having that percentage of negro population.
> I am willing also to have the percentage reduced. And hope the new census reports will be available.[4]

She asked that the letter also be delivered to Mrs. Salley.

On October 17, 1921, the board published a list of the states entitled to representation on the committee: North Carolina, South Carolina, Georgia, Florida, Alabama, Louisiana, Mississippi, Tennessee, Virginia, District of Columbia, and Maryland. Kentucky was excluded because it did not meet the 15 percent threshold, and Kentucky leaders indicated that they were having no problems integrating women of color into their leagues. There was extensive conversation about whether the chairman should be a Northerner or a Southerner. There were a number of letters declining the chairmanship. Julia C. Lathrop of Rockford, Illinois, became the first chairman. In this capacity, she received numerous correspondences from the state leagues identified for participation inquiring about the functioning and ultimate goals of the committee and expressing, in some instances, their hesitance in participating despite their acceptance of the premise.

New Albany, Miss.
Jan. 18, 1922

My dear Miss Lathrop:

I fear that I can be of no assistance to you. Though I have spent my entire life in Mississippi and though I have long wanted to do something for negroes—especially those in my own community—I must say that I do not know where to begin attacking the problem of suffrage for negroes in the South.

President Harding, in his famous Birmingham speech, expressed the conviction of the educated people of our state when he said that the negroes that are fit for the suffrage should exercise it. At the same time we agree with Mr. Batton Smith, one of our Southerners who is a student of the negro problem, when he says: "I believe it will be best to bend all friendly and progressive efforts, North and South, on three objectives; namely, the stopping of lynching, the improvement of negro education, and the extension of economic opportunity. At this stage none of these purposes can be aided by emphasis on Negro suffrage, though they can be greatly delayed thereby." This excerpt is from the Outlook, Nov. 9, which contains opinions that you may find of interest.

I should think that our Committee might begin by securing expressions similar to those found in the Outlook referred to above.

I can readily give you the most valuable sources of information in Mississippi. I have been in correspondence with all of our welfare agencies and have secured places on programs for all of our leaders who speak on the negro problem.

In answer to your questions, I think that the Committee should have copies of the laws and the figures mentioned in Question 1. I can readily secure the copies of the suffrage laws in Miss. There are no local regulations of any importance to our investigation. I do not know exactly what to say in answer to question 3. However, my better judgment is that we should confine our investigations for the first year to more general conditions. I believe it would be wise to include the cities with negro populations over 15%. We ought to try to see the problem as a whole, as nearly as possible.

Please believe, my dear Miss Lathrop, that the thing I'd like best in the world to do is to make a small contribution to the welfare of negroes here in the South. For this reason you may count upon me to help you in every way that is within my limitations of strength and ability. I am ready to give much time to this committee work.

Yours sincerely,
Blanche Rogers[5]

A year after its introduction, the committee was fundamentally inactive. In a memo from Chairman Lathrop to the national board, she outlined recommendations for consideration, if the committee was to be effective.

Report of the Special Committee on the Study of Negro Problems
Made by the Chairman Miss Julia Lathrop to the National
Board at its Baltimore meeting April 19th, 1922

I believe that The Committee should be continued.

Whatever may be the organization and membership of the Committee, however, cooperation with other organizations appear to me a basic necessity. The Inter-Racial Committees and the earlier University Commission on Race Questions, the rural extension work of the U.S. Dept. of Agriculture, different as they are in scope and approach, all afford valuable suggestions and offer avenues of cooperation and observation. While I fully realize that this Committee is one for study and report to the League, I am confident that in this as in all other matters in which the League has interested itself the laboratory method of study and experiment will be more or less followed. I believe that cooperation and consultation with reliable negro organizations is essential—otherwise we shall be misunderstood and our fairness questioned—methods, of course must vary, and must be determined locally and not from the outside. . . .

The census figures available indicate a gradual but unquestionable improvement in negro welfare in the decade beginning in 1910. Although many difficulties must be surmounted before the problems of the negro can be solved, I am confident that the League of Women Voters is in a position to help greatly toward more rapid and substantial progress in the decade we have just entered.

> Yours very sincerely,
> Julia C. Lathrop[6]

In 1922, there was continuing conversation about expanding representation beyond the states with 15 percent Negro populations to also include cities with 15 percent. Miss Lathrop's assertion was that "changes in the Committee should be made only at the instance of those who are already members and I note you are in favor of including cities with negro populations over fifteen percent."[7]

Miss Lathrop received correspondence from several people who declined to attend the scheduled committee meeting in Atlanta. Her frustration in attempting to constitute the committee along with the ambiguity of its charge from the national leadership at times discouraged Miss Lathrop. In a letter dated June 8, 1922, the national league president requested that despite her frustrations, Miss Lathrop continue as chairman of the Special Committee on the Study of Negro Problems. She acknowledged the poor participation and the reluctance of state leagues to participate:

> I never have known why so few states responded last year, but I can assure you that Mrs. Cunningham, who is now in Texas for her vacation, will provide all eligible ones to appoint a real member on your committee as soon as we have your consent to serve.[8]

Because of the lack of response to the request for the designated states to identify representatives, a letter from the national office on behalf of

President Park was sent to the presidents of those states urging their participation.

> 532-17th St. N.W.
> Washington, D.C.
> July 12, 1922.

My dear Mrs.

Mrs. Park has asked me to write you requesting that you name a member to represent your state on the Special Committee on the Study of Negro Problems or re-affirm your previous appointment.

Miss Lathrop, who served as Chairman last year, reported to the pre-convention Board meeting in Baltimore that only three members of the Committee had ever replied to any communications from her on the subject of the work at hand. Such a lack of response is a handicap no chairman can overcome so please ask your representative, as she was not one of the ones who responded, to take the work of this Committee to her heart and help to make it possible for the League to make a study of this real problem which will be a valuable contribution to the subject.

> Sincerely yours,
> Executive Secretary

[Handwritten note]: "Sent to presidents of States on attached list."[9]

The lack of activity of the committee was noted by several Southern presidents as an explanation for their inability to identify representatives, which put the committee's existence in jeopardy. While some viewed it as necessary, it did not seem to be a priority for all.

July 14, 1922

Mrs. Minnie Fisher Cunningham,
532 Seventeenth St.
Washington, D.C.

My dear Mrs. Cunningham,

A Chairman was appointed last year to serve on the Special Committee for the study of Negro Problems. She wrote several times for information or instruction and received no answer to her letters. So the plans tentatively made were dropped.

If the Committee is to be active this summer we will make an appointment at once. If, however the work will not begin until fall we would prefer to wait until the members of the League return from their vacations. The appointment can be made at the September Board meeting.

Our former Chairman is not available as she will be in Colorado for some months.

Very sincerely yours,
Lavinia Engle[10]

Upon the resignation of Julia Lathrop as chairman, the national leadership experienced difficulty in identifying and appointing a new chairman. Multiple possible reasons for this emerged: the committee was not a part of the adopted program, it did not receive any funding for its work, and it suffered from the perception that it was "interfering" with the autonomy of the Southern state leagues.

October 27, 1922

Mrs. Daniel Miller,
Baltimore, Md.

My dear Mrs. Miller:
Miss Lathrop has advised Mrs. Park that she will be unable to serve as Chairman of the Special Committee for the Study of Negro Problems this year and the National Board will have the matter of a Chairman under advisement at the meeting in Chicago in November. As soon as the appointment has been made you will be notified and some arrangement for arriving at plan for the Committee's work will be devised.

In the meantime, because of your interest in this subject, you will not want to miss the article in the Literary Digest of October 20th on the Report of the Commission on the Negro in Chicago. This Commission was appointed by Governor Lowden after the terrible race riots in 1919, and its report is probably the most important publication on the subject that has been printed. If you can secure a copy it will no doubt be a great help to you in whatever work the Committee undertakes.

Sincerely yours,
Executive Secretary[11]

After the Chicago meeting, a letter was sent to Mrs. D. D. Carrol of Chapel Hill, North Carolina, all state members of the special committee, and the Florida league president indicating that Miss Lathrop had accepted the presidency of the Illinois League of Women Voters and as such was not available for the chairmanship of the special committee. The letter included a request for suggestions of a number of names for this position to be listed in order of their "desirability." It indicated that the board was "especially concerned to find the right person for the place because the whole usefulness of the Committee depends so much on the ability of personnel."[12]

October 3, 1922
Miss Julia Lathrop,
Rockford, Illinois

My dear Miss Lathrop:
    The executive Committee in Boston last week had up for discussion the subject of that Special Committee on the Study of Negro Problems, which ought to be doing such good work and is not doing anything, because there is no chairman and no leadership.
    I was instructed once more to beseech you to accept the chairmanship of this committee and if you find that your health has not improved sufficiently to take up this in addition to your other plans in the autumn I was then instructed to take up the matter of securing Miss Sophanisba Breckenridge [sic].
    It may interest you to know that the *Woman Citizen* has agreed, per your suggestion, to carry a series of articles on lynching if the Committee will undertake the compiling of this material.
    Miss Sherwin's report to the Executive Committee was to the effect that you thought I was Acting Chairman of this Committee. I corrected this to Miss Sherwin and would like to correct it to you also. I had been acting this summer on the authority of the Executive Committee, simply to get the names of the state representatives. I thought everybody connected with the matter had this clearly in their minds and am sorry that there should have been any mistake.
    Always with the very best of good wishes for your health and happiness, I am,

Faithfully yours,
Executive Secretary[13]

Records indicate that the request for Miss Breckinridge to serve as chairman was made, and she declined chairmanship in a letter dated October 31, 1922.

Green Hall
The University of Chicago
Chicago, Illinois
October 31, 1922

Dear Miss Sherwin:
    I was greatly moved by your letter. You know how interested I have been since college days in the question of the relations between the white

and colored people. And I was very much honored that you thought I could be of service in that connection. It is, however, impossible for me to take up the chairmanship now. I am committed to undertakings that render me wholly ineligible for such responsibilities. I feel less distressed at my inability than I otherwise would feel if I shared your confidence. I am like poor old Moses in one respect that I have no hope of leading others on the way by which they enter the Promised Land; I can only go toward it myself and rejoice if others are going my way.

Cordially and
gratefully yours,

S. P. Breckenridge[sic]

Miss Belle Sherwin
National League of
Women Voters,
Department of Training
for Citizenship[14]

Bessie McD. Bricken from Alabama wrote to Mrs. Minnie Fisher Cunningham on October 5, 1922, apologizing to national league leaders for her failure to appoint someone to the Committee to Study Negro Problems, and her words captured the racial attitudes of most politically active Southern white women. "Unfortunately, many of our women do not see the responsibility or feel the obligation to work at this."[15]

In the midst of this internal strain, external organizations were interested in the work of the league on this matter. Miss Virginia Roderick from *The Woman Citizen* sent a letter on October 21, 1922, inquiring about "the progress of the League Committee on the Study of the Negro Problem in compiling material for us to use."[16]

Amid the apparent confusion surrounding the function and activity of the Special Committee on Negro Problems, Minnie Fisher Cunningham, executive secretary, who later became the chairman of the committee, sought guidance from the national leadership. Her recommendation was to assign the committee as a subcommittee to education to make it more palatable to leagues being asked to participate. The topic would therefore be embedded in a more generalized topic consistent with the adopted program, take the focus off the real purpose of dealing with the issue of race, and hopefully gain traction toward completion of its goals, as ambiguous as they were.[17]

With the number of questions regarding the committee's charge increasing and the excuse of lack of activity attributed to not being able to identify representatives, President Park requested that a letter be sent to participating state presidents detailing the progress of the committee thus far.

December 8, 1922

REPORT ON ACTIVITY FOR THE ORGANIZATION OF THE SPECIAL COMMITTEE ON NEGRO PROBLEMS

Following a conversation with Mrs. Park in New York, Miss Lathrop wrote, with Mrs. Park's approval, urging that I send out a letter to all of the states entitled to membership on this Special Committee, and after securing the appointment of the Committee Members to arrange for the Committee to elect its own chairman.

I immediately sent the first letter asking for appointment of a new member or reappointment of the person who had previously been serving on the Committee. I did not receive a complete set of names for the Committee, one or two of the presidents stating that it was impossible to secure workers at that season of the year and while people were so interested in the primary elections.

In the meantime Miss Hauser reminded me of the action of the Executive Committee with reference to the appointment of Miss Breckenridge as Chairman of this Committee that would make it impossible for me to proceed with a plan to have the committee elect its own chairman until the Executive Committee had reviewed the situation.

Taking these two facts into consideration it seemed best to wait until September to send a second letter to the State Presidents urging the appointment of the states' committee member. This letter was sent on September 19 and responses are now beginning to come in. A complete list of the states entitled to membership on this committee and the results as gained so far follows:

North Carolina—Mrs. D. D. Carrol, Chapel Hill

South Carolina—Mrs. J. B. Salley, Aiken

Georgia

Florida

Alabama

Louisiana

Mississippi—Miss Blanche Rogers, New Albany

Tennessee

Virginia—Miss Adele Clark, 601 Va. Ry. & Power Bldg., Richmond

District of Columbia—Mrs. W. F. McDowell, 2107 Wyoming Ave., (tentative)

Maryland—Mrs. Daniel Miller, 1520 Bolton St., Baltimore.

Respectfully submitted,

Minnie Fisher
Cunningham
Executive Secretary.[18]

Many of the affected states continued to send correspondence indicating their inability to identify representatives or their trepidation about the purpose of the committee. A letter from the Mississippi league in New Albany, dated December 6, 1922, indicated that they could not suggest a chair for the committee. A letter from Maryland, dated December 4, 1922, indicated that the board had discussed the work of the committee, and "our feeling is that the Chairman should be a person who would confine the activities of this committee to work that may consistently be taken up by the league."

> For example the question of fair play for negroes in the Courts would be a matter of legislation as it would mean the abolishment of the fee system for sheriffs. The question of riots is a matter for the police and not the League.
> These examples are my own but the sentiment was that of the Board. Miss Gertrude Well [sic] & Mrs. Palmer German [sic] of North Carolina and Mrs. Walter McNab Miller of Missouri would be southern women and at the same time clear headed.
> Sincerely yours,
> Lavinia Engle[19]

A letter from the Florida league indicated their relief at finally being able to identify a member for the committee.

Dec. 9, 1922

My dear Miss Cunningham,
    It is with more than pleasure that I write to tell you that at last Florida has a member for the Special Committee on the Negro Problem. I feel that we cannot be too grateful and am almost holding my breath for fear she will withdraw as have the others.
    The address is Mrs. Harriet Longdon of Daytona Beach, Florida. At present she has had little or no information as to what is expected of her but is willing to do her best. I shall indeed appreciate having her informed officially what has been done (if anything) by this committee so far. I will explain the nature of the committee to her, its formation, etc.; but I know that she would appreciate instructions from headquarters.
    Yours sincerely,
    Mrs. J. B. O'Hara,
    President
    Millie O'Hara[20]

In 1923, Miss Blanche Rogers of New Albany, Mississippi, became chairman of the Special Committee on Negro Problems. This took courage and commitment and a fundamental belief in the cause. The following Western Union telegram was sent to Miss Rogers May 5, 1923:

> Will you consider taking chairmanship of Leagues [sic] Special Committee on the Study of the Negró Problem of which you are a member but which has not been very active. Two hundred dollars provided to cover clerica [sic] expenses. Please reply to hotel Fort Des Moines, Des Moines, Iowa. Minnie Fisher Cunningham.[21]

This was the first indication that any funds were dedicated to the work of the committee.

No women of color were representatives on the Special Committee on Negro Problems. At a Thursday afternoon conference at the Des Moines convention, the national leadership and leaguers of color met to discuss their concerns. The meeting was attended by Mrs. Maud Wood Park, Miss Belle Sherwin, Miss Mott, Mrs. Cunningham, Mrs. F. W. Hardy, Mrs. Adele Clark, Mrs. Huston, Mrs. C. Beck, Miss Julia Lathrop, Mrs. E. C. Grady, Mrs. B. F. Bowles, Mrs. Nevine (T. J.), Mrs. S. Joe Brown, Mrs. Alice Webb, Mrs. Ida Wells-Barnett, and Irene Goins.

In the *Report of the Special Committee*, dated April 14, 1923, and presented to the national league leadership at the Des Moines convention, a group of integrated Illinois league members presented the following recommendations. Miss Lathrop, who had previously served as chairman of the committee and now served as president of the League of Women Voters of Illinois, one of the state leagues that supported integration in membership, presented the report.

Green Hall
The University of Chicago

Miss Lathrop's report. Saturday afternoon.

Realizing that education is essential for efficient organization, as planned by the National League of Women Voters, and knowing that no group of American women need and desire the advantages of such education more than the Colored women, we the undersigned feel that the very best means of reaching this group will be through the following channels:

We therefore beg leave to submit for your consideration the following suggestions:

First—Cooperation through connection with local Leagues of Women Voters.

Second—Training in citizenship in Colored Colleges and Normal Schools.

Third—Training of leaders in Citizenship Schools.

Fourth—Distribution of literature.

Fifth—Cooperation with already organized agencies, such as National Association of Colored Women, and Inter-Racial Committees, to the end that a more friendly feeling may be created between the races.

Mrs. Alice Webb

Irene Goins

Mrs. S. Joe Brown

Mrs. E.C. Grady

Per Mrs. Hardy[22]

A follow-up letter was sent to Miss Blanche Rogers, the new chairman, for her information. The letter contained references to the recommendations listed above.

Washington, D.C.

May 5, 1923

Miss Blanche Rogers

New Albany, Mississippi

My dear Miss Rogers:

You have not heard from me before because I have been unavoidably delayed and have lost a piece of paper which I meant to send you when I wrote. The Board was perfectly delighted to know that you will serve as Chairman of the Special Committee on Negro Problems and I was instructed to write and express their appreciation for your willingness to help in this way. I was also instructed to send you the enclosed letter from Mrs. Brookings on the subject of negro education and to suggest that you make the trip with Mrs. Brookings for the purpose of continuing the study which she began on this subject.

The enclosed letter from the Phelps-Stokes people was referred to you for your information and I was instructed to send you a list of the informal suggestions for co-operation which a group of negro women who attended the Des Moines Convention presented at a little conference with Mrs. Park, Miss Lathrop, Miss Adele Clark, Miss Nora Houston, Mrs. T. W. Hardy and I had with them. It is this list of suggestions which I have unaccountably mislaid and I am horrified at myself because I was guarding it more carefully than any other one paper I had in my charge. I am taking steps to get a copy of it forwarded to you at an early date.

With this letter and its enclosures I am also sending the suggestions for the continuance of the committee which Miss Lathrop made at Baltimore last year. I think they will be useful and I know Miss Lathrop will be glad to serve in an advisory capacity to you in this work if you care to call on her.

With sincere gratitude to you for undertaking this Chairmanship, I am,

Sincerely yours,

Executive Secretary[23]

On June 13, 1923, Miss Rogers wrote to Mrs. Cunningham to request further clarification of the charge of the committee. She indicated that Miss Lathrop had not given her clear direction of the status of the committee's initiatives or its steps for moving forward. She was confused about whether the priority for the board was citizenship or something else. Was the special committee to deal with the problems of Negroes in the League of Women Voters (internal) or problems of the Negro in society (external)? Could they be separated?

If you will only help me to make a beginning, I think that I can then go forward . . . I feel I should not proceed until I know definitely the purposes of the investigation. There was never a more opportune time in the South to start a movement to better the conditions of Negroes.[24]

The ambiguity about the purpose of the committee continued. Miss Rogers received a response to her query of June 13, 1923, from Elizabeth J. Hauser, secretary, indicating the reluctance of the board member responsible for standing committees to assume responsibility for this committee, and the tone of the letter to place the responsibility for defining it to the committee chairman was interesting. This affirms why the previous committee had difficulty gaining traction. It is also reflective of the dissonance within the organization about the level of aggressiveness to use in determining the amount of time and energy they proposed to devote to the issue of race.

June 26, 1923
Dict. June 25.

Miss Blanche Rogers,
New Albany, Mississippi.

My dear Miss Rogers:

On Friday last Miss Sherwin and I talked over the probable activities of your Committee because of a request which Miss Sherwin had had from Mrs. Cunningham in connection with your letter of June 13 to

Mrs. Cunningham. Neither Miss Sherwin nor I understood that special committees were under her direction as the standing committees are. It seemed to us that as Secretary I ought to go back thru the official records and your copies of all action which has been taken in connection with the Committee on Negro Problems, together with copies of the reports so far made by Miss Lathrop, of which, if my memory serves me, there have been but two in addition to the report made at Des Moines, copy of which I sent you some time since at Mrs. Cunningham's request. Miss Sherwin and I thought after you had this information you would be in a better position to judge what the scope of the committee was designed to be, though we are quite frank to say that in our opinion that never has been clearly outlined. It is our custom to encourage initiative on the part of committee chairmen and we believe the purpose of your Committee may be better developed thru your own suggestions perhaps than any other way.

I am just now quite occupied getting ready for a meeting of our Executive Committee and will ask you to wait until my return from that meeting before I send you the above mentioned material. I am sure that a little additional delay now will not matter since there have been so many unavoidable delays in connection with this work in the past. I am sure we are all very glad to know that you are ready now to begin in earnest upon it.

Yours most cordially,
Elizabeth J. Hauser,
Secretary[25]

While the special committee's inability to gain momentum was a source of constant conversation due to its lack of clarity on its charge as internal league issues or external societal issues, for the national leadership, issues of race and membership were being essentially ignored. It was clear that in 1924, the national league leaders, while not officially supporting separate leagues, did nothing to support or encourage integrated membership, nor did they overtly discourage state and local leagues from engaging in such practices. The official response from national leaders to inquiries about separate leagues was that they were only cursorily aware of the existence of such leagues. While there is evidence to support that women of color attended national conventions from the league's inception, the first mention of an actual colored delegate to the convention was in 1924. This begs the question of her treatment in terms of full participation, lodging, and attendance at invitation to league events.

By the time of the seventh annual convention, held in St. Louis from April 14 to 21, 1926, the Special Committee on Negro Problems was changed to the Special Committee on Inter-Racial Problems, indicating a philosophical shift and an attempt to narrow the scope of work.

Problem of Work
for
The Special Committee on Inter-Racial Problems
Adopted by the Executive Committee in 1924 and
by the General Council, 1925
National League of Women Voters

I. That the Committee formally advise educational institutions for Negroes, and existing organizations of colored women of the citizenship training work undertaken by the League, and offer an advisory service.

II. That the Board request the Committee on Education to:

(1) Continue and complete the study of Negro Education

(2) Get in touch with the trustees of various funds for promoting negro education and discuss the possibility of including citizenship training in the teacher training courses and social service training—a Week's Institute in each college.

III. That in the states in which the colored vote is a material and accepted fact, the state presidents be asked by the National president to arrange for ballot marking classes for colored women during the week prior to the election. Such classes to be conducted by women and scrupulously guarded from any imputation or suspicion that they are being held to influence the votes of colored women for or against any candidate or ticket.

IV. That in states where the inter-racial commission functions the state presidents be asked to study the effectiveness of this agency with a view to the desirability of co-operation.

V. That the chairman of the committee be instructed to send to each member of the committee the names and addresses of interested women and organizations in her state as such names become available in the file.

VI. That the committee itself be reorganized so as to include representatives of the Second, Third, Fourth and Sixth Regions, and a number of specially interested women of both the white and the negro races.

Supplementary.

VII. In addition to the above program, it has been suggested at meetings of the committee in 1926 and 1927, that colored women leaders in clubs and other organizations be advised of the League's program of work in Public Welfare in Government, as well as the Citizenship Training, and that literature of the League, especially on the Public Welfare items of the Program, be made available to study groups in such organizations—clubs, Y.W.C.A.'s, Church groups, &c—and that League speakers offer to explain the program or items on it to such groups.

[Handwritten note]: This has been mimeographed and copy sent each committee member.[26]

In 1926, the Illinois State League of Women Voters elected a black woman, Margaret Gainer, to membership on its board of directors. Gainer, also a member of the Illinois State Federation of Colored Women's Clubs, directed the latter's citizenship department, which included the program of the Illinois league. Several clubwomen in the Chicago area were league members. The Douglass League of Women Voters, a black unit of the league in the city, was headed by Irene Goins, a leader of the Illinois State Federation, as well.

The "Negro problem" was not the only problem the league faced regarding women of color. In 1926, two years after Congress passed and Calvin Coolidge signed a measure guaranteeing full American citizenship for all Native Americans born within U.S. territories, the national league was confronted with the responsibility of defining its course of action on behalf of Native Americans. The years 1926 and 1927 saw activity on the question of the "Indian problem," as chronicled in the file on Indian affairs. That this action occurred is of note. That issues related to membership of both Negroes and "Indians" were perceived as "problems" for the organizations was predictable. The league established a 1925–1926 fellowship for a woman graduate to study "the American Indian problem." This decision was prompted by a league study revealing the dearth of authentic material on the general "Indian" problem.

There were two "Indian" leagues in Wisconsin. Again, league bylaws made no provision for segregated leagues, but the same philosophy that allowed for the creation of separate colored leagues served as a foundation for Indian leagues. As correspondence revealed, the Wisconsin league decided to take action in the face of inaction at the national level. The philosophy of acquiescing to state and local leagues designed to address the membership of black women was used as a basis of action in the case of Indians.

The national leadership seemed as hesitant to address these issues as they were the issues of colored women. An April 29, 1927, Western Union telegram was sent from Mrs. Hooper to "Mrs. [*sic*] Belle Sherwin," care of the National League of Women Voters headquarters, Washington, D.C.

> Most urgent and vital indian problems in our state and in other states need immediate attention to relieve injustice and suffering we earnestly urge your council to hasten investigation of indian affairs and request that you put indian matters on your study program.[27]

A response to Mrs. Hooper was sent on May 13, 1927, on behalf of Miss Sherwin and indicated that while the telegram "had the attention of the Board of Directors at its post-Council meeting," it would be "impossible that the study be added to the study program." The study had begun two years ago under scholarship and was now being undertaken by the Institute of Governmental Research in Washington. Mrs. Hooper was provided with the name of the director, Mr. Lewis Merriam, and no further action was taken by the national board.

In an April 2, 1927, letter to Miss Florence Harrison, national board member, the Wisconsin league indicated the reason it decided to take action when the national league would not.

> I want you to understand this situation so the National will know we are not interfering in any way with general federal legislation. Our only method of securing an investigation of the conditions in Wisconsin is to secure a senate [sic] investigation of Indian affairs. If that is done we feel sure it will bring out the grave situation here and that we will be able to get some help for the Indians. . . .
>
> We have in Wisconsin what I believe no other state has; two Indian Leagues of Women Voters, and one of them owns their own club house, which is more than most any other League in the country can say. These women are asking our aid in making conditions bearable on the Reservations. . . .
>
> There are comparatively few of the states which have the Indian problems but where they do have them they certainly feel that the League of Women Voters must do their part in trying to remedy the conditions among the Indians.[28]

Despite the urgency expressed in the communication from the Wisconsin league, the newly named Special Committee on Inter-Racial Problems did not adjust its scope of work to include the issues raised about Native Americans. In their subsequent report, dated July 1927, in response to a request made in the post-council minutes to check up on the progress made on the execution of the recommendations adopted by the board in 1924, the chairman read the program of the committee and cited outreach activities to make interracial contacts, such as her attendance at the conference at Eaglesmere. Because a part of the program had been referred to the Education Committee, she called on the chairman of that committee to make a short statement. Earlier records indicated that the board always wanted to include the Special Committee under the Education Committee, but there had been opposition because the education committee did not feel this was its responsibility.

The following excerpts are from the July 1927 report of the Special Committee on Inter-Racial Problems, presented by Adele Clark:

The chairman expressed the desire to hear from Mrs. Cellhorn of Missouri, and Mrs. Ramsay of Illinois and from other States where there was negro membership in the League either as colored league units or individual membership. There was insufficient time to have adequate reports on these subjects and on the experiences of Alabama, Virginia and Georgia. . . .

So far, it has been ascertained that in the Third Region inter-racial work has been done in the main by informal conferences between league officers and committee women and leaders of the negro women: in co-operation with Church and club groups and Y.W.C.A. groups, and in assisting and furthering government agencies—State, county or city departments and institutions, the work of which affects colored people. In the Second, Fourth and Sixth Regions, and in one State in the Seventh Region, there have been in some instances league membership held by negro women individually, and in others colored leagues formed with representation on the general county or State Boards. . . .

[At the conclusion of the report was the following informal note:]

On the occasion, recently, of Miss Hauser's—the vice chairman of this special committee—being in Richmond, it was arranged for her to meet some of the colored women leaders for an informal discussion of the League program and for them to tell her of the work they were doing in social welfare and other areas. While no very definite results were accomplished, it was quite a gratification and an encouraging circumstance for these women leaders of their race in the South to meet a National league officer from another State and to feel that the league was taken an interest in their work.[29]

The report included specific information from those states that were to be represented on the committee. Alabama reported distributing literature to colored groups "seeking information along non-partisan lines." North Carolina had a major league legislative project regarding the acquisition and operation of "State of the Negro Industrial School for Wayward Girls originally established by Negro Women's Clubs" in the state. Virginia reported one local league taking an active part "in the effort to raise the salaries of negro women teachers." Virginia also reported that they were successful in preventing the consolidation of the boards of the white and colored industrial (reform) schools by the legislature under the auspices that the consolidation would "have resulted in negro members of the boards governing the negro schools losing their positions on those boards." Missouri reported the organization in ward and city groups of Negro leagues with representation on the board. Chicago reported that it "has ward League groups among colored women and has had valuable experience in conducting citizenship classes." Maryland reported, "A splendid piece of co-operative work is being done by a colored women's civic organization here in Baltimore. The League has made one particular piece of work the securing of suitable women on all boards of institutions." They continued, "We have made some headway and now have women (colored women) on the Boards of the more important institutions dealing with colored people."[30]

The chronology of reports from the Special Committee discloses that the league, instead of taking the revolutionary step to include women of color as "full" members and leaders, made the strategic choice that support of Southern white women was more important than Negro aspirations. This mirrored society at this time.

A REVIEW OF THE HISTORY AND WORK OF THE
SPECIAL COMMITTEE ON INTERRACIAL PROBLEMS
NATIONAL LEAGUE OF WOMEN VOTERS
1927

Chairman—Adele Clark

Vice-Chairman—Elizabeth J. Hauser

Membership: The Committee was composed originally of a member from the league in each State having a negro population of fifteen percent, and embraced States in the 2nd, 3rd, regions. It was later extended to include representatives from States in the 2nd, 3rd, 4th, and 6th Regions in communities in which there were [large] negro populations.

States now included:

Alabama, Florida, Georgia, Louisiana, Mississippi, North Carolina, South Carolina, Tennessee, Virginia, District of Columbia (3rd Region), Maryland, Pennsylvania, New York (2nd region), Ohio, Kentucky, Indiana, Illinois (4th region), Missouri (6th Region).

History

The Special Committee on Inter-Racial Problems was formed in 1921 by the Board of Directors at the time of the National Convention in Cleceland [*sic*]. A resolution by the delegates from the 3rd Region in a conference of that region requested the formation of such a special committee, the chairman to be selected by the National Board, and the membership to be composed of members appointed by the State League Boards from each State in which there was a negro population of at least 15%. Miss Julia Lathrop was the first chairman, Mrs. Minnie Fisher Cunningham succeeded her, and upon the resignation of Mrs. Cunningham the present chairman was appointed by the Board.

During the biennium in which the present chairman has served there have been informal meetings of the committee at the time of the National annual conventions or the General Council. This followed a custom of the committee in former years.

During the St. Louis Convention, 1926, the committee met with several colored delegates from Illinois and Missouri. Reports were made of inter-racial work undertaken in several States.[31]

This abbreviated history does not underscore the difficulty in making this committee fully functional. The ambiguity of the purpose and progress of the committee continued throughout its existence. What was unclear was whether the actual goal was to address Negro problems in society or confront the concomitant issue within the league. The league's strategy thus far was to position the issue of its relationship with race under the broader umbrella of education and other social issues.

A questionnaire was sent out to all state leagues in 1934, but most did not reply, nor did the states that responded always do so thoughtfully and accurately. The ineffectiveness of the special committee to fully execute its charge was evidenced in the infrequency of its meetings, all of which occurred informally at the national conventions, with no activity in the interim. The questionnaire was an attempt to determine the need for the continuation of the committee.

League files housed a response to the questions asked by the committee with no attributable information about its state of origin or the date in which it was received in the league office. The answers were handwritten, and it is unclear as to whether this represents the totality of the questions.

QUESTIONS
INFORMATION DESIRED BY SPECIAL COMMITTEE
ON INTER-RACIAL PROBLEMS,
NATIONAL LEAGUE OF WOMEN VOTERS.

1. Has your League appointed a member to represent you on the special Committee on Inter-Racial Problems, of the National League of Women Voters? ("Not this year as yet")

2. Please give the name and address of the committee member from your State, if one has been appointed, and if not, please indicate when appointment may be expected. (No answer)

3. Has your State League or any of your local Leagues, through the Inter-racial Commission in your community, or in co-operation with other groups, such as the Y.W.C.A., church or clubs, undertaken any study or work along inter-racial lines? ("Yes, the League officers representing the League have in many instances done so.")

4. Is the negro vote—especially the negro woman vote—a material factor in your State or community? (It has been stated to this committee that in Illinois, Indiana, Ohio, Oklahoma, Missouri, and in parts of New York and Pennsylvania, it is a factor). ("No")

5. Has there been any inter-racial co-operation in putting into effect laws on child welfare, maternity and infancy hygiene, mothers' pensions, juvenile court work, probation work, school attendance laws, child-labor laws, etc. in your community? ("Not beyond consultation and information given to negro women and League leaders.")

6. Do any negro women in your state hold positions on State for city boards of negro institutions, schools, reformatories, or hospitals, or as probation officers, police women, matrons in police stations, public health nurses, etc.? ("Yes.")

7. Have any negro institutions or groups in your State asked assistance in citizenship education work? ("Yes—especially, YWCA groups.")

8. Have any laws on inter-racial subjects been proposed or passed in your State since women were enfranchised, and if so has your League taken any position upon them? (No answer).

9. Has the assistance of your League been requested by negro women upon any laws or ordinances or rulings of boards affecting any of their activities—for instance, their salaries as school teachers, public health nurses, etc.? ("Yes")

10. Has your League assisted in or made any investigation as to the condition of colored women and children in industry? ("Not as a racial problem.")

11. Has there been any experience in your League of colored women organizing in League units or joining existing Leagues? ("No")[32]

A review of the history and work of the Special Committee on Inter-Racial Relations from 1927 contradicts some of the information in the 1934 report and speaks to some of the problems getting to the task, which is mentioned in several letters to the national board. Additionally, the committee's report for 1934 does not reflect the change in its name proposed in 1928.

SPECIAL COMMITTEE ON INTER-RACIAL PROBLEMS
4/17/34

HISTORY OF THE COMMITTEE: The committee has seldom, if ever, met as a committee and its function has been almost entirely limited to the informal assembling of leaders of the league and colored women in the League and sometimes outside it at the time of the National Conventions. This was the case in 1922 in Baltimore, in 1923 in Des Moines, in 1924 in Buffalo, in 1925 in Richmond, in 1926, in 1928 in Chicago and in 1930 in

Louisville. For reasons which I have not been able to recall or discover, there was no attempt at a meeting in Detroit in 1932.

Mrs. Minnie Fisher Cunningham was the first chairman of the committee and set up a plan of operation chiefly emphasizing the importance of securing adequate facilities for education of colored children and youth. The files of the League will reveal correspondence as well as the detailed plan prepared by Mrs. Cunningham, who was obliged to retire from her office in the League before the end of the year 1924. In 1925 Miss Adele Clark became chairman of the committee, in which capacity she has served informally and as consultant on negro women's problems ever since that time. Miss Cornelia Adair, when chairman of the Committee on education, was helpful in attempting to carry out some of the proposals made by Mrs. Cunningham. The new president also undertook correspondence in behalf of those plans. They were, however, general in character and their execution depended in large part on the response which could be secured from the persons addressed and the ability of the committee to function as the committee.

From 1926 on practically the only evidence of activity on the part of the League in relation to the Inter-Racial problem has been the attendance of Miss Clark on a series of meetings of the Inter-Racial Committee of the United States. Since 1930—unless records not at present available are found—it would appear that there was neither money for travel or time on the part of the chairman available to permit of even that slight connection.

During the years 1931, 1932, 1933, and to date 1934 the Depression has caused the problems of unemployment and relief to dwarf the particular questions of education and suffrage of negro women as they were originally raised. . . .

PROBLEM FOR THE LEAGUE OF WOMEN VOTERS: The question now is whether the league should attempt to continue a committee which is practically defunct through lack of means and personnel—a committee related to one of the largest and gravest problems which the country must face eventually.[33]

Conclusion

While the reports of the committee always recounted its origin, there was never justification given for why the 15 percent threshold was chosen or why that threshold would apply only to Southern states. Because of the national leadership's reluctance to deliberate the issue of race, the emphasis of the work of the committee camouflaged the issue of race under the program areas of education, voter information and citizenship, and employment.

Although the special committee was headed by prominent league leaders—Julia Lathrop (1921), Minnie Fisher Cunningham (1921–1925), and Adele Clark (after 1925)—no fundamental changes in the league's organizational structure or priorities changed as a result of their efforts. The demise of the special committee was slow, yet methodical. The lessons learned are clearly and accurately reflected. The optimism of the group of women at the 1921 convention was not realized or supported by the actions of league leadership. The rose-colored glasses that they donned in their initial encounter were replaced over the years by the amber-colored glasses of reality with the League of Women Voters.

Notes

1. Terborg-Penn, 1998, 155.
2. Library of Congress, LWV Folder, Special Committee 1921–1923, Box I:50, Box II:100.
3. Ibid., Letter #1.
4. Ibid., Letter #2.
5. Ibid., Letter from Miss Rogers when she was a committee member.
6. Library of Congress, League of Women Voters Folder, Special Committee 1921–1923, Box I:50.
7. Ibid.
8. Ibid.
9. Ibid.
10. Ibid.
11. Ibid.
12. Ibid., Filed 1922, December 2.
13. Ibid.
14. Ibid., Filed 1922, November 22.
15. Schuyler, 2006, 132.
16. Library of Congress, 1921–1923, Filed 1922.
17. Ibid., 1922, November 22.
18. Ibid., 1922, December 8.
19. Library of Congress, League of Women Voters Folder, Special Committee 1921–1923, Box I:50.
20. Library of Congress, Filed 1922, December 18.
21. Ibid., Folder, 1922.
22. Ibid., Filed 1923.
23. Ibid., Filed 1923, May 10.
24. Ibid., 1922.
25. Ibid., Filed 1923, July 20.
26. Ibid., Filed 1926.

27. Library of Congress Box II:188.
28. Ibid.
29. Library of Congress Box II:188, Inter-Racial Committee.
30. Ibid.
31. Ibid.
32. Library of Congress File on Negro Problems, File Box II:188.
33. Library of Congress Folder Box II:100.

CHAPTER FIVE

Through Amber-Colored Glasses

Lifting as we climb, onward and upward we go, struggling and striving, and hoping that the buds and blossoms of our desires will burst into glorious fruition ere long. . . . With courage, born of success achieved in the past, with a keen sense of responsibility which we shall continue to assume, we look forward to a future large with promise and hope. Seeking no favors because of our color, nor patronage because of our needs, we knock at the bar of justice, asking an equal chance.

—Mary Church Terrell, 1940

Introduction

The dual burden of race and gender was quite apparent during the debate over suffrage. Women of color who chose to participate in the suffrage movement and later affiliate with its successor organization, the League of Women Voters, were confronted with two realities: the fact that the white women of the movement prioritized gender over race in accomplishing its goal of full suffrage in a segregated organizational structure and that to ensure that the cause included them, they needed to access the resources of an organization such as the league, despite its overt attempts to discourage their full participation.

The experience that women of color had with the league paralleled the experiences that confronted them in the greater society. They navigated the nexus of race and gender in the organization and in society by recognizing that their realities did not allow them to view the league through the proverbial rose-colored glasses—glasses of white women—that allow people to see the world as it should be, but a lens of color, which was ever present. Because of society's inability to move beyond the issue of race, viewing the organization through amber-colored glasses more accurately reflected the hope, of women of color, that the league would be truly committed to full suffrage and access, even given the realization that historically the movement sacrificed the needs of women of color to accomplish the needs of white women.

This contradiction in principle and practicality was emphasized by suffragists of color from the beginning of the movement. In 1898, Mary Church Terrell delivered a speech before the National American Women's Suffrage Association entitled "The Progress of Colored Women," and in 1900, she gave a thirty-minute presentation before the same group entitled "Justice of Woman Suffrage."[1] Her remarks addressed the fragile balance between race and gender from the perspective of women of color. Terrell had the opportunity to become acquainted with many of the leaders of suffrage organizations, including Susan B. Anthony, Alice Paul, Carrie Chapman Catt, and Jane Addams. She and her daughter, although sometimes mistreated by white suffragists or made to march in the back of the picket lines, marched with suffrage groups, picketed in front of the White House, and pointed out to some of their white counterparts the inconsistency of their unenthusiastic stance about suffrage for black women.[2] Terrell, along with Mary McLeod Bethune and Nannie Helen Burroughs, was visible in the suffrage movement and held out hope that the needs of colored women would be addressed as well.

> The condescension they directed at black women was one of the means they employed to remind us that the women's movement was "theirs"—that we were able to participate because they allowed it, even encouraged it; after all, we were needed to legitimate the process. They did not see us as equals. They did not treat us as equals. And though they expected us to provide firsthand accounts of black experience, they felt it was their role to decide if these experiences were authentic. Frequently, college educated black women were dismissed as mere imitators. . . . If we dared to criticize the movement or to assume responsibility for reshaping feminist ideas and introducing new ideas, our voices were tuned out, dismissed and silenced. We could be heard only if our statements echoed the sentiments of the dominant discourse.[3]

As the NAWSA transitioned into the League of Women Voters, leaguers of color knew the organization was flawed. They hoped, however, that their inclusion would bring about needed change in the league's priorities. Throughout league history, their resilience and their actions on equal rights and equal opportunity ensured that they were not invisible.

Mary McLeod Bethune (1875–1955). (Science History Images/Alamy Stock Photo)

The league's 1947 Statement of Principle embodied a philosophy that women of color were drawn to despite dissuasion from participation in the organization.

> Believing in the dignity of the individual and that freedom and prosperity can be stably maintained within our democratic society, the League of Women Voters is dedicated to work unremittingly to support and strengthen that form of government of the United States. The purpose of the League is to promote political responsibility through informed and active participation of citizens in government, to the end that government of the people, by the people and for the people shall not perish from the earth.[4]

Most accounts of the league focus on the organization's legislative accomplishments. Overt responses to issues such as civil rights and race relations were consistently avoided by the national league leadership. There were, however, discernable turning points in league history revealing the organization's philosophy on issues of race. As the organizational focus changed over the years, it was apparent through the program adoption process at each convention cycle that the league found it easier to address race on the global stage than to take any overt action domestically. At the time of its greatest growth in membership, 1945–1964, the league supported a progressive public policy agenda as citizens rather than as women.[5] The 1950s and 1960s saw the greatest activity on the issue of domestic racial equality stimulated by legislation and Supreme Court decisions, yet a great deal of the league's resources in the 1950s were devoted to confronting the elements of the national conversations on Communism.

The league agenda of the 1950s, through its omissions as well as its priorities, mirrored the strengths as well as the weaknesses of its progressive tradition.[6] Many leaguers tout the organization's civil rights activism as representative of it being far more progressive than other organizations and consequently in the vanguard of the civil rights movement. League documents indicated that clearly the league was not, especially on an organizational front.

> While many individual members did actively participate in desegregating restaurants and other public facilities, their efforts in desegregation were personal rather than as members of the League of Women Voters. Thus the League fulfilled its progressive legacy. Most Progressives had not been concerned about civil rights; neither was the League of Women Voters.[7]

Looking through amber-colored glasses proffers a more comprehensive accounting of the history of the League of Women Voters from the perspective of women of color. The efforts of that first wave of courageous colored women who pressed themselves into the league and accepted the responsibility to effect social, economic, and political changes for the race paved the way for the second wave.

Two Realities

Mary Church Terrell was one of the most outspoken activists on the dichotomy of gender over race. Her experiences and legacy are important because her advocacy on behalf of women of color in the League of Women Voters carried beyond her initial advocacy in the suffrage movement. Throughout the duration of her affiliation with the league, she was keenly aware that she existed in two very distinct realities. She repeatedly reminded women what it was like to be a colored woman in the United States in one of her most publicized works, *A Colored Woman in a White World*.

But the white women of England and the United States have only one burden to bear, after all, the burden of sex. What would they do I wonder, if
they were double-crossed so to speak as the colored women of this country
are! If they had two heavy loads to carry through an unfriendly world the
burden of race as well as that of sex?[8]

With the cooperation of women such as Terrell, the league routinely col-
laborated with women of color for access to the black community. This
occurred despite the organization's inattention to restrictions to their full
participation as members and recognition that the experiences of women
of color, while similar in some respects, were quite different in others.

As the league cautiously and often covertly shaped its positions on race
and gender, outside organizations reached out to the league to share
information and resources, because its reputation and credibility on
legislative issues led them to believe in the league' s ability to effect
change. In December 1944, the national league office received a copy of
"The Negro in the South," a report of the Student Planning Committee in
a survey course on the Negro (Sociology 185) at the University of North
Carolina, Chapel Hill, distributed by the Southern Regional Council,
Atlanta, Georgia. The preface of the report indicated that the work was
completed in a six-week survey course on "The Negro" under the direction of Dr. Howard W. Odum of the University of North Carolina. The
class consisted of sixty graduate members. After the class, the committee
of ten graduate students continued its work, meeting with Dean James T.
Taylor of the North Carolina College for Negroes. They emphasized that
they were not researchers, sociologists, or specialists, but "consumers of
research."[9]

The students chose areas of study in education, housing, political and
civil liberties, economic opportunities, cultural participation, and suggestions for Southerners, for the Negro, and for the North. These areas were
consistent with the league's adopted programs, and the report was forwarded in the hopes that the findings would be useful to the
organization.

On April 25, 1945, the league received a letter from the National Negro
Congress signed by Mary McLeod Bethune, Stephen H. Fritchman, Adam
Clayton Powell Jr., Henrietta Buckmaster, Lewis Morrill, Max Yergan, and
Helen Gahagan Douglas asking for support for a statement about integra-
tion of the armed forces.[10] The league's support was solicited as part of a
"selected group of leaders, representing a cross-section of American life."[11]
There is no indication that league leaders signed on. This inaction was
consistent with the league practice of not taking a stand on racial matters,

even though the proposed platform of the 1946 convention intuitively aligned with the request.

PROPOSED PLATFORM

The platform represents positions taken by the League as a whole in fields of government.

I. GOVERNMENT BY THE PEOPLE REQUIRES:
- A. The protection of the citizen in his constitutional rights, especially those of freedom of speech, religion, assembly, and press.
- B. Removal of legal and administrative discriminations against women and minority groups.
- C. A system of free public education with equal opportunity for all and adequate protection for academic freedom.
- D. Legal protection of all citizens in their right to vote.

To This End the League Has Supported or May Support:

1. The extension of suffrage to the District of Columbia.
2. Abolition of the poll tax as a prerequisite to voting.
3. Registration systems designed to facilitate voting and protect against fraud.
4. Specific legislation designed to ensure women equal guardianship, jury service, independent citizenship. Opposition to the equal rights amendment.
5. Federal aid to public education administered by state departments of education.[12]

This seventeenth convention saw the first serious discussion by delegates about discrimination within the organization's operation when the league was confronted with discrimination in convention hotel selection, as reported in a *New York Times* article, "Race Bias Taken Up by Women Voters." The article indicated that Mrs. Maxwell Barus, president of the New Jersey league, had presented a resolution to the convention that the league only patronize hotels "which accepted all delegates without discrimination as to race" at its biennial conventions. The motion was carried by a voice vote. The article noted that the genesis of this action was the treatment of two Negro delegates to the convention. These delegates, Mrs. E. C. Grady of St. Louis and Mrs. Joseph Snowden, who represented a unit of the Cook County, Illinois, league, were forced to stay with friends because they were unable to get accommodations at the hotels where the other delegates were staying.[13]

This convention's delegates were also confronted with two other issues related to racial discrimination. Two motions were presented: one to obtain consideration of a blanket item calling for "protection of minority groups against discrimination" and another to request an addition to an agenda item of a section against racial discrimination in immigration and against lowering quotas.

> Mrs. Don Datisman of Indiana, offering the anti-discrimination item, explained that it had been rejected by the league's national board to shorten the legislative program and also on the ground that other items, such as the one against discrimination in employment made it unnecessary.[14]

Anna Lord Strauss, presiding president, justified the league's current work in helping educate the women voters of many other nations and concluded the convention by stating:

> Our nation is still a testing ground for representative government and the eyes of the world are upon us . . . We have only begun to assume our responsibility, long overdue, for leadership in world democracy.[15]

Again, given the opportunity to prioritize the elimination of domestic discrimination, the league leadership chose to focus on global issues.

An assessment of the lack of progress in addressing issues of race and voting was evident as the league approached an organizational milestone.

> The thirty years after the ratification of the Nineteenth Amendment have been called decades of discontent for feminists in the United States . . . For African-America women, discontent was compounded by disillusionment. The mainstream of the women's movement had failed to seek common ground for political action between blacks and whites. Race, which often determined class, took priority over gender during the decades of discontent.[16]

By the beginning of the 1950s, there was an increase in the number of state and local leagues requesting guidance from the national leadership about the inclusion of women of color as "full" members. The recorded minutes from the national board meeting (April 28 to May 1, 1950) reflect the tenor of the conversation. Although the board did not take a position on integration at this meeting, it did suggest that groups not be divided into Negro and white groups.

> It was agreed that it was desirable to have all racial and religious groups represented in League membership, but the problem of southern states

was recognized. The approach in many areas of the South was construct-ive and indicative of a real desire to move ahead, and was subject to serious discussion at state and local League conferences. It was agreed that some Leagues were not well enough established in the community to seek Negro members, but that serious consideration be given to Negroes seeking the League. Opinion was expressed that at some point, education must become active in this area and that action could lead to education. This has been borne out to be the experience in Oklahoma which had taken in Negro members in the face of threats that it would ruin the League, which result has not materialized.[17]

The historic explanation for the attitude of national league leadership toward the exclusion of women of color was that the league consisted of privileged women who lived at the center and whose perspectives on real-ity rarely included knowledge and awareness of the lives of women and men who lived on the margins. Ironically, the majority of women of color who participated in the suffrage movement and later the league were also privileged, yet they still endured the condescension of white women.

Hope Amid Hollow Claims of Progress

It is the women of America—black and white—who are to solve this race problem, and we do not ignore the duty of black women in the matter. They must arouse, educate and advance themselves. The white woman has a duty in the matter also. She must no longer consent to be passive. We call upon her to take her stand.[18]

Women of color were hopeful throughout the suffrage movement and transition to the League of Women Voters that white women would note their parity in the struggle.

On one occasion when the members of the association were registering their protest against a certain injustice, I arose and said "As a colored woman, I hope this Association will include in the resolution the injustices of various kinds of which colored people are victims."
  Are you a member of this Association? Miss Susan B. Anthony asked. "No I am not, I replied, but I thought you might be willing to listen to a plea for justice from an outsider."[19]

Women of color dared to believe that the league, as a mainstream organ-ization, would recognize the importance of their inclusion. That, how-ever, was not the case. A stark contrast existed between intentional and unintentional action of the league's national leaders. Women of color were not defeated by this experience. Their choices for affiliation were invisibility, assimilation, or something in between.

> I have done this, not because I want to tell the world how smart I am, but because both a sense of justice and a regard for truth prompt me to show what a colored woman can achieve in spite of the difficulties by which race prejudice blocks her path if she fits herself to do a certain thing, works with all her might and main to do it and is given a chance.[20]

The league's lack of recordkeeping complicated the ability to discern, other than anecdotally, how many women of color this impacted. For the first decade of the league's existence, 1920–1930, no data on the number of members of color are on record. No figures on the number of local leagues are available earlier than 1945. This lack of data provided cover for the absence of decision-making. It also provided an environment conducive for leadership to ignore what, without data, could not be identified as a problem.

The national league continued to avoid taking positions on integration and civil rights throughout the 1950s. Zelia Ruebhausen, appointed in 1946 as an official observer at the United Nations, mentioned civil rights in an article describing a United Nations vote in support of a report condemning intervention in Hungary by the Soviet Union. Ruebhausen was particularly embarrassed by a comment from the Russian delegate to the ambassador from Ceylon saying that he would be "safer in the streets of Budapest than he would be in Little Rock." She concluded by reminding league members that,

> this question of how the United States treats a colored minority at home is a sensitive and important issue to the rest of the world where only one person out of four is white. If the United States is to exert leadership, it cannot do it by dollars alone. We must also live up to our beliefs in the dignity of man and the rights of all citizens to equal opportunities.[21]

Despite Ruebhausen's impassioned plea, the national board continued to avoid the subject at its next meeting. The secretary recorded, "At this time there does not seem to be a need for discussing integration, so it was agreed not to take time for it."[22]

At the 1950 convention, President Strauss addressed societal changes intended to bring about a sense of urgency to the league conversations on race. Shortly after that convention, local and state leagues began communicating, with more frequency, their concerns and requesting guidance from the national leadership. Most notably, local and state league leaders presumed to speak on behalf of women of color, when in fact their queries more poignantly spoke to the impact on their leagues and their standing in the community.

While the league was under pressure because of its internal posture on race, it was also being exposed for the hypocrisy of its external position. An article in the *New York Herald Tribune* showed that when the league leadership felt its program was "overloaded," issues of race became nonessential. The headline of the article, "Women Voters Reject Action on Civil Rights," called attention to the difference between the league's principles and its perceived desire for practicality. Three proposals for action on "civil rights issues for the 1950–1952 program failed to receive a necessary two-thirds vote from almost 100 delegates and alternates attending the league's national convention, although all received majority support."

> Although there was no discussion of these proposals on the floor, a number of delegates explained their opposition to reporters with the conviction that their adoption would "split the league right down the middle." Others felt that the items were too controversial for the non-partisan league.
>
> "That has nothing to do with it," Miss Anna Lord Strauss, retiring league president, said afterwards. "It's all a matter of program load. It has nothing to do with the subject matter. The whole thing in the league is how much program we can handle. That's what is being thought out."[23]

To respond to the increasing sentiment for guidance from the state and local leagues, the League of Women Voters of the United States published a draft of "How to Get and Keep Members Active, Interested and Permanent" in August 1953. The publication addressed all issues of recruiting and retaining members and included a section on "cross-section representation." This section suggested some interesting guidance and was the first national publication that appeared to leave flexibility for integration.

> It is not enough to say that League member-be open to women citizens of every section of the community. A planned effort must be made to obtain that cross-section. Differing backgrounds, ideas, experiences, and perspectives result in a dynamic League qualified to speak for the community as a whole. Ideally, all economic, social, nationality, political geographic, and racial groups should be represented . . . But it should always be remembered that a genuine interest in the purpose and program of the league is the most important reason for membership, not the fact that a woman represents a particular segment of the community.[24]

Leagues were instructed to analyze their membership distribution according to geographic, economic, political, national, racial, religious, and social affiliations, as well as approximate age group and whether they are housewives or work outside their homes. They were instructed, "Don't call each member and ask her how much her husband earns, to what political party she belongs, or from what country her grandfather came."[25]

After the distribution of the publication, numerous responses were received in the national office. Soon after the distribution of the publication, state and local leagues began to collect and report data on their Negro membership. Most of the reports were obtained from delegates at convention. One such report indicated that there was one Negro member at Kansas City, no Negroes at Shreveport, one Negro member of the Memphis league who attended two sessions, and two to three who attended the dinner at the YWCA.

State presidents attempted to connect with each other at convention to discuss the issue of membership integration and share strategies for avoiding what some perceived as an inevitable conflict.

One response in particular, on August 15, 1953, challenged the content of the membership publication and its impracticality of implementation.

> As for the insertion of a paragraph called "Open Membership": I had the feeling that this text might leave the impression that the League picks and chooses it members and that it would be legitimate to try to avoid the kind who will be inactive or not give much to the League. . . . What is more, our "open membership" policy is more than just a "cross-section" policy and needs mention in its own right—particularly for Leagues in the south or elsewhere where there may be a discriminatory attitude in the community toward minority groups.[26]

Turning Point—The 1950s

During the 1950s, the nation and the League of Women Voters were confronted by two major issues: the Red Scare and civil rights. The league embraced action on the former with the adoption of its Freedom Agenda and shied away from the latter.[27] The league would not risk its prestige on civil rights. Its tradition of finding consensus or avoiding the issue continued. For many local and state league members who were taking action, the national response was viewed as too much study and too little action.

The decade of the 1950s witnessed unwavering attempts by people of color to be acknowledged as first-class citizens and saw the league address the challenges of race and gender in its organizational structure in many instances through its silence. In 1950, a black lawyer, Mrs. Ashley Pickerson, inquired about joining the Mobile, Alabama, league. In 1951, after deciding that joining the all-white Mobile group might cause them "embarrassment," she organized an all-black group in Tuskegee and applied for local league status.[28] While League of Women Voters bylaws state that "any person who subscribes to the purposes and policy of the League is eligible for membership," Southern leagues would not disregard the fact that they were living in the Southern culture.

There was no overt recognition by the national leadership that race should be a priority consideration of the League of Women Voters, despite landmark legislation and Supreme Court rulings. While Article II, Section 1 of the league bylaws states, "Any person who subscribes to the purpose and policy of the League shall be eligible for membership," the internal organizational structure consisted of "second-class" leaguers—women of color. While many of the state and local leagues included, in some capacity, women of color, the national leadership chose to focus on other issues. Their decisions would lead to unanticipated consequences.

The year 1954 was pivotal for the nation as well as the League of Women Voters. By the time the convention opened, two of the most important issues of the postwar era—the Cold War, as exemplified by the Army–McCarthy hearings, and civil rights, as exemplified by the pending Supreme Court decision in the case of *Brown v. Board of Education of Topeka*, Kansas—were in the news. During the next four years, the league confronted the former but shied away from addressing the latter.[29]

After the Supreme Court's landmark decision in *Brown v. Board of Education (I)*, much of the attention in Congress toward education during the remainder of the Eisenhower administration focused on integration rather than increased federal funding for local schools. On the subject of school desegregation, the league was silent. Because of the controversies related to both race and religion that were tied to educational issues, the league's national leadership believed it was unable to develop a comprehensive national position on education that would satisfy its state and local leagues. Not surprisingly, the same concerns that prevented the league from having an active role in civil rights hindered its effectiveness in areas related to federal aid to education. Consequently, the league did not have a voice in the formulation of any national education policy.

Percy Maxim Lee served as president during this, one of the most pivotal times in the history of the league. She handled it with considerable skill and kept the organization moving forward while often skirting the issue of race. Lee was the first commuter president and spent two weeks a month at the national office. At that time, the league had an apartment on P Street. Changes in the league included the publication of the *National Voter* magazine in 1951 and the transition of the Overseas Education Fund to the League of Women Voters Education Fund in 1957.

At the twenty-first convention, held in 1954 in Denver, Colorado, members were still referred to by their husbands' names. The 1954 Convention delegate profile recorded that all board members were married and none worked outside the home. At this convention, which was critical to conversations on race, there was no mention of race. It was at this convention that the first attempt at controlling for long debates was made. By convention rules, each state would caucus and choose six spokesmen: "It is expected that each group will determine its own method for selecting the spokesman."[30] This could account for why blacks weren't chosen to speak from the floor or why issues of race were not fully addressed.

The review of President Lee's speeches indicates that her commitment to the rights of individuals was mentioned often, and she wanted the members to cooperate in leading their communities to action on civil rights. In her 1954 address, she stated:

> I have come to look upon the League not as just a worthwhile but somewhat incidental occupation, but as a vivid and vital expression of that imperishable idea that is deeply rooted in the American conscience . . . the idea of the dignity and worth and capacity of the individual human being. This idea does not need crisis-treatment at this time as much as it needs steady, commonplace, everyday application.[31]

Lee cautioned delegates that the league had no position on integration or segregation. She stated:

> Every effort must be exerted to protect the integrity of the League and its usefulness and at the same time promote the principles in which it believes. The league must find a way to exert a calm, unemotional and wise leadership in the search for solutions.[32]

Two weeks after the league's triumphant 1954 national convention and the opening of the Freedom Agenda office in New York, the Supreme Court of the United States handed down its landmark decision in *Brown v. Board of Education of Topeka*, Kansas. The League of Women Voters, an organization that prided itself on being responsive to current issues, was strangely silent. The issue of integration was not new to the league. Although the board from time to time discussed integration of the membership, the conclusion of every discussion always remained that integration of the league in the South would be impossible to achieve. The board left the matter to the state and local leagues for action that would be "appropriate" for them. The 1954 *Brown v. Board of Education of Topeka* decision provided an environment in which the league had to consider its internal philosophy and external actions regarding segregation.

In a letter from Tennessee, sent to the national office on May 27, 1954, regarding Negro membership, questions regarding the league's stance on this issue were raised. A handwritten note on the letter stated "good question." The state league was seeking guidance and materials from the national leadership on how to respond to the request for membership of "a large group of Negro women who do domestic work and other unskilled jobs." The letter noted that one of their leaders was currently a league member who wanted to start a unit in her neighborhood. While their request for guidance indicated a desire to "find a spot for these women so they can become effective league members as well as be benefitted by membership in it," meaning the league leaders still regarded membership of this group as a problem. Their primary question was "whether there is a place in the league for persons or groups of persons of no education."[33]

The letter was answered by the organization secretary. The letter contained many unsubstantiated assumptions about these women simply based on race: 1) They are uneducated; 2) Having them as members would not benefit the league; 3) They need remedial instruction. The letter raises the questions about how white leaguers saw their interaction with women of color. Many saw themselves as being altruistic and black women as being second-class citizens, never acknowledging the value that this group of women would bring to the league. The response to this letter begins:

> Your letter poses an interesting question, one which we often ask ourselves. We say the League should be a cross-section organization, but can it really be? Our belief is that it can, but it takes working at it.[34]

There were no documents indicating what follow-up action occurred.

Another correspondence from Tennessee on July 19, 1954, provides a contradictory philosophical response to the earlier query.

> Knoxville has never had a group of Negro women domestic workers organized into a discussion unit. We have had Negro members for several years now. These Negro members are school teachers, college faculty, domestic workers, etc. . . . They attend different ones fo [sic] our units and we hold our general meetings in places where we can have inter-racial groups.[35]

In 1954, only fifteen percent of the entire league membership came from the eleven Southern states. It was reported that there were less than one hundred members of color in the South. The Southern presidents agreed that their local and state organizations were simply not strong enough to challenge the racial status quo, even if the membership supported such a position. In order to avoid a battle with potentially devastating effects for the league, leadership decided that the league's position of neutrality would remain in place.[36] The presidents agreed that under league principle I—representative government established in the constitution—a state or local league could not adopt an agenda item that would result in a position favoring segregation because it violated the bylaws, which stated that membership was to be open.

The 1954 Supreme Court decision forced the league to engage in conversations it had heretofore not made a priority. Recorded minutes of the meeting of Southern presidents in Atlanta expose the ambivalence to take action. Representatives from leagues in Texas, Tennessee, Florida, Virginia, Louisiana, South Carolina, North Carolina, Alabama, Mississippi, and Arkansas were present. Highlights of the meeting were recorded and filed. Eleven state presidents attended. The only Southern state not there was Kentucky.

In a letter to Lee in preparation for the Atlanta conference, Mrs. William C. (Frances) Pauley, organizer, posed several questions:

1. In saying that you "uphold the Constitution of the U.S. as interpreted by the supreme court [sic]" are you saying the LWV is upholding the decision and thereby is opposed to segregation?
2. Is it fair to our membership to give the impression of being opposed to segregation?
3. How do you answer, "Have you negro members?" (I say "yes" in the U.S., "no" in Georgia and quickly add that our membership is open to any person who subscribes to the purpose and policy of the League.) But again is this fair to that part of our membership (perhaps a small minority) who are so opposed to <u>any</u> change in our [sic] "old Southern customs." (When <u>is</u> the LWV in the South going to face up to the facts of life? If only we had followed Anna L. Strauss' advice ten years ago, when she wanted us to have negro members!)
4. Now that we have taken a stand on the school amendment and are put in the category with the bi-racial groups will we stand by them to lend a hand in case they get into hot water? For instance the Governor says that the Southern Regional Council will be investigated under the <u>Subversive Activities Act.</u> Also

Jane (our first vice-president) and Phil Hammer have again been accused of being subversive.

5. If we get in a <u>really</u> hot spot ourselves where do we get legal help?[37]

An excerpt from a subsequent, July 1, 1954, letter to the national board also speaks to these issues. The contents of the letter pointed to the inconsistencies in league principle and practice in stating that the league allowed Negro members but had no position on segregation of schools. The letter also indicated concern for the impact on league membership if the league took a stand.[38]

The role of the league in the debate about segregation also became an internal struggle it could no longer ignore. How to address this situation without alienating state and local leagues that did not want to take action, particularly Southern leagues, posed a particular problem for the national leadership. A letter to Southern state presidents from Mrs. Lee was sent out July 9, 1954. According to her letter, the need for the two-day conferences resulted from numerous letters received from league leaders in the South "expressing grave concern over the role of the League in dealing with the problems raised by the Supreme Court decision on segregation." Most notably, there were no black voices in this conversation.

A July 14, 1954, letter from the president of the League of Women Voters of Kentucky explained why Kentucky was not participating in the Atlanta conference. The Kentucky board agreed that the Kentucky league did not face the problems that many of the Southern leagues faced with respect to the Supreme Court decision on segregation. She indicated that due to a tight budget, the board did not see where the expense was warranted. Additionally, she gave examples of how Negro students were already integrated into the University of Kentucky without incident. She stated, "I should say that more and more we feel ourselves more oriented to the Midwest than to the south."[39]

In preparation for the Atlanta conference, held on July 27 and 28, numerous requests for guidance from the primary conveners were generated. Despite not having her questions fully responded to, Mrs. Pauley and her planning committee drafted the following agenda. There is no record that any women of color were invited to attend as observers or speakers.

ATLANTA CONFERENCE AGENDA

July 27–28, 1954
Tuesday July 27, 9:30 a.m.–12 p.m.—Mrs. Lee presiding.
Welcome and brief introduction—Mrs. Pauley

Explanation of purpose and agenda—Mrs. Lee

General discussion by state representatives.

The purpose of this discussion is to examine the problem as it is emerging in each state, exchange experiences that have a common, useful application and define the key questions which may fruitfully be put to the outside consultants. It is hoped that problems of only League nature will be postponed until the next day. Some of the questions which will be asked of the state representatives are:

1. What is the general attitude in your state toward the Supreme Court decision? What is being done to promote understanding of the issue? 2. What plans are being formulated by the state administration to cooperate with the Supreme Court in working out an overall approach? Do you anticipate any unusual difficulties? 3. Is legislative activity imminent, either to implement the decision or to attempt to circumvent it? Will it be an issue on the November ballot? How largely will it figure in the fall campaign? 4. What are the forces in your state which are working or might be joined to work for a long-range solution?

Tuesday, July 27, 1:30 p.m.–3:00 p.m.

Further discussion and formulation of questions for consultants.

3:00–3:15 recess

3:15–5:30 Discussion by consultants of questions submitted to them. It is planned that the consultants will be experienced in the fields of law, social and political sciences and the press. It is anticipated that this discussion will be broad in its approach and not limited to the League of Women Voters.

Evening: Dinner with Mrs. Pauley

Wednesday, July 28 9:30 a.m.–5:00 p.m.—Mrs. Lee presiding

General discussion of the role of the League of Women Voters in regard to the Supreme Court decision. Some of the areas which will be examined:

1. How to promote understanding of the issue and practical, wise solutions. 2. Authority of the League in this field. Should there be a "League position"? 3. How to handle ballot issues. 4. How to handle candidate meetings if it seems wise to hold them. 5. Attitudes of other organizations and how to promote cooperation. 6. Responsibility of state and local Boards to League members. 7. Desirability of cross-section membership, Negro members 8. Public relations problems. 9. Practical political questions.[40]

On August 18, 1954, minutes of the meeting were distributed for discussion to league leaders. They were reminded that the stated purpose of the meeting was to analyze the league's relationship to the Supreme Court decision and clarify its position on segregation. The conference participants recognized that any indication of "favoring integration in the deep

Southern states would be difficult to reach without great dissension within the League." They believed that the conflict that would result with their state officials could jeopardize any contribution that the league could make in the community, particularly in Voters Service. The guidance from the national board and staff against adopting agenda items on integration were in some cases interpreted as an order.[41]

The minutes of the meeting of the presidents of Southern states indicated that the following state presidents were present: Mrs. L. K. Richards, president, LWV of Texas; Mrs. Harry Bainbridge, president, LWV of Tennessee; Mrs. Albert Simons, president, LWV of South Carolina; Mrs. Harold Walters, president, LWV of North Carolina; Miss Warren Piper, president, LWV of Florida; Mrs. Winston Brooke, president, LWV of Alabama; Mrs. Carl Marcy, president, LWV of Virginia; Mrs. T. C. Fisher, president, LWV of Mississippi; Mrs. H. Theo. Goss, president, LWV of Louisiana; Mrs. LeMon Clark, chairman, and Mrs. Delbert Swartz, member, Committee for a State League in Arkansas; Mrs. John G. Lee, Mrs. Robert F. Leonard, Mrs. J. D. Perryman, and Mrs. Henry L. Killen of the national board and Miss Dixie Drake of the national staff. Mrs. Lee began the conference by emphasizing the impact of the Supreme Court decision. She reminded participants that "it is not just the South's problem but the North, East, South and West are all involved and must share responsibility." She continued by reminding leaders that it was essential "that League leaders most immediately involved meet and agree on the role of the League." Most important to the conversation was that the integrity of the league and its usefulness be protected and the principles in which it believes be promoted. She asked that the problems be examined objectively and dispassionately and expressed the hope that the conference might merge with a uniform and mutually useful approach.[42]

Each state reported on the state's general attitude toward the Supreme Court's decision, what was being done to promote understanding of the issue, what plans were being formulated by the state administration to cooperate with the Supreme Court in working out an overall approach or to oppose or circumvent the decision, and whether unusual difficulties were anticipated.

On the second day of the conference, President Lee opened the morning session by asking whether the League of Women Voters had any authority to take a position on the question of segregation itself. The reaction of the participants was a thorough discussion of the league's current platform principles. It was unanimously agreed that under principle I, the league had authority to oppose segregation. A debate led to the contradictory point that the league would have no authority to oppose segregation because there "is not now on the Current Agenda or Continuing Responsibilities anything that would authorize action."

In essence, this caused confusion because it indicated that while the league had the authority to oppose segregation, it had no authority to take a stand. The minutes indicate that "there was general agreement that it was a fortunate thing that the League could take no position at the moment."

> It was agreed that the state Boards should advise the local Leagues to avoid taking any stand on segregation and unless they had overwhelming membership support and considerable support in the community that they not take action on controversial school issues.[43]

The conversation on segregation naturally transitioned to the topic of Negro membership. Six of the states represented at the conference reported having Negro members: Texas, North Carolina, South Carolina, Arkansas, Tennessee, and Virginia. Their numbers were recorded in the minutes of the conference. Texas reported five leagues with only four or five Negro members in each league; Arkansas reported one league in Pine Bluff with just a few; Tennessee reported four leagues with no specific number of Negro members; South Carolina reported one league in Charleston with twelve to eighteen; Virginia reported four leagues and a total state Negro membership of twelve; and North Carolina reported five leagues with seven being the largest number of Negro members, except Kingston [sic], which was about half and half.

Each state then reported specific activities and actions that promoted or discouraged Negro membership. In Texas, for example, the Negro members asked to join. They attended unit meetings in homes, and one league moved its general luncheon meeting place so they could attend. In Arkansas, most members were from the Negro college. They noted that this was not the initial group that broached the subject of membership. Georgia reported that it had no direct applications for league membership but they cooperated with "one or two organizations having negro members."[44] Louisiana reported having no Negro members but expected requests very soon. They noted that some leagues were ready to integrate Negro members, while others found that they were in areas which would not condone integration.

Tennessee's report reflected the inconsistencies within the state. Tennessee reported four local leagues with Negro members from Negro colleges. They indicated that in some instances, the Negro members asked to join, and in others, white people have invited them to join. Memphis was identified as having had particular difficulty in integrating Negro members; it had previously had forty to fifty Negro members in a membership of 200 but at this point had about twelve Negro members. Nashville had eight Negro members with a membership of over 300. The Negro members attended unit meetings in the university library but were prohibited from luncheon meetings, as there was no place where they could be served.

Mississippi reported having no Negro members but was anticipating some applications. Alabama had no Negro members and had received one application years ago that had been withdrawn. Florida had no Negro members. Jacksonville had a Pullman Voters League whose members attend the league meetings, which were not luncheon meetings. Voter service material on candidates was not given to them.

The South Carolina league's recounting of its encounters with Negro members publicly highlighted the issues these state leaders felt they had to address. Their solution harbored assumptions to full integration.

> Several years ago a request came from a Negro woman, who moved to Charleston from Cincinnati. The League Board felt they could not turn her down, so talked with several leaders in the community, including the newspaper editors. Finally, after two months of deliberation, they invited a dozen or so outstanding Negro women to join. It will never be easy and no one of the women has contributed a great deal because their political education is so far behind. When interested they work awfully hard. Charleston has not given up its luncheon meeting, even though Negro members cannot attend the luncheon. They can come in afterwards for the program. In Columbia Negroes come to open meetings and feel welcome.[45]

While many of the leagues represented had no Negro members, both Virginia and North Carolina reported having success with integration in parts of their states. Virginia had had Negro members for six years at the time of the conference. They were described to be "of a fine type," already community leaders. They did not participate in units, "but there are enough meeting places where they are welcome and they occasionally come." It was reported that a "meeting is never scheduled where they cannot attend,"[46] which contradicted the previous statement that they did not participate.

North Carolina acknowledged that it had Negro members in five out of twelve leagues, with a Negro board member in Greensboro. Showing inconsistency in state efforts, they noted that Chapel Hill, a university town, had never been able to get a Negro woman because, in their experience, the women seemed "to be afraid because their jobs might be at stake." Integration efforts in other parts of the state met with mixed results. For example, "a crusade to get a lot of Negro members was stopped in Greensboro several years ago by a frank statement of a Jewish member of the Board to the effect that she thought they should come in gradually, otherwise they would not be representative."[47] In Charlotte, some of the white members refused to be introduced to the Negro members, but there were instances where Negro members attended meetings in homes. The Negro members were well integrated in Charlotte. In Asheville, there was no problem at all. In Durham, the wife of the Negro lawyer who had represented the plaintiffs in one of the cases of entry to the law school was invited to join. Only one member resigned from the league. Kingston [sic] had about 50 percent Negro members, but none were elected to the board. The president was from an old Kingstonian [sic] family.[48]

Characterizations of actions or inactions regarding Negro members in many cases reflected stereotypical characterizations and adherence to Southern culture. Applications were not required for league membership, yet some leagues required Negro members to submit applications. Some leagues felt that the "political education" of Negro women was far behind that which was required to be a member of the league, yet no assessment was made or required of members of the league.

These indignities and insults and the assumption of inferiority reflected how women of color were continually treated within the league organizational structure. In making these statements, league leaders ignored the glaring contradiction in league principles and practice.

In summarizing the conference discussion on Negro membership, participants agreed that no application for membership could be turned down on account of race but that someone could talk with the person, who may then withdraw her application for membership.

> In case she does not wish to withdraw the application she must be taken in. Under our By-laws there is no way to circumvent that, and with that as a known factor you try to prevent anything happening that would be detrimental to the League. It can be helpful to accustom people to the idea verbally. The state Board has an obligation to prepare the local Boards for the eventuality.[49]

It was also agreed that the less change in the pattern of the league, the better, but with good league procedures, little change would be necessary. Additionally, participants generally agreed that time was a most important factor in meeting the problems involved in the segregation issue; that in most areas, opposition was in direct proportion to the Negro population; that based on their knowledge of the situation, integration should come slowly; that the League of Women Voters could do more by not entering into controversial issues but by sticking to specifics when they began to emerge; and that the need for calmness and a temperate attitude should be emphasized. They concluded that precipitating measures and taking hasty action in the educational field would not furnish solutions.

In the "Highlights" account of the conference, it was stated, "It was just as strenuous as you have learned to expect a League meeting to be."[50] Three important observations were shared with all participants: 1) The league had no position on segregation. The next opportunity to take a position would be at the next convention, but there was no indication that there was a desire to do so; 2) Some state leagues had already taken positions in the absence of a national stand. Those states felt that they had not weakened the league by their stand but felt isolated from national support in their endeavors; and 3) The whole temper of the conference was that leagues must be extremely careful in the ways in which they supported the decision of the court and not do anything that would lessen the effectiveness of the organization.[51]

After the Atlanta meeting, the national board agreed that a local league could not come out with a position favoring segregation since the league, according to its bylaws and principles, was an integrated organization. The following year, the *Report on League Interest in Integration* was sent to board members prior to the April board meeting, but the minutes made no mention of the contents of the report. In a section of the printed materials that addressed public relations, it was mentioned that there was great resistance in the South to integration and that it was becoming increasingly difficult for the league to remain neutral. "Failure to oppose integration will be construed as support for it," a staff member added.[52] In the spring and summer of 1954, Southern leagues grew concerned as they anticipated their role in communities resisting compliance to the Supreme Court decision. The national league leadership recommended that leagues facilitate full compliance.

The Mississippi state president, after taking consensus from her board, urged in June of 1954 that local leagues discuss the public school issue and take a stand for an "adequate public school system for all children." She had hoped to have a league position to announce publicly, but correspondence between herself and the national board made clear that neither the Mississippi president nor the national board stood unaware of the potential consequences of taking any stance on education. A letter to the national board announced her concerns.

The national board advised the Mississippi league to exercise great caution and warned the Mississippi president to make sure that when coming out in favor of public schools, the league should make it quite clear that the stand is for a public school system and not against segregation.

> Taking a stand in favor of the public school system would not authorize the League either to favor or oppose a particular plan to implement the Supreme Court decision until all local Leagues had studied it and again reached agreement on whether they wanted to support or oppose such a plan. Certainly the implementation of the Supreme Court decision . . . must be carried out in a thoughtful unemotional manner . . . Local boards, as well as, the state board should be careful that they have the support of the League members; otherwise, the League cannot be very effective. However, by bringing to bear the orderly democratic processes in which we are experienced, the Leagues in southern states can make a contribution during this period of adjustment.[53]

In 1954 in the South, the league image was no longer that of the fearless progressive organization it had been in 1920. That image had faded. The Atlanta participants understood the wisdom of the charted course of public silence. The league's posture toward the South did little to challenge its disinclination toward integration. Correspondence from the national board to Southern leagues conveyed little sense of urgency to be prepared for and assist in immediate compliance with the Supreme Court. They suggested adhering to the timetables of others, no matter how slow.[54]

The national leadership exercised a passive-aggressive approach on issues of race. Recognizing that the issue would not disappear and that ultimately the organization would have to take a position, leadership's conversation about the league's position intensified. On April 25, 1955, President Lee was invited to attend the Southwestern Regional Conference on Integration in Houston, Texas, on May 17; "as part of the work of the Commission on community assets available for integration, we plan to have a series of short statements by representatives from some of the outstanding agencies working in the field of human relations."[55] The invitation was also sent to the Houston league. There is no indication that the league participated in this event.

On May 5, 1955, President Lee replied to a letter from Bishop S. L. Greene, chairman of the Southwide Conference on Integration in New Orleans, Louisiana, who issued the invitation. She declined, indicating that she could neither present nor submit a statement for presentation "since the League of Women Voters of the United States has taken no position in regard to the implementation of the Supreme Court decision on integration."[56] Her explanation was that the league program was adopted by the convention every two years and that the convention had met in 1954, before the court handed down its statement in *Brown v. Board of Education.*

The league acted deliberately, but without a sense of urgency, in its stance toward integration both in society and within the organization itself. This is underscored in a June 27, 1955, letter from Mrs. Etta Wright, president of the League of Women Voters of Liberia, to President Lee requesting information from the league. Mrs. Wright indicated that they were organized in five counties and three provinces in the Republic of Liberia. The league sent materials and words of support for the organization's success. There is no indication how long this league continued to exist. The irony of the league supporting black members on the global stage but making no assertive efforts on the domestic front or in the organization as a whole was not lost on leaguers of color.

The issue of integrated leagues would be front and center for the remainder of the 1950s as local and state leagues continued to seek guidance from the national leadership. The confusion that occurred over the lack of a clearly stated position intensified as leagues were left to make their own decisions in light of this ambiguity. Such was the case in North Carolina.

> On October 24, 1955 Miss Vivian Irving, a high school teacher and member of the American Friends Service Committee, who has long been interested in the work of the League of Women Voters, became the first colored member of the Raleigh League. The president, the vice-president, and unit organization chairman were immediately faced with the question of how to help the League adjust to this new factor in our experience in a manner consistent with the principles of the League and with the future outlook of the new South which would still not be an unwarranted imposition upon personal attitudes of those members whose backgrounds have not prepared them to receive colored persons in their homes for meetings.[57]

Miss Irving's membership and acceptance was a source of intense conversation with the Raleigh board. Subsequently, six members submitted letters of resignation, expressing that integration "went against all southern tradition and the entire social structure of the South."[58] As reflected in the recommendations to the Raleigh board, presented on November 7, 1955, by the unit organization chairman, the situation was perceived as creating a problem, with the salient question being, "How can the Raleigh League best adjust to the admitting of colored members?" The three recommendations that were presented "were in no sense preconceived, but are the logical result of strenuous inquiry."[59] The first recommendation was to consider holding all meetings in public places. This would require a significant change in the league custom of holding events in members' homes and could possibly eliminate the social aspect of the organization. This was not recommended as an option. The second recommendation was to set up a unit at the YWCA that "both colored and white members could feel free to attend." This recommendation was also rejected, as it would leave the situation unresolved. The third recommendation was the one proposed to the board for implementation on November 7, 1955. In that scenario, each unit would identify one member who would be willing to use her home on a regular basis for league meetings. This was thought to be the least controversial solution, and it replicated such systems being used effectively by a variety of leagues nationally. The committee believed that it required the least amount of reorganization and maintained the league custom of meeting in homes instead of public places. The committee was confident that this plan was the only logical and proper one possible to produce the desired results.[60]

At the request of the North Carolina state president, the Raleigh league president sent a copy of the recommendations to President Lee and the national board indicating that the recommended item had been approved unanimously. The letter indicated the seriousness with which they took this matter and their belief that they could continue to serve the community.

> There are six bona fide southerners on our board, which has a full membership of 15. So that I believe this board can be considered a fair representation of the membership as a whole, and that any difficulties the local league may experience with regard to Negro membership need not be expected to undermine it seriously, certainly not to the extent that abandonment of our principles would have done in any such attempt to evade the issue as has been made in the past.[61]

A handwritten comment on the original letter indicated that this was a "good report." Dixie Drake, program-organization secretary, responded on behalf of Mrs. Lee on November 18, 1955. Her response was filed as "League of WV Membership Negro," along with a variety of other letters about race. It should be noted that also in 1955, there was an intentional discussion of admitting men as members.

In 1956, the national league received unfavorable national publicity when *The New York Times* published a story, "Voters Unit Split Over Racial Issue,"[62] detailing the resignation of eleven officers of the Atlanta, Georgia, league, supposedly over integration. Although the national league bylaws provided that membership in the league was open to anyone who subscribed to the policies and objectives of the organization, the Atlanta league, the sixth largest league in the nation at the time with over eleven hundred members, had remained segregated.

At the Atlanta league's annual meeting in March 1956, the first act of the newly elected president was to introduce a resolution that the local league's policy of excluding Negro members be continued. When the resolution was narrowly defeated, she, three vice presidents, the secretary, the treasurer, and five directors of the local chapter resigned. Citing "increasing centralization of authority on a national level" as her primary reason, the president issued the following statement:

> We feel that the integration of our League at this time will raise so many problems that the effectiveness of the Atlanta League will be seriously impaired and that we can no longer properly function in the political life of our community.[63]

Ruth Lurie, the national vice president, who was responsible for organizational matters, addressed the Georgia resignation in a report included in the April board briefing. Lurie wrote: "It is not at all surprising that the heightened tension in the South on the segregation question has been reflected in the leagues in some of these states."[64] She described the Atlanta controversy as a personality conflict between the Georgia president and the Atlanta board:

> Although the issue of racial segregation was publicized as the cause of this action, it comes as the culmination of a deep seated and long standing antagonism between the Atlanta and state board.[65]

She went on to mention that the Mississippi state president had recently resigned, leaving only a small board:

> It is possible that in a state as lagging and backward as Mississippi, we hastened the organization of a state League before the locals were ready to shoulder it.[66]

Race was not specifically mentioned as a part of the problem in Mississippi in the communication to the national office, even though it was discussed at the same time as the problems in Georgia. The attitude toward the demographics of league membership was also reflected in leaguers' opinion about the amount of energy that should be exerted toward the segregation-integration debate. Former first lady of the United States and former League of Women Voters vice president of legislative affairs Eleanor Roosevelt believed strongly that women deserved a place at the table when it came to politics. She did not distinguish by race. Her 1956 column published in the *Washington News* exposing the league's hypocrisy on issues of segregation for its own members engendered mixed responses from local and state leagues and an equally ambiguous response from the national leadership. Mrs. Roosevelt commented: "What an inconsistent people we are. Segregation in the League of Women Voters might make sense if all barriers to voting by Negroes were lifted."[67]

Since Mrs. Roosevelt's remarks specifically referenced Alabama, a letter was sent from President Lee to the Alabama league president in February 1956 assuring her that the national leadership had attempted to correct Roosevelt's remarks regarding segregation in the league.

> We felt that we should correct her impression and have written her today as follows: "In your column of February 24, as it appeared in the Washington News there is a comment about the League of Women Voters which is not quite correct. The League has no policy on segregation and its services are indeed made available to all citizens. I hesitated to call this to your attention but I thought you might receive some inquiries about League policy."[68]

As a result of the column, there were multiple requests for clarification on the league's position on segregation from the community at large and other organizations. In response to these queries, rather than acknowledge the unwillingness of the national leadership to act, the response invoked the states' rights mantra. The league exhibited the same tentativeness revealed by Mrs. Roosevelt's remarks.

> The League of Women Voters of the United States has no position on segregation of the races, in public schools or otherwise. I am enclosing a copy of our present national Program.
>   The state and local Leagues of Women Voters are practically autonomous in program matters, selecting those issues relating to state and local government in accord with the wishes of the membership. Usually only one or two items on each level of government are given attention during any program period. These are selected by the members in local meetings and in state and national Conventions.[69]

The 1956 convention, which marked the thirty-sixth anniversary of the founding of the league, was held at the Chicago Hotel Sherman. While many who had been longtime members of the organization would have preferred to "turn back the clock," the league found itself embroiled in internal controversies—controversies that mirrored the changes in society and would challenge the league's fidelity to its own principles. At the time, league traditions from its founding were still being adhered to. League board members were still being referred to by their husband's names. The 1956–1958 national board was still all white. The league was still collecting data on members who attended conventions, but race was not in the demographic data collected. Neither program nor practice conscientiously recounted perspectives through the lens of women of color.

To question whether race was an issue was to ignore a vital part of league history and its future. The program adopted by members at convention indicated no commitment to diversity. There was, however, emphasis on an international focus and the work of the league in the United Nations, particularly the Far East (Japan). To further marginalize women of color, article IV of the bylaws indicated that "only one local League in each community shall be recognized." That meant that "colored" leagues would have no standing in the organizational structure and, if they continued to function, would be relegated to becoming "units," as many of them technically had been from the beginning. In reality, this decision officially and intentionally eliminated colored leagues. There was concern that the league might not appeal to a wide variety of women, but many thought this could be overcome by proper use of materials and program items by local leagues.

The constraints on televised meetings and hotel accommodations, which required and often encouraged segregation, forced the league to make strategic decisions about how it presented itself as an organization. A newspaper article in the *Chicago Daily News* about the convention perpetuated the image of the league as a "white woman's" organization. The headline read, "No Orchids, Dances or Side Trips; League Plans a Working Convention."[70] There was a companion article that detailed how league spouses were "co-operative" in allowing their wives to relinquish the household duties to attend the meeting. It was noted that because of the nature of the membership, many leaguers had household help.

Information collected about the nature of league membership at convention reinforced the stereotypical image of the organization. In the 1956 survey of 971 of the 1,081 delegates to the league convention, it was noted that all but 25 of these 971 were married and they had an average of 2 children each.

Shirley Chisholm (1924–2005). (IanDagnall Computing/Alamy Stock Photo)

Their ages ranged from 23 to 74; 6 were 24 years old; 41 were under 30; 6 were over 70. The average age was 43; 637 at some point had business careers and 836 had some college experience. Twenty percent of the delegates surveyed were engaged in full- or part-time jobs, as secretaries, nurses, writers, teachers, researchers, psychologists, librarians, a TV reporter, and a branch manager. Thirty-eight percent found that their league responsibilities took from forty-one to one hundred hours per month, and 10 percent worked more than twenty-five hours a week on league activities. Forty percent were between thirty and forty. Thirty-seven percent had two children, 28 percent had three children, and 20 percent had four children or more.[71] The choice of questions in the survey provided a glimpse into what league leadership determined was important to know about its membership. The questions were devoid of any interest in collecting data on racial or ethnic diversity.

While 1956 marked the thirty-sixth anniversary of the founding of the league, the data of the survey did not indicate progress in expanding membership demographics. There were no statistics in the survey on women of color. When the secretary reported to the convention, she indicated that both "statistically and in narrative, they are a picture of the organization itself."[72]

The 1956 focus was on Communism. No priority discussion or action was given to the implementation of the tenets of the *Brown* decision, but there were announcements of league culture, such as "no smoking; no hats." A *Chicago Daily News* article from April 28, 1956, signified the priorities of the league at the time in an article entitled "This is No Pink Tea, Ladies." The reporter began by stating that even though the League of

Women Voters of the United States is "often called the most significant organization in the country," on "many controversial issues the league is silent, because the membership has not chosen those items for study and action." The reporter quoted a national league spokesman as saying, "We don't seek to expect unanimity among our members, but if there is a substantial difference of opinion on any issue, we simply don't take a position."[73]

The organization's lack of a stated position on integration posed a problem at the state and local levels. Local leagues continued to attempt to navigate the issues of segregation and integration and receive guidance from their state leagues in the absence of a solid policy from the national leadership.

Virginia leagues were particularly proactive in attempting to reconcile league principle and practicality, as demonstrated by a series of letters between Virginia leagues and the state and national leadership. One unquestionable example was the letter from the League of Women Voters of Hampton, Virginia, January 21, 1957, alerting the state leadership to its aversion to a hotel policy refusing to accommodate their Negro members at the state convention in Richmond.

The letter served to protest the treatment of its two board members and to request that a "uniform policy be established so that such embarrassing situations shall not arise again." The proposed policy would ensure that integrated leagues could attend state meetings "without embarrassment to Negro or white members." The letter indicated that at least two of the league's Negro board members felt that they should resign after the incident.[74]

The response to their request for a policy reiterated the fact that the league adopted such a policy at the 1946 convention. The board recognized, however, that "the practical aspects of carrying it out have been more difficult in the last year." The response concluded by reaffirming commitment to integrated membership. "Our Negro members are more important to us these days than ever when communication between groups is more difficult."[75]

The Virginia League of Women Voters continued to actively confront the issues of segregation in all venues while the national league sustained its passive role. The Alexandria League of Women Voters took a stand in the appointment of Negroes to the school board by urging the appointment of a Negro to the Alexandria school board. Their message to the board was that Negro representation would "contribute to the orderly implementation of the recent Supreme Court decision" outlawing segregation in public schools. Four names, including those of two Negroes, were offered in nomination for two school board posts that had become vacant on July 1. The two Negroes—Rev. Howard Stanton and Mrs. Edith Turner—were also backed by a number of colored organizations.[76]

Segregation at candidates' meetings had been the focus of considerable attention in Virginia since the last communication from the national leadership. The state custom had been that of segregating the audiences at these meetings. Just before the first meeting, the league was informed by the Defenders of State Sovereignty and Individual Liberties that unless the audience was segregated, as provided, they said, under section 18-327 of the Virginia code, a warrant would be secured against it for committing a misdemeanor. Attorney General William Hassan declined to issue a warrant, stating that in his opinion, the law did not apply to the league's meetings and that the league should continue such meetings on a nonsegregated basis, just as they had always done. The meetings were picketed since the NAACP was one of the cosponsors. The league continued to hold the meetings in a nonsegregated manner, but the issue did not go away.

The matter was filed as a field report on October 19, 1956. The report indicated guidance provided by the national board. The context provided indicated that the League of Women Voters of Arlington had a history of sponsoring joint candidates' meetings in school buildings. Guidance from the national staff reminded the league that it was "in no position to make a test case" because its actions would affect the entire league, both financially and in terms of integrity. It was recommended that if the Arlington league chose to proceed, they should seek legal advice about a "carefully worded written statement to be read at the beginning of the meeting, giving necessity for conforming to the law."[77]

Shortly after the first ruling, an alternate opinion was published in an Arlington newspaper which summarily removed the decision from the Arlington board. Virginia's attorney general ruled that audiences attending a series of debates between Arlington County board candidates "must be segregated by race."[78] The meeting sponsors agreed to comply with the ruling of the attorney general. Arlington was not the only community to face the challenge of nonsegregated meetings.

In 1956, Memphis faced a similar issue in sponsoring candidates' debates, not because of a legal ruling, but because the Peabody Hotel, where the event was to be held, had a policy prohibiting Negro guests. Because the league holds integrated meetings with white and Negroes attending, hotel management revoked the league's contract. Mrs. Keith Sherriff, the Voter Services chair, explained that the league was nonpartisan in making arrangements with the Peabody management. Thomas J.

McGinn, vice president and associate manager of the Peabody, said there had been a misunderstanding and hotel policy forbade Negro guests. He said the meeting could not be held there if Negroes attended. Mrs. Sherriff said efforts to arrange another meeting place would be made that day.[79]

The absence of a national policy on integration allowed for state and local leagues to pursue disputes on integration at their own discretion. By 1957, seventeen local leagues and eight state leagues had agenda items dealing with integration and discrimination that included schools and employment opportunities. These leagues were Little Rock, Arkansas; Berkeley, California; Washington, D.C.; Gary, Indiana; Montgomery County, Maryland; Minneapolis, Minnesota; St. Louis, Missouri; Des Moines, Iowa; Lawrence, Kansas; Webster Groves, Missouri; Portland, Oregon; Nashville, Tennessee; Alexandria, Virginia; Arlington, Virginia; Fairfax County, Virginia; Falls Church, Virginia; Madison, Wisconsin; Illinois; Kansas; Michigan; Missouri; Oregon; Virginia; and Wisconsin. In the Deep South, only the Little Rock, Arkansas, league had voted education to its agenda.[80]

These agenda items in many instances received an unenthusiastic response from members. A report to the national board, dated January 14, 1957, on membership in Virginia was representative of this reaction.

> We know definitely of about half a dozen people who have withdrawn from the League in protest against the adoption of the item, the admission of Negroes, or the referendum stand. My guess would be that there have been at least that many who joined as a result of our stand. How account for the other losses? . . .
>
> There was a real question whether the League's entering this highly controversial field would not be an effective barrier to organizing new Leagues. In one of the communities in which there was interest in the League, potential leaders did say that the mere question of the possible admission of Negroes would so divide the interested group that success was doubtful.[81]

Many of the conclusions regarding race were based on regional anecdotal information, not any objective data collection by the league. Even though it had the capability of conducting such research in partnership with universities and other organizations, it did not. To do so might have meant that the league would be further questioned about such data and the contradictions in league actions exposed.

The controversy confronting the league over its lack of a position on integration and the implementation of the *Brown* decision continued to call attention to the organization from both internal and external sources.

Dorothy Height (1912–2010) with Eleanor Roosevelt. (Everett Collection Inc/ Alamy Stock Photo)

Requests regarding the league's policy on inclusion of Negro women as members from outside organizations and researchers continued through the remainder of the decade and into the next. A consistent response was provided for all inquiries: "We cannot give you figures concerning Negro membership as our records are not kept that way." The response always included a statement that "there are Negro members scattered throughout the country, but it is not possible to tell you how many local Leagues have mixed membership. We do know from personal observation in visiting Leagues that there are Negro members in some Leagues in all sections of the country. We have no all-Negro Leagues."[82]

The response did not acknowledge the previously existing colored leagues nor provide any information on when they were disbanded. There was no explanation of the fact that despite collecting all types of data at conventions, the league did not keep data on race. By this time, the Special Committee on Negro Problems, which had become the Special Committee on Inter-Racial Relations, was extinct.

In an additional response to a request from a researcher, league policy was cited.

According to the By-Laws of the League of Women Voters of the United States "any person who subscribes to the purpose and policy of the league" is eligible for membership. . . . We have no way at all of knowing how many Leagues in the South—or anywhere in the country—have Negro members. Since no records are kept that would indicate race, the only way one could know would be personal knowledge.[83]

The response was always the same. The league did not keep such records. Given that queries on the participation of women of color in the league had been posed since its inception, the fact that such data was not collected seemed implausible. The opportunity was available. At each national convention, there was demographic data collected, but never on race. Race did not become a part of the data until 1978, when it was included in the report at the insistence of the two black national board members.

External forces also impacted the league's behavior and response. In a letter to the national office requesting materials on integration, the league's response was, "We do not have any on the subject. However, our Publications Catalog is enclosed and if you find other topics in which you are interested we will be happy to fill your prepaid order." The response implied that the conversation of race was not one that the league participated in; however, the league's internal struggle with race is well documented in its establishment of task forces and committees to address the issue since its founding.

Local and state leagues continued to engage despite national leadership's inactivity. The League of Women Voters of Pennsylvania participated in a National Conference for Human Rights, cosponsored by Honorable George M. Leader, governor of Pennsylvania, and Mr. David J. McDonald, president of the United Steelworkers of America. The premiere showing of the film *Burden of Truth* opened the conference. Produced as a project of the United Steelworkers of America Committee on Civil Rights, it graphically depicted the tragic effects of discrimination against Negroes.[84] Despite the participation of state and local leagues in activities informing and promoting integration, when the issue of civil rights surfaced, the national league leadership continued to restate that it had no formal position on segregation or civil rights.

Racial tensions intensified throughout this period as integration became a mandated way of life in many parts of the country. There was no attempt to reconcile spending so much time on the world situation without addressing the domestic situations. What becomes obvious is that the national leadership made a strategic decision to avoid what they perceived would be dissension in the organization.

President Lee acknowledged the extent of such feelings in the organization in 1958 when she said that "racial conflicts are as old as man [sic] . . . [because] man is his own worst enemy." She was undaunted by the scale of this problem, preferring to look upon the "growth and changing patterns of life" as common to everyone and offering "the league unparalleled opportunities for service and creative leadership."[85]

In her farewell address at the 1958 national convention, Lee once again felt a need to defend the league's position on school integration. Saying that neutrality was "the only tenable course," Lee pointed out that individual league members had worked "unobtrusively and undramatically to better conditions." While it was impossible to ignore the problem of integration, for Lee it would have been "disastrous to become involved in it."[86] In an attempt to reconcile principle and practicality, she stated, "The pursuit of liberty, equality and justice is still a mission incomplete."[87] Her commitment to the rights of individuals was mentioned often, and she wanted members to cooperate in lending their communities to action on civil rights.

Conclusion

The 1950s saw significant challenges with the implementation of integration originating from the *Brown v. Board of Education* U.S. Supreme Court decision. League members' arguments in the 1950s about a policy on segregation was in stark contrast to earlier policy considerations.

As the league approached the 1960s, there was some movement in its recognition that society was changing and that it had to change accordingly, albeit unwillingly. The twenty-third convention photo showed two black delegates. While some women were identified by their first names, the practice of identifying members by their husbands' names was still evident. It was, however, reflective of an inevitable transition. The national leadership of the league was still all white.

It is difficult to attribute motivation or intent or to overgeneralize the action or inaction of national league leadership. The League of Women Voters is a paradox in women's history—an association of women whose focus moved beyond women's issues to issues perceived to be in the public interest, yet who could not grasp the disingenuousness of not addressing the issue of race in its own organizational culture. To say that women of color who undertook the journey of affiliating with the league were looking through rose-colored glasses would be inaccurate. They were realists. They hoped that the league, with such noble principles, would value their membership and contributions on an equal footing with all other members. But they also understood the reality of the times. So, instead the lens they saw through was amber-colored—hopeful, yet realistic.

This is a part of league history that cannot be denied, no matter how big the rose-colored glasses we use. In 1944, the league pronounced that it was an association of members, and until 1960, it operated on bylaws adopted in 1946. Those bylaws, while not expressly excluding women of color from full participation from a policy perspective, did nothing to change the practices, fueled by lack of expectation and accountability from the national leadership, that all members be equally accepted.

Each decade presented new challenges. There were decades when the league's national leadership was more active in guiding state and local league actions on race relations internally and externally in what would become known as the "league way."

Notes

1. Terrell, 1940, 14–15.

2. Newman Ham, 2005, 15; Terrell, Mary Church, n.d., "Mary Church Terrell Papers," Library of Congress.

3. hooks, 2015, 12–13.

4. Statement of Principle, League of Women Voters of the United States, 1947.

5. Bucy, 2002, 1.

6. Ibid., 25.

7. Ibid., 177.

8. Gordon et al., 1997, 122; Mary Church Terrell, "Being a Colored Woman in the United States," Mary Church Terrell Papers, Collection 102, Box 3, Folder 53, 1, Manuscript Division, Moorland Spingarn Research Center, Howard University, Washington, D.C.

9. McDonald et al., 1944; North Carolina College for Negroes is now North Carolina Central University.

10. Library of Congress, Special Committee Folder.

11. Library of Congress, League of Women Voters Papers, Special Committee Folder.

12. League of Women Voters Papers Convention, 1946.

13. *New York Times,* 1946, May 2, Bess Furman.

14. League of Women Voters Papers, Convention, 1946.

15. League of Women Voters Papers, LWV Convention Transcripts 1946.

16. Terborg-Penn, 1998, 172; Gordon et al., 1997.

17. League of Women Voters Papers, Part I, reel 9; Bucy, 2002, 172.

18. Waisman and Tietjen, 2008, 677. Quote by Josephine St. Pierre Ruffin.

19. Newman Ham, 2005, 179. Quote by Mary Church Terrell, 1898.

20. Ibid., 30.

21. Ruebhausen, 1956, 1; Bucy, 2002, 175.

22. Minutes Board Meeting, 1958, September 8–10; League of Women Voters Papers, Part I, reel 11.

23. *New York Herald Tribune*, 1950, April 25, Judith Crist.

24. League of Women Voters Papers, *How to Get and Keep Members*, 1953.

25. Ibid.

26. Ibid.

27. Library of Congress Box II:667. At the 1954 national convention, the league concluded that its best contribution would be to develop a widespread awareness in regard to American heritage and individual liberty and its relationship to national security. This became a national initiative. A series of discussions ensued on the Bill of Rights and individual liberty in an atmosphere of the fear of Communism.

28. Library of Congress, League of Women Voters Files Drake to Pickerson, 1951, March; Dietrich, 1981, 11.

29. Bucy, 2002, 134–135.

30. League of Women Voters Papers, 1954 Convention Workbook, 128.

31. Osborn, 1994, 104.

32. Bucy, 2002, 172.

33. Library of Congress Folder, Special Committee on Inter-Racial Relations.

34. Ibid.

35. League of Women Voters Papers.

36. Young, 1989, 38–39.

37. Library of Congress Folder Special Committee on Inter-Racial Relations.

38. Ibid.

39. Library of Congress File, 1954 Container, 18.

40. Library of Congress Integration Folder, 1954.

41. League of Women Voters Papers; Bucy, 2002, 173.

42. Library of Congress Integration Folder, 1954.

43. Library of Congress, Integration Folder Minutes of the 1954 Conference, 7.

44. Ibid., 8.

45. Ibid., 11

46. Ibid., 13.

47. Ibid.

48. Library of Congress Integration Folder, 1954, 10–11.

49. League of Women Voters Papers.

50. League of Women Voters Papers, Highlights from the State Meeting, July 31, 1954.

51. Library of Congress Integration Folder Highlights, 1954, July 31, 2.

52. Board Briefing, Pre-Council meeting, 1955, 22–25 April; Board Briefing, 1955, 26 August; League of Women Voters Papers, Part I, reel 10; Bucy, 2002, 173.

53. League of Women Voters Papers Leonard to Fisher, 1954, June 16, Library of Congress; Dietrich, 1981, 8.

54. League of Women Voters Papers.

55. Ibid.

56. League of Women Voters Integration Folder.

57. Dietrich, 1981, 11.

58. Ibid.

59. League of Women Voters Papers. Letter to Mrs. Lee from President of LWV Raleigh, November 11, 1955.

60. Library of Congress Folder Interracial Relations.

61. Ibid.

62. Library of Congress. *New York Times*, 31, March, 1956; Bucy, 2002, 174.

63. "Voters Unit Split Over Racial Issue," *The New York Times*, 1956, March 31; Bucy, 2002, 174.

64. League of Women Voters Papers.

65. Ibid.

66. Board Briefing, 1956, April, League of Women Voters Papers, Part I, reel 10.

67. Library of Congress, League of Women Voters File, Segregation. Hand-written note, Roosevelt, Eleanor *My Day Article*.

68. Library of Congress File Segregation, Handwritten notes—Roosevelt, Eleanor, *My Day* article.

69. Library of Congress File Segregation.

70. League of Women Voters Papers, Convention Folder 1956.

71. Ibid.

72. Ibid.

73. League of Women Voters Files, *Chicago Daily News*, 1956, April 28, Helen Fleming.

74. Library of Congress File Segregation.

75. Library of Congress Interracial Relations File State Convention Report, 1956, April 18, 10.

76. Library of Congress Integration File.

77. Library of Congress File, League of Women Voters Papers, Voter Services, 1956, October 19.

78. Library of Congress File on Integration, 10.

79. Library of Congress File Segregation.

80. League of Women Voters Papers.

81. Ibid.

82. Ibid., January 30, 1958, was one year later—the date may have been a mistake. Handwritten note that this letter was filed under LWV members, Negro members, N.C. Files. Copy of the letter from April 4, 1956, was missing.

83. League of Women Voters Papers.

84. Library of Congress, League of Women Voters File Proceedings of a National Conference for Human Rights, 1958.

85. Osborn, 1994, 95.

86. League of Women Voters Papers, Proceedings, 1958 Convention, Atlantic City, New Jersey.

87. League of Women Voters Papers, 1958 Convention, 134; Osborn, 1994, 102.

CHAPTER SIX

The League Way

A woman is free if she lives by her own standards and creates her own destiny, if she prizes her individuality and puts no boundaries on her hopes for tomorrow.

—Mary McLeod Bethune

The 1960s has historical significance as the decade of turmoil, activism, and political change. It also presented the biggest challenge to the way the league functioned as more women of color saw the benefits of belonging to this mainstream organization. Membership in the league provided broader access to policy makers and opportunities that would allow these women to more expediently execute an agenda that would benefit people of color. As the League of Women Voters celebrated "Forty Years of a Great Idea" at its twenty-fourth convention in St. Louis, Missouri, in 1960, it could not have predicted that it would soon be entering a decade of rapid change and reorientation to its traditions, referred to by its members as the "league way."

Prompted by the civil rights movement, a totally new item appeared on the league program agenda in 1964: "Equality of Opportunity." This new topic led the league to consider, more intentionally, fair housing and educational and employment practices and eventually, in 1972, to support the Equal Rights Amendment.[1] Just as it had in 1944, this new activism caused another round of intense debate over what kind of organization the League of Women Voters should be. The national calls for greater involvement and action in promoting equality of opportunity were met in some, but not all, local communities with agreement. Toward the end of the 1960s, much of the advocacy for the league to take stronger positions came from an activist national board guided by President Lucy Wilson Benson (1968–1974).

While struggling with the externally imposed accountabilities for integration, the league attempted to minimize dissension among the membership by affirming that league membership reflected the common good. Still, well into the 1960s, visual depictions of the league did not encourage or invite women of color. The custom and culture of the league to use images and symbols of white members to represent the membership of the organization was still prevalent.

Throughout league history, there had been a strong connection with the National Council of Negro Women (NCNW). Convention minutes report that invitations were extended for NCNW representatives to attend as special guests but not to participate, even though some of the women of color were also league members. This relationship would become even more important as the "league way" continued to be challenged to adjust to the national movement for equality.

1960s

A June 5, 1961, request for membership figures from the president of the league of Kokomo, Indiana, engendered the same response given to such request in the 1950s—that those records were not kept in a manner in which they could be easily distributed from the national office. It was interesting that even at the twenty-fourth convention, the league found it important enough to collect data on marriage, divorce, and interests, but not race.

The league's history of transactional relationships with women of color was still apparent. Through the League of Women Voters Education Fund's (LWVEF) Inner City Project, local leagues and inner-city organizations worked jointly. Unfortunately, in many instances, because most league members involved in the project were white and had no direct connection to the communities they hoped to help, their efforts were seen as paternalistic and condescending. League leaders knew that to gain access and acceptance, given their lack of members of color, they had to unite with other organizations. These joint efforts regrettably were neither true partnerships nor did they result in the acknowledgment by league leadership that the organization needed to add voices of color to their membership.

While the fabric of society in the United States was changing rapidly and dramatically in the 1960s, the twenty-fifth convention in Minneapolis, Minnesota, held in 1962 with the theme "'61 was Lots of Fun," spoke only in a cursory manner about issues of race. The primary question still posed since 1954 was, "What are the Leagues in the south doing about the school situation?"[2] The mere mention of civil rights caused dissension when it came to consensus on program adoption. One of the "Not Recommended" items was civil rights. "Not Recommended," in league terms, means that the national board had discussed the issue and its impact on the organization and determined it not to be a priority for the league.

In 1962, in response to the relegation of civil rights to "Not Recommended" items, local leagues in Farmington, Connecticut, Tampa, Florida, Deerfield and Skokie, Illinois, and Grinnell, Iowa, all offered recommended changes for the league program. Farmington wanted the league to study and support legislation to end discrimination in the United States; the Illinois leagues wanted studies of measures to ensure protection of civil liberties and rights; and Iowa wanted a study of legislative means of facilitation and guaranteeing equal rights for all minority groups. The twenty-sixth convention's press release spoke to the fact that these controversial issues would be raised at convention. The outcome, however, was to stay the course.

In July 1963, President John F. Kennedy invited the League of Women Voters of the United States' president, Mrs. Robert J. Phillips, to attend a conference of women on civil rights. She attended and subsequently constructed a memo discussing the conference and the implications of civil rights for local leagues. Distributed to local leagues, the memo explained that "during the early part of the spring and summer when the civil rights movement began assuming the proportions of a social revolution, many people asked . . . what the League's stand on civil rights was." It continued that there "was no formal, explicit position at that time since civil rights had not gone through the usual league process of study, discussion, consensus and action."[3]

Although the matter of civil rights had come to the league's attention in 1954 in response to *Brown v. Board of Education*, the memo equated the league's lack of foresight in preparing itself to address civil rights to "various times in the past" when "the force of events presented the League with a situation in which it did not expect to find itself and faced with decisions it did not expect to make." It cited as similar instances "the bombing of Pearl Harbor, the crisis over civil liberties in the 1950s, and the intense international situation in 1956 at the time of Suez and the Hungarian uprising."[4]

Since the league lacked a position on civil rights, President Phillips told President Kennedy and local leagues that they could not support the civil rights act then pending in Congress. The league's first opportunity to put a civil rights-related item on its agenda would come the next year, at the May 1964 convention.[5] Issues of race or racial tension did not rise to the level of importance or priority, even though this was the height of the civil rights movement and the impending Civil Rights Act of 1964 and the Voting Rights Act of 1965 had become the topic of national conversation.

The national league leadership justified its decisions by endorsing a progressive human resources item along with its Voter Education Project. Such action permitted Southern leagues to explore civil rights-related areas at their own discretion. In consideration of the lack of consensus on the issue, the policy intentionally did not push any league into areas that might expose them to community criticism for which they were unprepared.

After civil rights became an undeniable issue for the nation, in 1963, the board asked President Ruth Phillips to issue a memorandum in the area of civil rights, even though the issue was not on the national program. Her guidance to state and local leagues was that

> We have no Current Agenda item; we have no national consensus; but we need not sit with folded hands. The crisis is national; the problem is local. In every League some sort of effort is needed.[6]

Phillips emphasized voter services, candidate information, and voter registration for minorities but made no mention of outright segregation. She did suggest that members could act as individuals in local communities and suggested that members might join human rights councils or other committees actively working on ending segregation. The national league leadership continued to support its earlier strategic decision not to begin this work in 1954, when it could have. In a *National Voter* article in September 1963, league leaders stated their cautious approach. They affirmed that the "civil rights" crisis was not new and that "the demonstrations these past months are the outward and visible signs that one minority group, the Negro is no longer willing to be relegated to second-class citizen status." The leaders further decided to debate what the role of the league would be beyond simply acknowledging the crisis. The league's default position was to study the problem.

> Should the League of Women Voters move into this critical area by adopting a civil rights Program item at the national level?
> The first requisite in work on such an item would be to gain an understanding of the nature of the problem in its various forms in different

geographic areas and of the role and responsibilities of the federal government . . .

No one can predict at this time what civil rights legislation will be passed by Congress . . . No matter what legislation is passed at national, state, or local levels, the task of community education to change attitudes will remain. Does the League have a role here?[7]

At the twenty-sixth convention, held on April 20–24, 1964, in Pittsburgh, Pennsylvania, the advance materials reported that for the first time in eight years, the league's national board recommended a new domestic subject for its national program, "Equality of Opportunity." Civil rights, however, remained a "Not Recommended" item. During that convention, in preparation for discussion on the floor, New Hope, Pennsylvania, and Pasadena, California, held a caucus on equal housing opportunity and civil rights.

The presentation of the "Proposed Program for 1964–1966" posed a challenge for delegates between study and action. Leaders questioned whether opportunities for education and employment, which this new program focused on, could indeed remedy the situation of second-class citizenship. Within the text of the proposed program, league leaders recognized that if the league adopted this item, they would "try to understand the problem and seek appropriate remedies."

Americans have become acutely aware not only of discrimination against racial and minority groups but of the existence of a broader group of people who are caught in a cycle of deprivation and hopelessness. It is becoming clear that direct and concentrated efforts are needed if we hope to deal with the unhappy situation of millions of Americans.[8]

The board proposed the "Equality of Opportunity" program in the belief that the emphasis on employment and education would be consumed under existing program concerns. The board believed that league concern for their other priority issues would address the critical focus of civil rights.[9]

On its face, the proposed program seemed like a positive shift, but the league history of being paternalistic toward blacks is evident in this statement and complicates its efficacy. The second paragraph indicates the underlying assumptions, totally dismissing any contributions made by its members of color and other collaborating organizations.

The third paragraph of the complete proposal emphasized vocational education remedies only, not higher education. Within the text, people of color are referred to as "deprived." This was an interesting word choice for an organization like the league. Finally, these issues became crucial because the nation was changing, and the league, if it wanted to remain relevant, had to change as well. Employment and education—particularly vocational education—would maintain their standing in league priorities because they were considered safe areas for discourse.

The 1964 convention exposed the league's duplicity. While dealing with the external challenges of civil rights and equality in society, the league was still ignoring its own internal relationship with women of color. The "National Board and Prospective Boarders" document offered a summary of characteristics of board members, whose characteristics, unfortunately, had not changed since the beginning of the organization. According to the profile, national board members or potential board members had served as presidents of their local leagues and/or state leagues, they were college graduates, and they were defined by their husbands' occupations. All were married and had an average of two children. "Having a minimum of household help," almost all cooked and cleaned house themselves, "with occasional assist from the male side of the family." Again, the nominees for the board remained all white. The nominating committee boasted that it received 251 recommendations for positions on the national board, yet no one of color was moved forward. League records do not indicate if anyone of color was even considered by the nominating committee.

Even though President Phillips attended as a representative of the ninety-three organizations President Kennedy invited to the White House on July 9, 1963, to rally support for his comprehensive civil rights bill that had been submitted to Congress, it was not until 1964 that the league adopted a study of civil rights as part of its national agenda. By the time this action took place, the civil rights movement was well underway. The league's position merely affirmed civil rights for Americans; this position had actually been covered by its platform in principle, but not practice, since 1920. While the league did ultimately support the Civil Rights Act of 1964 and the Voting Rights Act of 1965, its efforts in the area of civil rights were seen as coming too late to have the major impact they could have had if the league had been at the forefront.

By its 1964 convention, the league was receiving national television coverage of its convention proceedings. The thought was that this was a "coming of age" of women's political participation. The U.S. Information Service filmed the entire convention and used the films overseas.[10] As was league custom, local and state leagues held informational meetings and caucuses at this convention on subjects of interest to their communities and the league. On Tuesday, April 21, 1964, Sue Spetrino of the Ohio league facilitated such a meeting, entitled "Adventures of Living in an Integrated Neighborhood." This meeting was publicized as just an exchange of constructive ideas on a subject of interest to many league members. It was noted that few Southern leagues were interested in such meetings. Consistent with tradition, Mrs. Lelia D. Moten of Pennsylvania, a member of the National Council of Negro Women, was invited as a special guest. League leadership continued to see the importance of having this connection with women of color without dealing with real integration among its ranks.

President Lyndon B. Johnson spoke at the 1964 convention closing plenary. This was the first time a U.S. president addressed convention and shows the regard with which the league was held. His topic was the War on Poverty and the Great Society. His remarks, while compelling, were not enough to inspire the league delegates to include civil rights in its national program. The program item "Equality of Opportunity" did not receive the three-fifths vote necessary for adoption.

The focus of the conversation then changed to the adoption of human resources, which in the league's rationale would benefit all people, not just Negroes. They found this strategy to be more acceptable to league members. The following excerpted justification was offered in a press release.

American democracy is rooted in the concept of equality of opportunity. But in the United States today civil rights and economic opportunity are not equally accessible to all. That some minority racial groups are at a severe disadvantage is obvious; disadvantaged are the poorly educated, those displaced by automation, and persons living in depressed areas. These are the underdeveloped human resources of our own country.

The national Board proposes that the League limit its work in the next two years to the fundamentals of adequate education and its corollary, improved job opportunities. We would seek an understanding of the nature of the problem in its various forms and the speared and joint roles and responsibilities of federal, state and local government.

The League has the advantage of a national perspective because it works in all sections of the country and in a wide variety of communities. We would focus attention and work not on the needs of any one group but on all those in our population who are denied opportunity.

The self-perpetuating pattern of this situation can be broken only by education and employment opportunities, including an end to racial discrimination. Discrimination against Negroes, Indians, Spanish-Americans, Puerto Ricans, and other minorities reduces their employment opportunities, wastes their talents, inhibits their motivation, and limits their educational achievement. Although 78 percent of poor Americans are white, nearly half of all nonwhite citizens live in poverty.[11]

This release reveals the cavalier posture the league displayed in its commitment to social issues of the time and in its interactions with the black community. The comparison made to the work the league did for years with underdeveloped countries while ignoring the plight of people of color in the United States left enough flexibility for Southern leagues to opt out of any initiative.

At the conclusion of the 1964 convention, the league decided to limit the number of delegates per league. The 1964–1966 adopted national program focused on apportionment of state legislatures. The first U.S. secretary of Housing and Urban Development, Robert Weaver, addressed the convention. Once again, the league had an opportunity to take a stand and make a declarative statement on civil rights but failed to do so.

Mrs. Robert J. Stuart, league president from 1964 to 1968, assured the public that the league was an organization "of great diversity." Her remarks conveyed a diversity in thought and program, not membership. To attempt to reconcile this lack of diversity in membership with league priorities was inconsistent in principle. What was consistent, however, was the practice of having representatives of the National Council of Negro Women as invited special guests in the cities where conventions were held.

On the threshold of the passage of the Voting Rights Act of 1965, because of its aversion to take a position, the league found itself in the midst of the civil rights struggle without authority to take national legislative action. In her 1965 council address, President Stuart attempted to clarify the league's position and provide a blueprint for moving forward.

the eye-opening effect of the Civil Rights memo caused many of us to take a new look at our own communities and the League's relation to them. I suppose we've all been aware that the struggle for civil rights was just the outward and visible sign of a deeper and far more far-reaching malaise. But beginning with the summer of 1963 and continuing through the fall and winter, League conscience stirred and League interest quickened.

When program-making time came along, we had suggestions from more than 900 local and state leagues, and there were those who wanted a straight civil rights item; those who wanted a study of federal-state relations, and those who expressed concern about "human resources and educational opportunity." Then there were those who wanted to see congressional machinery improved, and it was clear that they were interested in this because they hoped that Congress would do something about "human resources, civil rights" or other issues which concerned them. . . .

Our principles make clear what League members believe about civil rights as well as voting rights, so we could have adopted a broad or a narrow item in this field, but as all League members are aware, we consciously limit our program so that we can be effective and we have to make choices. . . . Thus when we make a commitment in terms of League time and energy, we find that we almost inevitably adopt a program which is applicable and significant in all parts of the nation, and what we chose to work on, was the development of human resources.[12]

The league knew that access to the polls represented an acknowledgment of social equality and the potential for economic actualization. Despite the league's acquiescence to social pressures to embrace "Equality of Opportunity" as a program item, its symbols, photos, and publications until the late 1960s and early 1970s did not reflect any diversity. These symbolic representations of the league's attitude called into question the organization's true commitment to it members of color and had a strong influence on membership. State and local leagues, in spite of national inaction, remained active in their commitments. As an acknowledgment that disenfranchisement also disproportionately affected Native Americans, the Duluth, Minnesota, league adopted a study of the impact of equal opportunity as one of its program item on August 5, 1965.

In its October 1966 edition, *Ebony Magazine* included a six-page article, "The League of Women Voters: National Group Helps Stimulate Interest in Vital Public Issues." The article focused on women of color in the league and their challenges and experiences. The league was represented as a moderate alternative to what was perceived as the more radical organizations of the time. "In short, the League helps to bridge the information gap between governors and the governed, thus promoting individual effectiveness and dispelling the notation that you can't fight city hall."[13]

A primary purpose of the article was to show that women of color were in fact members of the league for a variety of reasons, not dissimilar to their white counterparts. They joined to learn more about and influence issues of the day; to ensure engagement of all eligible voters through the implementation of voting rights legislation; to better conditions for Negroes; to encourage reciprocity between league membership and other civic activities. The article spotlighted twenty women from across the nation—New Jersey, New York, Hawaii, Louisiana, Michigan, West Virginia, Washington, D.C., Florida, Indiana, Illinois, North Carolina, Rhode

African American Women with Sign Reading "Segregation Is Discrimination." (The author wishes to thank the National Association for the Advancement of Colored People for authorizing the use of this image.)

Island, Missouri, Iowa, and Georgia—with varying lengths of time in the league and varying responsibilities.

Quotes from these women gave insight into their relationship with the organization and their opinions on why women of color did or did not affiliate with the league. Many stated that some women viewed the league as an invitation-only organization. Others believed that energy devoted to league activities would diminish their impact in organizations already working diligently in their communities. Mrs. Gloria Marquez, board member of the Pound Ridge, New York, league stated:

> If Negro women join in meaningful numbers, they can play an important role in bettering conditions for all Negroes through their League work. They can also help white members of the League to more clearly understand Negro problems.[14]

Dorothy Height, who in addition to being a league member was president of the National Council of Negro Women, stated that she was having a

Mildred Madison. (Photo provided by Mildred Madison/George McKenney. Used by permission of Sharon Madison.)

hard time persuading her friends to join the league because "they can't see how working for a new state constitution, for instance, has much to do with the solution of their problems."[15] Also featured in the article was Mrs. Dora Needham Lee, who was eighty-five years old at the time of the printing and who had been a league member since 1948 and a suffragist forty-six years ago.

This type of visibility among black women should have substantially increased league membership. That the league and its members of color would be featured in this premier black magazine could have been used as a membership recruiting tool, but its value was compartmentalized.

For the three years since the passage of the Voting Rights Act, the league experienced internal conflicts both in the intensity of its actions on positions to enforce an equal opportunity agenda and on its stance toward integration in its membership. The events of 1968 were pivotal for the league internally and externally. The 1968 national convention buttressed the activist position that was endemic of the times.

Among convention materials was a list of suggestions to "erase racism" through the human resources item. In her speech to the convention, the outgoing president expressed a common league fear that younger women overlooked the league for more visibly active groups. She challenged the convention to tell "its story" better and "face the fact" that few people were joining the league primarily because it was a source of information, but rather they were joining because it was a "means through which they can work to achieve desired ends."[16]

In the press release for the 1968 convention, the league continued its practice of identifying the characteristics of its delegates as an indicator of its impact. The 1968 convention boasted 1,432 delegates representing 1,200 leagues from all fifty states, the District of Columbia, and Puerto Rico. More importantly, the press release emphasized that these delegates "voted overwhelmingly to call upon Congress and other branches of the government for immediate recognition of and constructive action to alleviate the domestic crisis of poverty and inequality."[17]

Nothing in this language specifically addresses race or integration or the enforcement and implementation of the two most powerful pieces of legislation passed in the 1960s. This ambiguity allowed local and state leagues to avoid addressing the issue of race because they could interpret this language to concentrate only on whites living in poverty.

The events of 1968 were pivotal for the league both internally and externally. Lucy Wilson Benson, league president from 1968 to 1974, led the organization through this tumultuous time. In 1968, the league received a $275,000 grant from the Ford Foundation's *Reducing Racial Tension* program to expand to four new areas its inner-city voter education project, *Inner-City Citizenship Education*

> where, through work on a common goal of achieving better housing and jobs by political action, Negro activists and the League's predominantly white middle-class members also hope to understand each other better.[18]

The program's focus was the problem of cities and racial conflict. Surprisingly, the board witnessed the appointment of its first woman of color to serve in a national capacity. Predictably, the demographics collected at convention still did not include race. Josie Johnson (Mrs. Charles W.) of Minnesota became the first black national board member when she was appointed in 1968. There are records of black leaguers convening in solidarity at conventions, as they recognized that there was strength in numbers. The communication between black leaguers and the national leadership increased dramatically. It is unclear whether each communication was responded to or just filed.

The decade of the 1960s ended with the league still masking its lack of desire to take the lead on the issues of race, either internally or externally, but indicating its commitment to the cause through its more benign

Dr. Josie Johnson (1930–). (Photo by Marty Nordstrom. Used by permission of Carol Nordstrom and Josie Johnson.)

partnerships. Lucy Benson spoke before NAACP in Jackson, Mississippi, in September 1969.

The 1970s and 1980s witnessed the national league leadership making some symbolic gestures in response to repeated calls for action to correct the internal struggle with its members of color. There were obvious interruptions at the national level, with the sustainability of any of the programs and activities contingent on the desires of the president and board at that time. With no obvious sense of urgency, individual state and local leagues responded to matters within the auspices of states' rights.

1970s

President Benson's skill in navigating the internal and external environments of the time facilitated a necessary cultural shift in the organization. In the 1970s, a management consulting firm was engaged to assess the league's operation. This would become one of many subsequent self-studies purported to guide the league into the future. There was no indication of who decided which questions were important and what was to be emphasized. Many of the questions were the same as those asked in the 1920s related to family, work outside the home, and age. Apparent value tensions for the organization surfaced in the conclusions. In addition to issues of equality, the league suffered from internal division over the Vietnam War, and many members sought a more visible role for the organization in women's rights and the social movements of the time. The proposed national program, Human Resources: Support of Equality of Opportunity, for education and employment was thought to address any needs members would have concerning the league's stance on civil rights, but this perspective was being questioned.

In the 1970s, there was little mention of the Special Committee on Inter-Racial Relations or whether it even existed; it was not funded, nor was there any evolution of its function to reflect the changes in society. The committee is not mentioned in the 1970 list of committees. It is difficult to discern if this happened in the 1960s because of the civil rights movement or in the 1950s as a result of *Brown v Board of Education*. Regardless, the committee seemed to just fade away.

The 1970s also marked a significant milestone for the organization—its fiftieth anniversary. Hillary Rodham, Marian Wright Edelman, Shirley Temple-Black (deputy U.S. representative, UN Conference on Environment), and senators Birch Bayh and Edward Brooke all spoke at the twenty-ninth convention. Dr. Dorothy Height (NCNW), Clarence Mitchell (NAACP), and J. Frances Polhaus (NAACP) were special guests. Along with the diversity of speakers, the league presented "Problems of American Indians" as an issue for discussion.

The 1970–1972 proposed program still positioned racial issues under the human resources program area, which included support of equal opportunity in education, employment, and housing. As was characteristic, the league dealt with some controversies openly while dealing with more sensitive issues covertly. Convention attendees were discontent with the league's powerlessness to take action on significant issues of the day, particularly as it related to the Voting Rights Act. As a result, the 1970 convention adopted a bylaws amendment enabling the league to act "to protect the right to vote of every citizen" without the formality of adopting voting rights in the national program. This unusual decision reflected member conviction that protecting the right to vote is indivisibly part of the league's basic purpose.[19]

A May 4, 1970, press release again detailed the characteristics of the "1,700 capable, energetic, loquacious ladies" who attended convention. Questions they responded to were about marital status, family, if they did their own housework, and what their husbands did for a living. The 1970–1972 nominating committee slate included the first known board member of color to be elected by the membership, Josie Johnson (Mrs. Charles W.). She had previously been appointed to the board in 1968, but this time she was running for election. Also at this convention, a group of black delegates presented their concerns to the national leadership in an attempt to ensure that their voices would be heard. By using the established league processes, they ensured that their method of interaction was considered both professional and polite.

In a memo to the national league leadership entitled "Concerns About the League of Women Voters by a Group of Black Delegates and Observers at the 50th Anniversary Convention," this group of leaguers made it clear that they felt the organization, through its procedures and programs, was not being responsive to the needs of all citizens. Their concerns were in response to proposed changes from the organization committee. Their memo addressed the need for the league to not assume that it knows what is best for all populations. "The League should know now that citizen needs must be defined by the citizens." It continued by addressing the changing member profile, which they noted should include more members who worked and younger members, and asserted that all should be valued.

> These new members are bringing to the League valuable and unique resources. They bring imaginative and vigorous leadership potential, particular commitments, an ability to work in partnership with a variety of people and a freedom from the stranglehold of arbitrary and irrelevant traditions. The benefit of this input to League program will be lost unless the League gives a higher priority to the need for this contribution. Its low priority has been evident. Youth involvement appeared in fourth place and the organizational methods in urban areas appeared in last place on the list of recommended League procedures.[20]

The group offered three recommendations to the national board: that it instruct the organization committee to develop methods for aggressively seeking from communities the information needed to make league programs more responsive, to report recommendations for approval to council 1971, and to follow through by assuming national leadership in guiding the operation. The memo concluded by reminding the league that its current method of engaging with communities of color was considered in many instances altruistic at best, condescending at worst.

> The League offers to the potential member the opportunity to learn. Implicit in the way this has been handled is the concept that the League is the teacher and the other segments of the population are the students. The

issues of the 1970's make that concept obsolete. There are learning experiences "out there" for the league, too.[21]

There was no indication in the league files that this letter was formally responded to; however, a "call to action" at convention resulted from the recommendations. Along with the letter from these black delegates, the election of Josie Johnson and Fay Williams to the national board served as a catalyst for more visible recognition of leaders of color at the national level. Records indicate that the league generated a list of black league members attending convention on May 11, 1970. This is the first indication that the delegate profile questions may have shifted.

A May 14, 1970, memorandum was sent to black caucus members by Christina Smith, a black staff member, providing the list of names of those black women who participated in the caucus and soliciting the names of any black women missing from the list.

Dear Sister,

Here is the list of those who participated in the Black Caucus.

The recommendations of the caucus have come before the Board, and are beginning to be dealt with.

One of the first needs and requests is to locate all of the Black women in the League. Therefore, we are requesting that you send to Christine Smith in the national office, the names and addresses of all of the Black League members that you know. In those cases where you have the League but not the address, please send that. . . .

Program-Organization Staff[22]

The thirtieth convention, held in 1972, continued to show some evolution in league culture as it attempted to adjust to the times. Despite the fact that the first meeting of the Special Committee on Negro Problems was held in Atlanta in the 1920s, there was still an apparent reluctance to deal with race by name in the South. The majority of the queries to the national leadership at this convention centered around the league's position on the war in Vietnam.

The 1972–1974 slate of nominated officers showed no indication that black women would continue in national leadership. These were the first convention publications that did not consistently list husbands' names, husbands' careers, and number of children. Husbands' names, however, were listed on committee assignments. The delegate questionnaire again reflected no questions that would allow for a disaggregation of participant data to indicate diversity. This was also the first public acknowledgment that there was really no typical league delegate.

This recognition of the changing nature of league delegates precipitated the call for examination of the organizational culture once again. The 1972–1974 league self-study was the first in a twenty-year series of self-examinations. League historians indicate that "it remains a landmark in LWV history, because the findings closely parallel later internal studies of the 1980s and 1990s."[23]

> The times they are a changing . . . As the report put it, when the League was founded, its central task was to legitimize a role for women in political life. This meant . . . that roles needed to be clearly delineated both so their validity could be established and so League members would know what was expected of them. . . . So one of the League's main problems at the moment is to avoid being trapped in yesterday's structures as it tries to fulfill today's demands . . . Society's demands . . . Women's demands . . . Members' demands.[24]

A report was prepared for the March 1974 national board meeting and appeared in the 1974 delegates' *Convention Workbook I* as part of background preparation for a Thursday afternoon discussion based on the study. The study was funded by the Kettering Foundation. The study consisted of an analysis of the 1972 annual report, 370 phone interviews, a Gallup Poll, case studies of four leagues, and interviews with 114 former members. While much emphasis was on membership, long-range financial planning, and communication, the self-study did not consider race as one of its primary focuses; it was as if the issue had disappeared. The emphasis was to assess the league's "public standing."

A member profile was generated that was not unlike the previous characterizations ascribed to league members: four in ten were over fifty, with only 7 percent under thirty; 87 percent were married; over half had been in the league at least five years; their personal politics matched national proportions; and most had previously been active in other volunteer activities.[25]

Having this information did not facilitate a noticeable change in league culture or operation. Subsequent convention delegates continued to reflect this members' profile, and the issues that the league continued to prioritize did not focus on domestic diversity.

The 1974 convention was pivotal for the organization on a number of fronts. The program focus was on passage of the Equal Rights Amendment. There were a number of documents in the convention materials that spotlighted the fact that an internal conversation about race was occurring. A requested document listing the number of black women officials in the United States was generated. When the 1974 convention amended the bylaws to provide that all league principles could serve as authority for action, the separate amendment on voting rights which had been added at the previous convention was no longer needed.

In a move that would fundamentally change the League of Women Voters, convention 1974 voted to admit men. This occurred despite the fact that women of color were still struggling to be accorded the rights of full membership in many state and local leagues and had no expectation from the national leadership that this would happen. There was never anything in league bylaws that formally excluded women of color, so the need to admit men by an action of convention could be justified. To have any adoption at convention addressing issues raised by women of color was anathema to the principles and would expose the league for how it really operated. In future conversations, many leagues felt defining diversity as including men met their obligation.

It was also at this convention that bylaws were changed to emphasize that "only one" local league in each community shall be recognized by the board of directors. This summarily dissolved any of the vestiges of colored leagues that had been allowed to exist earlier. Theoretically, this should have aided the integration of members of color into the organization. Despite issues within the league, the 1974 delegates were becoming more diverse. This convention for the first time mentioned delegates from Puerto Rico and the U.S. Virgin Islands. The increase in diversity was not a result of intentional outreach by the national leadership, as indicated by the comments from the women of color who attended the convention. The black caucus at the June 1974 convention indicated the need to work collectively to bring about change.

At the luncheon meeting on Thursday, May 9, 1974, national board members and staff were present to listen to the concerns of the group. Some members of the leadership made statements to the group. Members of the caucus, recognizing that the surge of civil rights legislation of the 1960s had briefly made racial justice a priority on the national league agenda and made possible the recognition of the black caucus in the league, now felt that their efforts had been "stalemated by assigning responsibility for the Black Caucus to state boards." The members of the caucus realized that this delegation of authority would minimize the importance of their recommendations and lead to inconsistent or nonexistent attention to critical issues. Leaders of the caucus strongly expressed these sentiments to the league's national leadership.

Integration has lost the unity of voice and moral purpose that captured League conscience in the '60s. We feel the strong support of the national League has scattered in disaffection, despair and plain combat fatigue.

The dedicated Black leaguer is still active, still struggling, though still largely isolated from the power positions in the LWV. We must not allow to develop a mutual void of distrust. The mood is not yet despairing—not yet—but it is bleak, lonely, and a pall of disenchantment pervades.[26]

While not as optimistic as they had been previously, the caucus members believed that the presence, sharing, and participation of national board and staff members in the luncheon meeting added a hopeful and encouraging dimension. The group determined that "the only way to give relief to the swelling tide of emotions was to end with all leaguers present joining hands in one full circle and singing 'We Shall Overcome.' "[27]

It is questionable that the national leadership would have given full attention to this matter had it not been that Dorothy McKinney was on the national board at the time. In a June 1974 memorandum to the national board, she provided a summary of the meeting of the black caucus at the 1974 convention. "The caucus was representative of 20 states and of as many viewpoints, portfolios, and perspectives. There was no typical Black delegate. There were women with full-time paid jobs and those who had never held employment outside the home and all levels of League involvement were represented."[28] The concerns of the caucus centered around three areas: the need for more action in the human resources field, the need for black leadership development, and the inclusion of black leadership at all levels of the league. Caucus members identified how their concerns manifested in their treatment as league members.

—consideration of the notion that one needs a Ph.D. to participate effectively in the LWV
—complaints that only one Black involved at the national board level
—general disenchantment with the LWV, involving the feeling of a gap between principles and action.[29]

Black league members expressed frustration with their portfolio assignments relegating them solely to issues aligned to the black community, "where nice white ladies are afraid to visit. Fear of rape was felt to be the same for any woman regardless of race."[30]

Caucus members also addressed the issues of the structure of league meetings, which were scheduled during the day, prohibiting many potential black members who worked on a full-time basis from attending.

Additionally, caucus members reported feeling that meeting places discouraged their participation.

Black leaguers felt that their competence was constantly being questioned and that they must prove themselves, thus "making necessary the development of survival techniques."

> —one member (the only Black member from Palm Springs) though vice president, was unable to recruit or interest other Blacks concerning membership in the League. She also noted that the fact that though she has worked successfully with the Black community in pupil assignment and busing plan and served as liaison to Black organizations in community action, she felt the assignment from League local board unfair but was motivated to do a good job in spite of inequities in portfolios.[31]

Caucus members conceded that there were benefits to league membership.

> Attention was called to one local League president (California) who, while working full time felt that involvement in League was stimulating and excellent preparation for political involvement and leadership.[32]

Because black league members were also frequently members of black organizations, their role as liaisons presented an important contribution. Black members provided voice to encourage coalitions of black organizations with the league at the national level. Caucus members warned that it was important for the league not to drain off black leadership in other organizations.

There was a general consensus of a need for more opportunity for this kind of dialogue. Lavonne Henter of Nevada, Margeurite Kisseloff of New York, and Ann Brown of California were designated to speak for the caucus on the floor of convention. In support of the statements by the black leaguers, one leaguer felt that white leaguers had predetermined roles for blacks, "all the way from Sammy Davis Jr. to Mary McLeod Bethune."[33]

A motion was made, seconded, and passed that the national board provide funds and directions to convene black membership in order to create opportunities to consider issues raised by black delegates. The record of how much was allocated was not readily available, nor was there any clear expectation from the national leadership on how the work of this group would be presented to the membership or acted upon.

In 1976, the league adopted the formation of the Endangered Species Committee, mandated to study and prepare alternative choices for the future direction of the league and address the phenomenon of the vanishing volunteer. The *Endangered Species Committee Report* recommended strategies to generate more young leaders who had lost patience with the "mirror gazing" of the league.

The remainder of the conventions in the 1970s continued to include a diverse group of speakers who represented the programmatic priorities of the league. Convention 1978 changed from Illinois to Ohio because Illinois would not ratify ERA. This move should be noted because there is no indication that conventions were ever moved because civil rights were not being enforced. The 1978 delegate profile indicated the trend of women going back to work. "Almost a third of the delegates are part of the workforce with almost half of them (40%) having taken on paid jobs in the last five years."[34] The national board continued to display a lack of diversity. At this convention, a Native American caucus was convened. The recommendations from that caucus were not in the convention folder.

1980s

The conventions held in the 1980s continued to address issues of race in society through the league's positions on human resources; equal access to education, employment, and housing; urban policy; and the promotion of the fiscal well-being of cities and the quality of urban life. To indicate that the issue of race should still be a priority with state and local leagues, the League of Women Voters of Nashville hosted a desegregation caucus. Consistent with the national league's inclusion of special guests of color to affirm its commitment to diversity, special guests included Marion Berry, D.C. mayor, and Eleanor Holmes Norton. In the league publication *A Great Idea Through the Years: 1920–Present*, the organization credited itself with being at "the forefront of the struggle that culminated in the passage of the Voting Rights Act Amendments of 1982."[35]

The 1980s witnessed an increase in the number of members of color elected to the national board, including Edith Bornn (U.S. Virgin Islands, 1980–1982), Julia T. Richie (Michigan, 1982–1986), and Julia A. Holmes (New York, 1982–1986). By the 1982 convention, under the Presidency of Dorothy (Dot) Ridings, the league was forced to question its reason for being for the first time since 1944.

The 1982 convention mandated the development of a strategic long-range plan by an outside consultant and a committee of local, state, and national leaders. It was a response to shrinking membership and persistent national league deficits. As had become the practice, the characteristics of the delegates were publicized. The release indicated that there was really no typical league delegate. Activities and interests of the delegates spanned too broad a range of subjects to provide any categorization. More than 80 percent of the women participated in other civic and community organizations.

The delegate questionnaire from convention 1982 consisted of twenty questions. There were 506–515 responses, with the number of responses varying by question. The questions were consistent with previous questionnaires: length of time in the league; current league position; league activity: how many hours per week; how many other organizations the member is active in; whether the member has ever held elective office (and if yes, on which level of government); whether the member has ever been appointed to public office (and if yes, on which level of government); whether the member has ever run for public office (and if yes, on which level); employment (outside the home); political affiliation; sex; age; race; education; household income; marital status; children; geographic area; community size; how many national conventions the member has attended; what the member's primary source of information on issues is.

There is no indication who actually selected the questions, whether staff or board members. The questions on the questionnaire had evolved and no longer emphasized husbands' occupations. This particular questionnaire did include a question about race. The race category had 515 responses (white, 491, 95.3 percent; black, 14, 2.7 percent; Hispanic, 4, 0.7 percent; Oriental, 3, 0.5 percent; other, 3, 0.5 percent). It is unclear why this particular questionnaire addressed race, but it could be attributed to the request of the black caucus to be able to identify progress on their recommendations to the organization about equity in membership. It could also be attributed to the fact that the national board now had two members who made sure the conversation of race in the league was central.

The 1982 research again spotlighted enduring themes: the league needed to modernize; local leagues needed staff; members needed to feel connected to the whole; the number of priorities needed to be limited; resources needed to be used more efficiently; and the league needed to better communicate its purpose to the public. At the core of these themes was how the league recruited and retained members. In directions to the board at the 1982 convention, one member summarized the sentiments of many: "I think the membership campaign will be great: all minorities and the elderly should be 'mainstreamed' into active membership."[36]

The Story of Two Julias

Both Julia Holmes and Julia Richie served on the national board from 1982 to 1986. Their activism on the board resulted in a significant cultural shift in the relationship between the organization and its members of color. At the 1984 convention in Detroit, Michigan, they held an informal meeting with minorities who were delegates. There were twenty-three delegates, including Holmes and Richie, who attended the informal sessions. Their records indicate that there were "10 minorities who were not in attendance." In addition to networking with other delegates of color, their agenda focused on current convention activities, years in the league, levels in the league, league portfolios, and reasons for joining the league.

Holmes and Richie reported that black league members shared the same enthusiasm in being at convention as their counterparts. They collected and disseminated information highlighting the work of black leaguers. They found that black leaguers had fewer years of participation, with terms varying from one to three years. There were, however, six delegates from the group with terms longer than three years. These members—Iris G. Reeves, Corneida Lovell, JoAnn Price, Geneva Maiden, Cheryl I. Smith, and Adrienne Latham—were identified to serve as mentors for newer caucus members.

Caucus members reported having experience at varying levels of the league. There were four delegates who had participated at the state level, either with board positions or off-board responsibilities at the state level—Iris G. Reeves, Corneida Lovell, and Bette Lawrence and Julia Holmes. Their reasons for joining the league were consistent with those of other convention delegates. Eleven delegates had become members because of local programs their respective league had offered at the time they joined. Eight delegates had become members through their friends' invitation. Two delegates had become members after attending league-sponsored events.[37]

They used the information gathered to better inform all conversations at the national board level on issues unique to leaguers of color. After the tenure of the two Julias, JoAnn Price (Maryland, 1986–1988) became the lone black member on the national board.

The organizational behavior of the league in the 1980s was reflected in its many board decisions. During this time Dorothy S. (Dot) Ridings, President (1982–1986) inaugurated the exhibit program. Between 1982 and 1984, the Human Resources and Social Policy, which had served as the province for those controversial issues related to civil rights and race, began to make a transition. Following the August 1984 meeting of the board, four major board committees—Advocacy Issues, Communications, Finance and Administration, and Membership and Organizational Development—were established, under which all program activities were to be conducted.

The board gave direction that Washington, D.C., should be the site of every other convention. In 1986, the reliance on the delegate profile questionnaire to profile members was eliminated. There is no clear indication of why this was changed. Also that year, Grant Thompson was named the league's first male executive director.

A new logo was designed for the LWVUS to signal that the organization was changing with the times; it included a gray background with a red check. Publications exhibited more diverse depictions in symbols and messaging.

The June 1988 convention report, *Long Range Plan of the League of Women Voters, 1988–1992*, anticipated that the league's culture would need to continue to evolve if the organization was to remain relevant. The committee recognized the external realities of changing demographics and work patterns, the aging society, changing family and employment patterns, and shifting population distribution/characteristics. They reported that minority populations, including Hispanics and Asians, were growing at a faster rate than the rest of the U.S. population, and the minority middle class was increasing. While specific membership and outreach strategies were not outlined, the need for a more inclusive tactic was stressed. One tangible goal was to achieve a 2 percent net growth in membership each year.[38]

1990s

The 1990s witnessed an increase in the league's activities toward an inclusive membership. In 1990, Gracia Hillman became the first woman of color to serve as executive director. The year 1992 witnessed the second of only three contested elections for national leadership. Becky Cain was elected president. For the first time in the league's seventy-year history, the thirty-ninth convention nominated a male league member from Maine—Alvin M. Moss Sorrento—to be on the national board.

Conclusion

> Black women played an active and valuable role in electoral politics of the 1920s, but their role is, too often, overlooked as if it was an unimportant, even impotent factor in the profound political changes underway.[39]

This sentiment typified the struggle of women of color to be fully recognized for their contributions to the League of Women Voters.

This new activism, much of it spurred by the reform climate of the 1960s, caused, just as the 1944 convention, another round of intense debate over what kind of organization the League of Women Voters should be. The 1960s witnessed the continued struggle for civil and human rights and the passage of the Civil Rights Act of 1964 and the Voting Rights Act of 1965. A paradox existed in the league's response to the growing civil rights crisis of the 1960s, and the organization's national leadership directed its energies to equality of opportunity and built a solid foundation of support for equal access to education, employment, and housing. In the Southern states, most black women—and black men—still faced impediments to voting well through the 1960s. Correspondence with the national office indicates that most efforts to address race problems were targeted to Southern leagues, with minimal attention paid to the fact that many Northern leagues were just as segregated. Where Jim Crow laws and black codes sought to prevent their suffrage, women of color persevered, yet these women were not monolithic in their thoughts and actions. In the introduction to her book, *Witness to Change: From Jim Crow to Political Empowerment*, Sybil Morial recalled that "in the 1960s and '70s, she started a civic league to register African-Americans to vote, because she couldn't join the League of Women Voters."[40]

Should the league have been forward-thinking and progressive? Indeed, and not only when absolutely forced to be. The 1970s witnessed the continuation of the war in Vietnam and the resignation of the nation's thirty-seventh president, Richard M. Nixon. The 1980s saw the league focus its attention on the passage of the Equal Rights Amendment (ERA). The 1990s and the early twenty-first century would see a resurgence in the priorities associated with diversity. In the context of these major shifts in the social fabric of the United States, the league had its own internal struggles regarding how to address the concerns of its members of color, particularly black and American Indian. This was an obvious invitation to self-analysis, not to recreate the living past.

The league has been successful at many things, but not in addressing its internal issues with race. The formal and informal structures in place in the League of Women Voters uncovered countless value tensions. Examining these value tensions allows us to analyze the evolution of the relationship between the league and its members of color as a precursor to moving forward. Those women of color who, through perseverance, forced the league to take a candid look at itself and its relationship with them carried the weight of history that would propel the league into the future.

As Maud Wood Park stated at the Des Moines convention in 1923, when the league was only three years old, "An organization, like an individual, needs to see itself as a whole from time to time."[41] Moving forward, the "league way" would be further challenged under the weight of the history to come.

Notes

1. Ware, 1985, vii.
2. League of Women Voters Papers filed in LWVUS office, Convention Workbook, 1962, 8.
3. League of Women Voters Papers filed in LWVUS office, Basic Document—Not Recommended Items, Spring, 1962.
4. League of Women Voters Papers filed in LWVUS office, Basic Document, Press Release, Sunday April 12, 1964.
5. League of Women Voters Papers filed in LWVUS office, Basic Document, *Presentation of Proposed Program 1964–1966.*
6. League of Women Voters Papers filed in LWVUS office; Stuhler, 2000, 273.
7. League of Women Voters Papers filed in LWVUS office.
8. League of Women Voters Papers filed in LWVUS office, Convention Folder, 1964.
9. League of Women Voters Papers filed in LWVUS office.
10. Osborn, 1994, 123.
11. Ibid.
12. Stuhler, 2000, 274–275.
13. *Ebony Magazine*, 107.
14. Ibid.
15. *Ebony Magazine*, 108.
16. League of Women Voters Papers filed in LWVUS office, Convention Folder, 1968.
17. Ibid.
18. Ford Foundation Annual Report, 1968, 4.
19. League of Women Voters Papers filed in LWVUS office, Convention Folder, 1970.
20. Ibid.
21. Ibid.
22. League of Women Voters Papers filed in LWVUS office, Convention Folder, 1970 (names listed in appendices).
23. Neuman, 1994, 41.
24. League of Women Voters Papers filed in LWVUS office, Convention Folder, 1970.
25. League of Women Voters Papers filed in LWVUS office, 1974 Self-Study and Convention Workbook.

26. League of Women Voters Papers filed in LWVUS office.

27. League of Women Voters Papers filed in LWVUS office, Convention Folder, 1974. Minutes from May 9, 1974 luncheon with Black Caucus and Lucy Wilson Benson.

28. League of Women Voters Papers filed in LWVUS office, Convention Folder, 1970. Memorandum June 1974, from Dorothy McKinney to National Board.

29. Ibid.

30. Ibid.

31. Ibid.

32. League of Women Voters Papers filed in LWVUS office, Convention Folder, 1970.

33. League of Women Voters Papers filed in LWVUS office, Convention Folder, 1974.

34. League of Women Voters Papers filed in LWVUS office, Convention Folder, 1978.

35. League of Women Voters Papers filed in LWVUS office, Convention Folder, 1982.

36. Ibid.

37. League of Women Voters Papers filed in LWVUS office, Convention Folder, 1984 (names of black league delegates in appendices).

38. League of Women Voters Papers filed in LWVUS office, Convention Folder, 1988.

39. Gordon et al., 1997, 135.

40. Morial, 2015, 107; *Ebony Magazine*, 1966.

41. League of Women Voters Papers filed in LWVUS office, Convention Folder, 1923.

CHAPTER SEVEN

The Weight of History

This is the story of a colored woman living in a white world. It cannot possibly be like a story written by a white woman. A white woman has only one handicap to overcome—that of sex. I have two—both sex and race.

—Mary Church Terrell, 1940

To say that the past influences the present and the future is to capture the evolution of the League of Women Voters as it moved into the twenty-first century. That progression highlights the continued existence of the struggle to legitimately address issues of race and diversity in its membership and organizational priorities. In the fall of 1987, a conference on Afro-American Women and the Vote, cosponsored by the League of Women Voters of Massachusetts, sought to detail the tensions within the organization as it dealt with the issues of its relationship with its members of color. Papers presented at the conference analyzed common themes while posing questions for further research. These papers resulted in a widely distributed publication, *Afro-American Women and the Vote: From Abolitionism to the Voting Rights Act.*[1] The work was mindful of the leadership role both black and white women played in advancing civic engagement in the black community but also described the difficulty black women had in prioritizing the need for such joint efforts in the League of Women Voters.

The conclusions of the conference posed fundamental questions about the League of Women Voters' internal operations, policies, practices, and traditions, which often did not reflect the principles it espoused, as well as about the priorities it identified as external issues for emphasis and the guidance provided by the national leadership to state and local leagues. One persistent question remained dominant: How can there be an obvious history of second-class membership in an organization devoted to upholding first-class citizenship?

Throughout league history, the organization was revered as its founders philosophically envisioned it—an "everywoman's" organization. In practicality, however, it was anything but. On June 16, 1998, this changed with my election as the first national president of color. As I would soon learn, there is a price to be paid for breaking barriers. To be the first and accept the responsibility to secure the legacy of service and sacrifice of those upon whose shoulders I stood required me to carry the weight of history.

This chapter addresses some of the considerations, conversations, and contradictions that led to this milestone for the league and how the organization accepted or rejected this progress. I served two terms as president; the first term (1998–2000), I was nominated by the nominating committee, and the second term (2000–2002), I used league policies, principles, and practices to run from the floor. Each term brought its own challenges along with significant benefits, both for me and the organization.

The League as an "Everywoman's" Organization—Part II

Throughout its history, the league as an organization has struggled with issues of gender and race, with gender always triumphing as the priority. Those issues manifested through the tension between league principles and practicality. The composition of the league's national leadership symbolized the organization's response to diversity or lack thereof. The characteristics of the 1950s board, which were still evident when I was appointed to the board in 1994, illuminate the organization's subliminal messaging about its leadership.

THE NATIONAL BOARD AND PROSPECTIVE "MEMBERS"
The average League membership of the 19 women who are either on the national Board or nominees for it, is 21 years . . . Sixteen have served as presidents of their local Leagues and eleven as presidents of state Leagues. Others have held various offices in their local and state Leagues, including Director, Vice President, Education Chairman and Legislative Chairman. Three have held special national posts representing the League at the United Nations and on the U.S. National Commission for UNESCO.

Sixteen are college graduates, three have M.A. degrees and one is a Ph.D. Eight have been teachers. Other previous professions include business women, newspaperwomen, research assistant, occupational therapist, librarian and social worker. Husbands include lawyers, businessmen, professors, surgeons, engineers, federal government executives, a judge, investment counselor, newspaper editor, and musicians. Sixteen have traveled outside the United States, 13 to parts of Europe. All are married.[2]

Absent any codified criteria for service at the national level, this description embodied the informal standard.

Despite its symbols, images, and messaging, the League of Women Voters became my organization of choice, just as it had for the women of color who'd come before me. I recognized the divergence of gender and race in defining myself as a league member. The organization's embrace of the plight of women of color who chose to be league members underscored the recognition that in an ever-changing demographic society, the League of Women Voters, in order to remain relevant, must unreservedly embrace diversity. The practicality of this conceptual shift was reflected in the seventy-fifth anniversary theme "Many Voices, One Vision," whose significance gave rise to diversity as a priority for the league.

Each president dictated the tenor of the organization's position on controversial matters. The league's commitment to prioritizing diversity depended on the philosophy of the national leadership of the time. Because Percy Maxim Lee had been president during one of the most tumultuous periods of league history in its reckoning with its position on race, her remarks to the League of Women Voters of Connecticut were especially telling in their absence of any reference to the league's inaction on issues of race. She indicated that during her tenure (1950–1958), she considered the attacks on the league's credibility during the McCarthy years the most significant.[3]

The league's 1997 resolution on the woman suffrage statue—a statue of Sojourner Truth that would be placed in the Hall of Statues—issued by President Becky Cain (1992–1998) reflected this thinking. The ultimate decision to support the placement of the statue was the result of much discussion and was not without controversy, but it reinforced Cain's commitment to diversity.

Resolution Regarding the Woman Suffrage Statue
October 30, 1997

Whereas, women won the right to vote after a 72 year struggle led by suffragists, women of all backgrounds, who traveled hundreds of thousands of miles and worked countless hours to mobilize citizens for political action;

Whereas, the League of Women Voters recognizes that many women of color, and in particular, Sojourner Truth, were a significant part of the historic struggle of the woman suffrage movement;

Whereas, the League of Women Voters honors the contributions of all women who led the fight for woman suffrage;

Whereas, the League of Women Voters believes that it is important that women not repeat the mistakes of the past that separated black and white women who were pursuing the same goal of achieving the full participation of all citizens in our democracy;

Whereas, the League of Women Voters recognizes that symbols often carry strong messages and believes that concerned groups should work together to heal the divide associated with the relocation of the Portrait Monument;

Now therefore be it resolved that the League of Women Voters joins with other organizations in calling for a new, inclusive woman suffrage statue that would honor the contributions of the leaders of the woman suffrage movement, including Sojourner Truth.

Now therefore be it resolved that the League of Women Voters calls upon the Congress of the United States to expand the membership of the Congressional Woman Suffrage Statue Commission from 11 to 15 members, to include four additional members of the public with knowledge of the woman suffrage movement and of women and the arts; and to consult broadly with the historic national women's organizations that participated in or were organized out of the woman suffrage movement, as well as contemporary national organizations organized for the advancement of women, in recommending an alternate statue for permanent placement in the Rotunda of the United States Capitol.[4]

Evolution or Revolution?

Moving into the twenty-first century, the league's national leadership, guided by program adoption at each convention, made strategic organizational decisions. These decisions, often impelled by events in society, simultaneously gauged the fluctuation of the status of women in the workforce and volunteerism. What was explicit was that in the more complex issues, such as race, there was an obvious conflict between advocating for change in the broader society while not changing the league's internal culture. The impact on women of color in the league was often misrepresented, misinterpreted, or misunderstood. The pace of implementing needed change was continually questioned.

The league was often reluctant to use its extensive organizational prominence and integrity to serve as a catalyst for change. Throughout its history, there were attempts to evaluate organizational culture and purpose. In addition to the major structural change that occurred in 1946 following the election and change in direction at the 1944 convention, the league engaged in a number of internal studies, which resulted in minimal subsequent changes. Throughout the 1950s, the league could also be challenged on its internal racial policies through its passive lack of welcome of nonwhites rather than its formal exclusion. Colored Women Voters Leagues and the Colored Women Republican Club were among early separate deliberative vehicles encouraged by the league from 1920 through 1955.[5]

The University of Michigan conducted a major study of the league from 1956 to 1958. A league internal committee examined ways to streamline the league from 1968 to 1970. A 1972–1974 league self-study employed survey experts who relied on such tools as Cantril's Ladder and the Gallup Poll. And in 1978, the *Endangered Species Committee Report* provided another internal assessment. A series of strategic plans, including the most recent "Transformation Roadmap" of 2018, chronicle the inconsistent attempts to prioritize diversity, equity, and inclusion. Current researchers attempting to understand the dynamics within the league and the dichotomy it represents also conclude that the organization has been intentional in its reluctance to evolve.

> The League of Women Voters' dragged response to pressures for racial integration was rejected by all levels of its membership in the 1960s without backward glance. Over time, the League's members elected Carolyn Jefferson-Jenkins of Colorado in 1998 as the first black American to serve as League president; she is still active in her local chapter. But national selection of black leadership has not been repeated, and trends toward white dominance remain stubborn. As of 2002, 5 percent of League members were "of color" in spite of an official association policy that encouraged racial diversity.[6]

The choice of evolution over revolution has allowed the league to continue to consider organizational changes and their consequences as a balance between principle and practicality. Changing an organizational culture as entrenched as the league's requires a commitment, both ideological and with regard to resources, at all levels of the organization.

My Story

> Feminist thought and practice were fundamentally altered when radical women of color and white women allies began to rigorously challenge the notion that "gender" was the primary factor determining a woman's fate.[7]

When I joined the League of Women Voters of Cleveland, Ohio, in the 1980s, it was because the league's reputation, integrity, and access to the political environment provided an additional conduit for my continued advocacy and activism for equitable engagement of all citizens. My membership was initially a transactional relationship but would later become transformational. My league affiliation allowed me to expand my sphere of influence and leverage the vast influence of the league to broaden my engagement, outreach, and access. Additionally, it allowed the league to access the value I brought to the organization.

My pathway to the national presidency was both traditional, in that I had been an active league member at the local, state, and national levels and had served on the national board since 1994 and as second vice president, and nontraditional, in that my election would represent a cultural shift in the organization. The election of the first black president, whether perceived as evolution or revolution, was acknowledged as a new day for the league. Reaction to my election was varied; many members, partners, and funders perceived it as a new chapter for the league, while others found it to be a disconcerting change in the organizational culture. It was an indication that the league was moving into the twenty-first century and was finally recognizing the need to become more diverse and reflect the changing demographics of the nation.

On Friday, February 28, 1998, I received the call. The league's nominating committee was in retreat and had selected me to run for the presidency of the league. The chair of the committee called to see if I would accept the nomination. Accept? Did I have a choice? This was a life-defining moment. To be president of a seventy-eight-year-old organization that was perceived to be white and elitist? To be able to guide this organization into the twenty-first century? To be the first black president? To be able to carry my grandmother's legacy of civil rights and social justice advocacy on the national and international stage? To recognize one more time that the purpose of my existence was bigger than just me? These thoughts all went through my head in the moments before I responded with a resounding "yes." I recognized the enormous responsibility I had just accepted, as well as the tremendous opportunity. What about my family? What about my job? How could I do all of this? Would my health sustain? Would I be overcommitted? As I collected my thoughts and remembered my prayers, I knew this was my destiny.

There were initiatives afoot to run a slate of officers from the floor at that 1998 convention who would challenge my nomination to the office. This was the first indication that my credibility as a league leader would be challenged. I, and obviously the nominating committee, thought my nomination resulted from merit, but the rumblings among some delegates were that perhaps this was a symbolic gesture to prove the league's commitment to diversity. This disparagement was disputed by my work at the local, state, and national levels that equaled the qualifications for advancement of other national presidents.

On June 16, 1998, a new chapter in league history began when I became the first woman of color to serve as a national president. This accomplishment was bittersweet because on June 10, 1998, my mother passed away. Because of this family emergency, I was unable to fully participate in the convention, but I was able to return for the election, which served as a tribute to her memory. This was an extremely emotional time for me—the death of my mother, the rumors of challenges mounting from the floor, the pressures of being a pioneer. Carrying the weight of history would soon materialize.

While each league president carried the weight of leading such a complex historic organization, unlike the others, I felt the weight of history and of representing the legacy of the women of color who'd had to balance gender and race as they'd labored in the league throughout its history. It was a different weight, one that can only be understood by someone who has the weight of race and gender on their shoulders. My accomplishments in the league became eclipsed by my race.

Many leaguers refused to recognize the significance of my election, while other external organizations applauded this as an historic event. Civil rights, social justice, and black organizations, recognizing the challenges I was to face, embraced, supported, and applauded me. Opportunities emerged to consider what had once been uneasy alliances for league partnerships with a variety of diverse groups. Though there were many challenges, they were outweighed by the support these organizations provided.

My election raised many questions and exposed the contradiction between the league's desire for progress and its fear of change. That fear was unwarranted; I was a league member, committed to the organization and its principles but determined to realize those principles for all of its members. One conversation that surfaced was that "she is going to make this a black organization." Despite the impossibility of that happening in an organization that was never more that 5 percent women of color, would increasing diversity have been so bad?

Against the backdrop of a preponderance of images and symbols of white suffragists, I assumed the responsibility that the position required, always remembering the sacrifices of the women of color who were not in these images. There were occasional publications spotlighting women of color beginning in the late 1960s, but that was the exception, not the rule. The primary question for me was, what could I do with the platform I had been given? While straddling two worlds, I was always defending the right to be in a leadership position and the right to speak for the league.

As a racial-barrier breaker, there were certain truths I had to grapple with; the most important was that being a woman of color was my identity, but not my only concern. Inevitably, as a constant, it was expected that I would explain how it felt to be first. I used this opportunity to

Becky Cain Transferring Power to Carolyn Jefferson-Jenkins. (Meg S. Duskin. From *The Voter*, September 1988. Used by permission of the League of Women Voters and Becky Cain.)

1998 Board. (Photo by Chad Evans Wyatt. Used by permission.)

promote the need for greater diversity in the league by responding, "I am league president because I have labored at every level of the organization—local, state, and national. The fact that I am black is a bonus."

I chose to focus on the opportunity that existed to transform the league into a twenty-first-century organization. The efficacy of the members who saw me as "league member first" was responsible for my election. From the outside, it was a changing of the guard. From the inside, it was the changing of an organizational culture.

When I became president in 1998, I symbolically had my formal office photo displayed in color, in stark contrast to the photos in the hall of presidents, which were in black and white. Unfortunately, when I returned to the league national office in 2014, I found that the photo had been redone in black and white, losing the symbolism of the gesture.

A Matter of Principle

You may not control all the events that happen to you, but you can decide not to be reduced by them.[8]

Addressing internal political issues was not new to the national league presidency. The league history, while subject to external influences and internal change, reflected that for the most part, the league adhered to its founders' values. This was both advantageous and disadvantageous to the organization. Its relationship with its members of color was the most visible area where the league was continually forced to confront itself and its principles. The end of my first term as president presented one such challenge.

The league uses a nominating process whereby a nominating committee recommends a slate of officers and board members to the convention delegates for election. Per *Robert's Rules of Order*, after the report of the nominating committee, the floor is open to further nominations. If there are such nominations, there is then a contested election. The nominating committee is composed of four members elected by the previous convention and three members appointed by the board (LWVUS bylaws). The nominating committee, according to bylaws, "is charged with the important responsibility of identifying future leaders." The committee traditionally presents a single slate of officers and directors to the annual meeting or convention, although there is no bylaws requirement to do so.[9] League bylaws, which define the league's purpose and function, provide an operating framework for nominations from the floor. The bylaws are meant to protect the organization and its members and to provide assurances that rights will be protected, responsibilities and powers defined and limited, and the goals of the organization stated and implemented.

The league's nominating committee decided not to nominate me for a second term as president, 2000–2002. There was only one other time in league history when there was a one-term president, and it was recorded that the decision was at her request. I had made no such request. Absent what I believed to be any substantive reason for my ability to continue as president, I decided to use the league's bylaws and processes to run from the floor.

Having served on the nominating committee, I was keenly aware that the committee's criteria could be both arbitrary and subjective. The chair of the committee sets the tone for discussions about nominees. Once notified that I would not be nominated for a second term, I had a decision to make. Instead of challenging the system, the easiest thing to do would be to retreat, but that is not the league way. The organization's fundamental doctrines and continued existence were based on challenging, when necessary, a perceived injustice. This irony was not lost on me. To just accept a decision without substantive explanation would be uncharacteristic of any league member.

My nomination from the floor would be only the third time in the league's eighty-year history that leadership would be challenged using the very procedures the league lived by. In 1944, a "substitute slate" of three officers, headed by Anna Lord Strauss, defeated the three nominated officers, while the rest of the "regularly nominated slate" for the board was elected. The nominated officers had supported a revision of the bylaws developed under the outgoing president, Marguerite Wells (1934–1944). In 1992, the nominated slate of officers and board, headed by Becky Cain, was elected after a contested election for president, second vice president, and director. The challenging candidates had served on the previous board, headed by Dr. Susan Lederman (1990–1992).[10]

With the 2000 league election, the organization faced a twenty-first-century challenge to its ideals. I was joined in this challenge to the nominating committee's leadership slate by the first vice president, Margaret Brown (Wyoming), and second vice president, Faye Sinnott (Illinois). While the 1998–2000 board was the most diverse in league history, the 2000–2002 board was almost all new. The nominating process appeared to be an effort not just to replace me, but the majority of the board. Traditionally, the nominating committee considers the need for a balance between new and old to maintain continuity and institutional memory.

The messaging surrounding the election materials distributed at convention gave deference to the nominating committee's choice: "In 2000, the sitting president Carolyn Jefferson-Jenkins will challenge Beverly McKinnell, Minnesota, the nominee for President. Jefferson-Jenkins was elected president in 1998."[11] Of particular note is that I was challenging the nominating committee's choice and not that I was being challenged as the incumbent.

When I chose to run again, I had a job to finish. Just as Carrie Chapman Catt pronounced the league's mission to "finish the fight," I, too, had a fight to finish. Upon accepting the presidency in 1998, I, along with the board, developed a ten-point plan. Seventy percent of that plan had been accomplished during my first term. I believed that the remaining 30 percent could and would be accomplished during a second term. In the conversation that emerged at convention, those accomplishments were being overshadowed by a small group of members who chose to make the election less about substance and more about race.

As a trailblazer, I chose to accept this challenge of pushing the boundaries of league culture. My reelection theme was *Believe*. I focused on the language of hope. I was not running against anyone, I was running for the league. I, like many other members, wanted to continue to believe in the league and its principles, believe that we could be a better organization, believe that we could remain relevant, and believe that we could make a difference. My reelection campaign chairs, Gerry Cummins (Colorado), Jean Armstrong (Louisiana), and Dr. P. Paulette Bragg (Georgia), made sure that the reelection team remained focused on the positive aspects of the league and this process. The team refused to engage in the character assassination or personal attack of the opponents, despite the fact that I was the subject of innuendo and personal attack. A "Personal Letter to Delegate Concerning Nominating Committee's Choice" was placed on the chair of each delegate during the initial plenary session. The letter posed two questions: "What is the effect of this challenge to the nominating committee recommendation?" And, "How will it impact the League?" The authors of the letter purported to identify and define the issue at hand.

> The fact that the current president has gone to the media (who are always looking for conflict with inferred racial undertones to sell papers) with her challenge, is not putting the good of the organization first. Surely the TOP numero uno qualification for the LWV presidency is to put the organization FIRST. The act of going to the media is like producing a negative campaign ad. It is saying that the individual is more important than the organization. Perhaps a reason the nominating committee chose to nominate someone else this time was that they saw over the past two years that the current president was more interested in her own power than the organization. This is apparent in the attached June 13 media interview published in the Cleveland Plain Dealer.
>
> The presidents [*sic*] performance was evaluated by a diverse nominating committee over two years. It was a long deliberative process. Having attended most (if not all) Board meetings, they were privy to observations and insights that the general members were not. League practice is not to air negatives about volunteer performance. If a president is not renominated by the committee which we elect, there must be compelling reasons. They have tried to keep the nomination and election at a respectful, clean level the same that we ask of our elected officials campaigns. Their decision was not taken lightly.
>
> This is the second time in a decade that this difficult decision was made. In the first instance, the sitting president accepted the decision gracefully for the good of the League.
>
> We encourage the delegates to vote for the slate recommended by the nominating committee, trust in their two years of first hand observations, and not allow this convention to be caught up in negative campaign tactics and racial inferences. The latter would be most unfortunate for the LWV.[12]

The inaccuracies in this letter regarding process, motivations, and intent were countered by a member of the nominating committee in a response to a local league president who wanted further explanation.

The ELECTED members of the Nominating Committee interviewed all of the sitting board members at our October meeting—except Carolyn. I got wind that she had not been scheduled Thursday night (prior to the Board meeting). I spoke to two members of the elected nom com and noted their apparent oversight. One later told me that the chair felt that Carolyn had been interviewed the preceding fall. (At that time, Carolyn was asked if she intended to run again, but apparently that was pretty much the extent of the interview. As I understand it, by the way, at that time she hadn't decided.)

We as a nominating committee had only just completed the Board interview questions recently—basically in time to be included in this meeting's Board preparation packets. Clearly, Carolyn wouldn't have been on a level playing field with the rest of the Board, since the questions used for the rest of the board had not been developed at the time they talked to her. I suggested that the two members of the nom com I spoke with to recommend interviewing Carolyn, or to have the elected members of the Nom Com formally tell her that they felt she had been interviewed at the prior time. Apparently neither action was taken.[13]

The league miscalculated the external impact this challenge to its principles would have. It is unclear who raised the issue of the league election and race with the media, but much to the organization's chagrin, this election became a national conversation. The focus on race and the deviation from previous league practice seemed to attract the most media attention. The national league leadership was so internally focused that it did not expect external attention on a league election. Not since league conventions were televised in the 1950s and the sponsorship of the U.S. presidential debates that lasted until 1988 had a league event received such national media attention. Once the national board recognized the magnitude of the media coverage—where the news articles were circulated by the Associated Press and discussed by league members nationally—the league leadership hired a Public Relations firm to work with the nominating committee and its slate of candidates.

The questions I was asked from the news media were in response to comments they received when interviewing some league members. Most wondered why I, as the first black president, was only being given an opportunity to serve one term. As there was no substantive explanation for not renominating me and the league traditionally had presidents serve at least two terms, the conversation became preoccupied with race.

My desire for privacy was juxtaposed with the necessity of standing by principle. I used a grassroots effort to campaign—the same grassroots efforts that were the very foundation of the league. As permitted by bylaws and policies, I purchased the organization's membership list and sent a letter to members indicating my intent to run for reelection so that it would reach the league presidents and members at the same time as the news of the nominated slate.

Interestingly, in terms of the league's ideals, there was no outrage when there was talk of challenging me as nominee in 1998, but there was some outrage when I decided to challenge the system by running from the floor. In addition to challenging the tradition, I was accused of "playing the race card." Contrary to this assertion, both I and my campaign team were intentional in not referencing race, instead focusing on substance. I campaigned on my record as president and my vision for the league.

The league recorded that 5 percent of its membership was comprised of people of color. It was still characterized as an organization of middle-aged, educated, and middle- to upper-class white women. One of the counter campaign arguments was that I was more style than substance, which totally disregarded any of my accomplishments as a league leader. Their narrative, while drawing attention to the league, marginalized the fact that I was a long-time league member, that I was qualified to be president, and that I followed the league's own rules in choosing to run from the floor.

Despite attempts to discredit me and the process, many league delegates were determined to ensure league integrity in the election. For example, the delegates from the League of Women Voters of North Carolina posed a number of questions to the nominating committee.

QUESTIONS FROM NC LEAGUE MEMBERS TO NOMINATING COMMITTEE, CAROLYN & BEVERLY:

1. There is "character assassination" of Carolyn and Board members whisper but say they can't give particulars because "it is not the League way" or they're under a "gag order." You'll have to say something because this is pushing people toward Carolyn, when we should be getting a balanced picture of the 2 candidates.
2. Was [name redacted] fired or did she resign as Carolyn says & Board accepted unanimously her resignation? How was lawsuit settled? Firing is a red flag. If fired, was there any documentation of her performance?
3. How is Carolyn hard to work for? Is she tough or unfair? Give particulars.
4. What were Carolyn's objectives when she took office? Did she achieve any of them?

5.   Give particulars about why Carolyn is not a team player. Could she have been trying to lead in a new direction that old Board members not want?

6.   Is Carolyn a leader with a vision that we should embrace, and are old League establishment members just against vision & change?

7.   Give rationale for extreme action against Carolyn (not nominating for another term). You must give reasons and examples.

Each of us pays $21 to LWVUS. We want answers.[14]

There have always been dissenters at convention and conversations about accepting the nominated slate or holding authentic democratic elections. When it comes to electing leadership, the league had become too complacent in not challenging processes and traditions and too comfortable in accepting internal processes that contradicted its principles.

The characterization of this election challenge took several forms: some viewed it as a welcome change to the process characterized as "ascension" to the presidency, while others viewed it as conflict within the organization. However, this episode, as one leader put it, meant the league ironically had trouble dealing with its own political situation. The league is hardly the only organization that has had such difficulties, but it did seem more ironic in light of the league's role as advocates for the political process. This same opportunity to hold democratic elections had been available throughout the life of the organization. The fact that there have only been three times in its nearly hundred-year history that this process was used is interesting. In each of those three times, the league was embarking upon significant cultural change in the organization.

A schism emerged among delegates as to how to interpret this occurrence. To perceive running for office from the floor as confrontational is a fundamental misunderstanding of the league's principles. Many members viewed it as consistent with what the league stood for. The league had clear "Campaign Policies for Candidates for LWVUS Office," which were adopted by the LWVUS Board of Directors on October 16, 1994. The policy followed the 1992 contested election and resulted from a conversation that "becoming a League officer should not be an anointing, but a democratic process as outlined in the League principles."[15] This became an ongoing discussion in subsequent years. The policy outlined in detail the roles of alternate slates and individual candidates in securing member contact information and soliciting funds, as well as of campaign expenditures and distribution of resources. All candidates were required to sign a Fair Campaign Practices form, which was submitted to the convention parliamentarian. The parliamentarian was charged with issuing a ruling on any dispute arising from implementation of the policies.[16]

The Fair Campaign Practice Principles were revised for the 2000 election. The practices purportedly aligned with the league's belief that candidates for national office should conduct campaigns in accordance with the identified principles. Those principles included not engaging in unfair or misleading attacks upon character. Of particular note is the principle that indicates that "candidates will not be part of any appeal to prejudice."

> —Candidates will neither use nor be involved with the use of any campaign material or advertisement that misrepresents, distorts, or otherwise falsifies the facts regarding an opponent. Candidates will clearly identify (by name and address) the source of all advertisements and campaign literature published or distributed.
>
> —Candidates will publicly repudiate support deriving from an individual or group whose activities would violate these "Fair Campaign Practice Principles."[17]

Since, as the incumbent, I still had the responsibility to lead the convention, my attention was devoted to doing just that. During convention, I was uncharacteristically challenged on parliamentary procedure. At the 2000 convention, I replaced the league's customary parliamentarian because she voiced a preference and openly campaigned for the nominated slate, which called into question her ability to render decisions impartially.

Before the votes were cast, a presidential candidates' debate was held. Each candidate outlined her vision for the league. My focus was on the accomplishments of the league under my tenure and my vision for the organization into the twenty-first century. I restated that I was not the conventional league leader, because the league needed more than convention to remain relevant in the twenty-first century. I was apolitical when it came to my personal advocacy but not about issues, justice, fairness, and equity. I had a vision of a diverse league and an agenda to help make that happen—the member-developed and board-adopted "Future Plan." This twenty-first-century strategic plan dealt with the league's impact, visibility, and organizational development.

I challenged the status quo, using the rules that had been designed by the organization to maintain its integrity, and won. It was a matter of principle. My reelection was a referendum on the league's ability to withstand a challenge and move forward. It symbolized the league's espoused values of embracing a democratic process. The league prided itself on being an incubator of democratic political norms, seen most clearly in the structure and process that formed their political voice. I was reelected with 60 percent of the vote.

Based on what was perceived to be an affront to league processes, some of the board members, who had been elected as a part of the nominated slate, intentionally created an environment to delegitimize, or render ineffective, my presidency. At the first post-convention meeting, the board voted to reverse the long-standing practice of allowing the president to appoint additional members to the board and established a new process, not supported by bylaws, to allow themselves to identify and appoint additional board members. The board voted to limit my ability to make decisions and restricted my travel. They determined that local league requests for visitations by the president were to be accommodated by staff.

There is a price to be paid for breaking barriers, but the support that I received from many leaguers, and particularly leaguers of color, gave me the strength to endure what was to come. I received one particularly consequential letter from retired Judge Jean Murrell Capers, both a long-time league member and the first Negro (her preferred term) woman to serve in the Cleveland City Council in 1949. She was reelected four times and from 1977 to 1986 was a Cleveland Municipal Court judge. Judge Capers had been an informal mentor to me in the Cleveland League of Women Voters. Her encouragement, in my early years, had kept me engaged. Reconnecting with her on a speaking engagement in Cleveland shortly after the 2000 election reminded me why my efforts remained a matter of principle. Judge Capers's letter, inviting me to a speaking engagement on Government and Women, was inspirational and aspirational. At age eighty-seven, she was still a champion for social justice and equality.

August 29, 2000

Dear Dr. Jenkins [*sic*]:

It was truly a breath of the finest intellectual air to see and hear you at the recent Cleveland League of Women Voters Annual Luncheon. I know what I must do, now, since I have allocated time to work with the League. . . .

I joined the Cleveland Chapter when that was the only Chapter in Cuyahoga County—in 1945 when I finished Law School and ran for City Council for the first time. I had planned to run for Council simply because the person in the position wasn't interested in doing the work which was necessary. Cleveland was then Republican, of course, as were most northern cities. This was still during the period when the members were women who did not work since that was not the fashionable procedure for women in society. The latter made all of the difference in the world as to the positions on issues which the League took since the women, all college graduates or Finishing School graduates, studied the laws with regard to the issues and took the position the women felt best—not the position that the "unseen decision-makers" provide and act as though it were that of the League. . . .

I'm interested in Women of Color in Leadership positions as was Dr. Bethune's legacy—which has not been followed. I worked with Dr. Bethune from 1945–1952 when she retired from the Council and the late Mrs. Vivian Carter Mason of Norfolk, Va was elected after the late Dr. Dorothy Boulding Ferebee, M.D. served the one year following Dr. Bethune at Dr. Bethune's request. Had Dr. Bethune been living, I would have known you and about you since that was the major thrust of Dr. Bethune—that Women of Color throughout the United States would know each other in order to be inspired by and through them. . . .

Goodness! I've rambled far too much if you haven't put this missive down. Anyway, please let me know about your coming since it will be the most important gathering in Ohio for 2001. It will be presented by the Harriet Tubman National Clear Sight Foundation, an educational foundation. If it weren't so important for our young women, I wouldn't do it. At 87 ½ I need to be at home in my rocking chair. But if someone had not done it for me, I wouldn't have had it as hard/easy as I did.[18]

Judge Capers concluded by thanking me for listening, but it is I who needed to thank her for all of the trails she blazed, the challenges she overcame, the legacy she left. She died in July 2017 at the age of 104.

Despite the initial resistance to my reelection, I continued to fulfill the responsibilities of the presidency using the established policies, practices, and traditions of the organization. My focus continued to be on the completion of the ten-point plan and ensuring movement forward for the organization into the twenty-first century. Beginning in 2000, "Issues for Emphasis" were no longer selected at conventions, and at the 2000 convention, the league adopted a concurrence to add support for restoration of the federal payment to the District of Columbia. The league offered the first national candidate debates online through its internet-based voter education program, Democracy Network (DNet®). In 1998, the Democracy Network was tested and then launched nationwide in January 2000. This website was a major effort to provide information regarding elections to citizens across the nation.

Judge Jean (Eugenia) Murrell Capers. (1913–2017) © 1991 *The Plain Dealer.* All rights reserved.)

As the league continued to reinvent itself, many changes were occurring, and "Making Democracy Work" was prioritized. This initiative included increasing voter turnout, encouraging campaign finance reform, and promoting civic education, diversity of representation, civic participation, and voting representation for the residents of the District of Columbia. During the same period, LWVEF activities included "Running and Winning," a program that encouraged young women to consider careers as political leaders as well as community dialogues on water resources, energy, and health care.

A hallmark of the new century was the commitment of the league to increase the use of electronic communication to league leaders across the nation. A monthly electronic newsletter was launched, and the league's membership database became available electronically for direct updating by league membership chairs.

At convention 2000, the per member payment (PMP) for student members was set at one half the regular rate and direct member input on program planning was implemented. For the first time, all membership brochures were produced in Spanish. Despite some resistance among the ranks of delegates, the league launched one of its most aggressive national diversity campaigns under my leadership.

The league adopted updated positions on trade and the UN in 2001 and 2002. The league was instrumental in the enactment of the Help America Vote Act of 2002 and the bipartisan Campaign Finance Reform Act of 2002. The league worked to renew the Voting Rights Act and filed a number of amicus briefs relating to campaign finance reform issues,

2000 Board. (Photo by Sam Kittner. Used by permission.)

racial bias in jury selection, and Title IX. The external political environment also impacted the work of the league. The 2000 election and hanging chads, as well as the reinvention of the electoral process, consumed much of the league's attention.

My remarks to the delegates of the last convention over which I would preside served three purposes: to remind leaguers to remain true to the organization's principles; to show that challenges to the status quo, using the structure established by the league and focusing on its mission and vision, can indeed make an organization stronger; and to challenge the organization to live up to its potential as an organization dedicated to the democratic process for all.

> The State of the League of Women Voters in the 21st Century
> Remarks by Carolyn Jefferson-Jenkins, President
> 46th Convention
> June 17, 2002

Thank you very much! It is great to be here with so many wonderful and committed League leaders from across the country. I am particularly pleased that all 50 states, the District of Columbia, the U.S. Virgin Islands and the Commonwealth of Puerto Rico are represented. Welcome! You are the heart and soul of the League. Your communities, your states and your county all owe you a great and lasting debt.

It has been my privilege to serve as your President for the past four years. I have been humbled by this honor—the fulfillment of the mandates of the members—and energized by the possibilities that lie before us. We are all volunteers who give of our time freely to the organization whose mission, vision and principles have attracted us. And because I use every opportunity to espouse these ideal—indulge me while I do so now.

"The League of Women Voters, a nonpartisan political organization, encourages the informed and active participation of citizens in government, works to increase understanding of major public policy issues, and influences public policy though education and advocacy. We believe in: respect for individuals; the value of diversity; the empowerment of the grassroots, both within League and in communities; and the power of collective decision making for the common good."

The story of the League of Women Voters is the story of a consistent cycle of resistance, resilience and renewal. Decade by decade we have survived—and sometimes thrived. In the words of our founder Carrie Chapman Catt

"Meantime, there will stand the league of Women Voters, the big, composite, nonpartisan body, with its clarification place for partisan complexities, its common meeting ground for the furtherance of principles, ideals and issues. It is a vast experiment."

Stand she said we will and stand we have. Study before action are the watchwords of the League of Women Voters on issues. They also characterize the league's examination of itself as a federated structure. Study before action has guided our organizational evolution.

Over the 82 years of its existence, the League has undertaken many self-studies in various efforts to remain a vital organization. Some have led to reform and change while others have been shelved and disregarded.

Let me provide an historic context for the challenges we face today— lest you think they are new. In the 1920s all but two states belonged to the League of Women Voters. Local leagues had no vote at Convention and any communication from a local League to the national League was required to go through the state League. By 1924, the League was organized in 346 of 433 congressional districts, the District of Columbia and Hawaii.

The early days were wrought with growing pains and a continual attempt to re-organize with the League's modified focus and agenda once the 19th Amendment was passed. Like many nonprofit and for profit organizations, the League barely survived the Depression.

In the early 1930s, the national leadership saw an overwhelming need to reexamine the organization so the "Committee on the Realignment of the Program" was convened in 1933. Restructuring, however, took another decade to accomplish. The League was not ready for change.

By 1942, the League had no choice but to change to survive. It had become ingrown and rigid with state boards standing in the way of communication between the national board and local members. Membership was declining and the financial situation was odious. The League members realized that "as the price of survival" the League had to refit itself to the time and occasion.

Historians report that the 1944 Convention marks the birth of the modern League. The 1946 Convention adopted a new structure for the organization. The League adopted and revised bylaws. The organization's name was changed to reflect the restructuring. The National League of Women Voters was reconstituted as the League of Women Voters of the United States. Its primary objective, as rephrased, was to promote "political responsibility through informed and active participation of citizens in government." Also eliminated was the injunction that every woman should enroll as a registered voter and party member.

The Convention adopted the policy and reforms that, according to Percy Maxim Lee, who joined the national Board in 1944, saved the League from dissolution. While ostensibly doing well, we once again found a need to study ourselves. The 1956 convention resolved upon a study of the balance needed between national security and protection of individual liberties. Internally, there was still a concern about the "inactive" member.

The 1956–58 University of Michigan survey of League membership prompted then league President Julia Stuart to refer to the finding as a "cultural shock front." The role of women in society was changing and the civil rights movement was intensifying. In response, the 1960 leadership attempted to employ the League's strengths while recognizing its limits in a crisis atmosphere where the irresistible urge of many members was "to do something about every crucial problem that plagued society." In spite of the attempts to maintain focus, the League agenda proliferated. The debate about the League becoming a single issue or a multi-issue organization surfaced.

Still the grassroots felt left out and their interest subverted. During the 1968–70 biennium, a "Structures and Procedures" Committee examined ways to streamline the League and gathered grassroots suggestions at regional meeting. Enter the 1970s, a time when numerous "women's groups" were emerging. The 1972–74 League Self Study was the first in a practically continuous 20 year series of self-examination.

At the 1974 Convention, the LWVUS board worried that the League was "trapped in yesterday's structures and must fight the idea that there is a 'League' way of doing things." Leaders complained that members were largely inactive. Local members complained that local leadership would "dole out only specific, narrowly defined and often boring tasks." The result was dissatisfaction all around leading to overworked leaders (oftentimes busy at busy work) and underused, disenchanted members.

The 1976 study resulted in the "Endangered Species" Committee mandated to prepare "alternative choices for the future direction of the League and address the harried vanishing volunteer." The Endangered Species Report generated yawns; leaders had apparently lost patience with mirror gazing. The League was not ready for change.

In 1982 the League was forced to question its reason for being for the first time since 1944. The 1982 convention mandated the development of a strategic long-range plan by an outside consultant and a committee of local, state and national leaders. The long-range plan was a response to shrinking membership and persistent national deficits. The research turned up themes that are not new to us: the League needs to modernize; local leagues need staff; members need to feel connected to the whole; focus on a few priorities; use resources efficiently; communicate League purpose to the public.

The League was not ready to change. In the 1990s, Making Democracy Work was leadership's attempt to restore a focus to league priorities. Organizational issues and questions continued. Old themes were echoed in the 1993 "Crossroads" plan and the 1999 "Future Plan." You have heard the old adage that states "that those who do not learn from the past are condemned to repeat it." What has the League learned? Members of the League must learn to study the past to prepare for the future. Knowing that radical change has occurred before should give us the courage to change again. Resistance, resilience, renewal.

The fundamental change that occurred in 1946 was not without pain. It was at this time that the league changed from a federation of states to an association of members. The demonstrated solidity and resilience of the League in its first fifty years, however, give reason for confidence in its ability to rise to the demands of the future. Its enduring principles have stood the test of time.

If the past is a prologue it may be said with confidence that the League of Women Voters in the 21st century must be and will be as vital and constructive a force in serving the public interest as it has been in the years before. The membership itself determined what the League would be. The evolutionary trends that have been set in motion have led us to this point—to this day.

We heard the message of the need for organizational change repeated decade by decade. We have heard, but have we responded? I love this excerpt from the *Chicago Daily News*, clearly reflecting a league made vital from its 1942 renaissance—though not without challenges. "This is no Pink Tea, Ladies!" *Chicago Daily News*, April 28, 1956. The reporter wrote:

"The League of Women Voters of the United States often called the most significant woman's organization in the country opens its national convention here Monday. When its national convention ends next Friday, elevator operators and other employees in the Sherman hotel will probably be saying the usual things about leaguers: 'They aren't as flutter as most women.' 'They sure don't laugh and squeal on the elevator the way a crowd of women usually does' or 'They're a bunch of brains.' Some observers will inquire 'Just what IS the League of Women Voters?' Here is a possible answer: 'It is the offspring of the woman suffrage movement, organized in 1920 by the same leaders who had just attained votes for women. It was intended to be a temporary movement to give women knowledge and confidence to exercise the franchise intelligently. The idea of disbanding faded when the job proved big and continuous.'"

As we entered the 21st century we have been challenged to retool our organization. We have made the hard decisions that will guide the future of the League. You spoke, we listened. We re-examined our priorities and reprioritized our future. The process is not complete, but amazing changes have taken place. At the dawn of the 21st century, the league is pursuing its mission and values in ways which are both familiar and new. The League of the 21st century is online, community-based, diverse, democracy-focused, action packed.

Since Convention 2000, a substantial number of programs, activities, events and initiatives have taken place on your behalf at the League of Women Voters of the United States. Most items are highlighted throughout your convention book, but there are several significant items I would like to emphasize. Because the "Future Plan" our strategic framework was adopted at Council 1999, I will report in those categories.

Organizational Development—website redesign, Capwiz for members, clearinghouse, funding solicitations and membership, recruitment on the web, expansion of listservs, establishment of the concept of a Governance Committee to review the League's processes and procedures, the addition of tactics to the strategic plan, prototype member data entry on the web, the acquisition of DNet®, improved legal protection of the League and DNet® trademarks, board development activities prior to board meetings, Kettering Leadership Institute, LeadershipPLENTY®- Pew Foundation, the National Voter readership survey, Diversity training and leadership development at Council and Convention, "Members News and Views" newsletter, new membership brochure for the first time in 7 years—both English and Spanish, growth of off-Board task forces, web and fax/mail based stud, updates and concurrences, emphasis on evaluation, expansion of funding base reestablishing previous relationships, service on committees and commissions including the appointment of off-Board members to represent the League, National Civic Leagues City Charter Revision Committee Coalition for Justice, improved responsiveness to members, strengthened professional capacity for staff, progress in establishing the Barbara Stuhler library (chaired by Beverly McKinnell), establishment of strategic partnership with *Governing* Magazine, etc.

Visibility—League was mentioned on *The West Wing* and *Scrubs* television shows, there was continued improvement of the "National Voter," an increased number of press releases, testimony before the U.S. Senate, U.S. House of Representatives and the Carter/Ford Commission, Democracy Net (DNet®) will be featured on "Rock the Vote," "7UP," and the Grammy's 30 city national tour called "Step-Up." League is an endorser of the Declaration of Independence Project, 100 media mentions per month, over the past two years, we have had coverage on CNN, *Alan Keyes Show*, NBC, MSNBC, Fox News Channel, C-Span, *Washington Post*, *New York Times*, *Christian Science Monitor*, *Washington Times*, *Los Angeles Times*, *USA Today*, *Congressional Quarterly*, Associated Press, Reuters, Knight Ridder, Scripps-Howard, Newhouse News and Copley News Service, Voice of America in 7 countries, numerous interviews on NPR. I served as moderator (Denver location) for the event we served as national co-sponsor of with "The Better World Fund," UNA-USA, and the UN Foundation, readership surveys, Judge, Good Housekeeping Good Government Award, Coalition for Free TV, Global News Network, Brazilian PBS Documentary on Racism, co-sponsored *Selma Lord Selma* an ABC film production about Martin Luther King Jr. and the Civil rights movement.

Impact—Voter integrity assistance with the 2000 presidential election, international expansion of program in Latin America and Africa, translation of League materials into Spanish and Portuguese, revised "Choosing the President" and participated in call in talk shows, created "Navigating Election Day," a new league publication for new voters, continuation of "Take a Friend to Vote" initiative, Judicial Independence Project, Election Systems Study Task Force, UN Update Task Force, extensive lobbying on the Hill for election reform and campaign finance reform, election administration survey to members, Election Administration Reform Symposia, increase in the number of coalitions to include Americans for Reform, the revitalization of the Motor Voter coalition, National call-in days successful, NAACP Blue Ribbon Commission on Voting, ABA Commission on Public Financing of Judicial Campaigns, WomenVote increased presence in communities of color, lobbying on the Hill on other League priority issues such as health care, reproductive choice, tax reform, electoral college, ABM Treaty, and environmental issues, increase in the number of state and local leagues using DNet®, over 10,000 candidates currently in DNet®, more Leagues participating in 2002 than ever before. To date DNet® has received over 6 million hits and 900,000 page views for 2002. All candidates for federal, statewide and state legislatures have been posted in 22 states. AOL is presenting DNet® content in their election center. Universities where I have presented on behalf of the League include: University of Virginia, UC Berkeley, UC San Bernardino, American University, Princeton University, Georgetown University, George Mason University, Milwaukee Area Technical College, Cleveland State University, University of Leiden, The Netherlands, and the University of Sao Paulo, Brazil.

This is an impressive list, given some of our challenges. When I joined the league, the world was a much different place (what was going on when you joined?). We are moving in the right direction, however, we face a great risk. Will we allow cultural entrenchment to paralyze the League? What we are currently experiencing can be graphically depicted in one of today's best sellers *Who Moved My Cheese?* by Spencer Johnson, M.D. (1998). Dr. Johnson addresses the subject of change with a great quote from A.J. Cronin.

"Life is no straight and easy corridor along which we travel free and unhampered, but a maze of passages, through which we must seek our way, lost and confused, now and again checked in a blind alley. But always, if we have faith, a door will open for us, not perhaps one that we ourselves would ever have thought of, but one that will ultimately prove good for us."

Who Moved My Cheese? is a story about change that takes place in a maze where four amusing characters look for cheese—cheese being the metaphor for what we want to have in life. Two mice named Sniff and Scurry and two little people, beings who were as small as mice but who looked and acted like people today, Hem and Haw. I won't tell the whole story but rather refer to the lessons learned. Each of us has our own idea of what Cheese is, and we pursue it because we believe it makes us happy. If we get it we often become attached to it. And, if we lose it, or it is taken away from us, it can be traumatic. The "Maze" in the story represents where you spend time looking for what you want. It can be the organization you work in, the community you live in, or the relationships you have in your life.

The lessons learned are referred to as "The Handwriting on the Wall" and I think you will find them appropriate: Change happens (they keep moving your cheese; anticipate change—get ready for the cheese to move); monitor change (smell the cheese often so you know when it is getting old); adapt to change quickly (the quicker you let go of the old cheese, the sooner you can enjoy new cheese); change (move the cheese); enjoy change (savor the adventure and taste the new cheese); be ready to quickly change again and again (they keep moving the cheese).

If we are to believe the "Handwriting on the Wall" what challenges will we face as we move toward 2020? The 21st century finds us experiencing both financial and ideological tension. What does the League do next? Campaign Finance Reform and Election reform legislation have been or will be passed by Congress. What does the League do next? Can you answer succinctly? When asked this question we need to be able to answer in a short, concise way that people understand and that makes people want more.

Every generation has to challenge an issue—a burden no one else has to carry. Our generation has the burden to ask the hard questions: What do we want to become as an organization? How can we help citizens become full participants in our democratic society? How will we share leadership? What are the lessons we must learn? Please ask yourselves, what do you deserve from this organization? And, what commitment are you willing to make?

The answers to these questions lie in the League's mission. The answers also lie in the League's membership. We must invigorate our membership, because, in the final analysis, our strength and ultimate success will be found in the thoughts and actions of our members. We must address these challenges by design—not by crisis. The League must have a look, a voice, a purpose, a presence that is reflected at all levels and in all activities.

The League must continue to build citizen participation in the democratic process—even in the League. We must continue to study key community issues at all levels of government in a nonpartisan way. We must continue to value diversity and exemplify inclusion over exclusion. We must continue to act with trust, integrity and professionalism. We must continue to acknowledge our heritage as we seek our path to the future. We must capitalize on the new spirit of volunteerism in the United States to grow and to empower this organization. Civil liberties, equity issues, civil rights issues, women and ethnic minorities in elected office, health care, environmental issues, technology, coalition building, leadership development, diversified funding strategy, comprehensive marketing plan.

We must promise, like our predecessors did in the 1930s and 1940s that we will change, so that we can "finish the fight" that started in the 19th century when women first came together for the right to vote. We must understand that demographics will drive much of the political debate in the coming decade. We must position ourselves to embrace that, or we risk being left on the sidelines of history.

What we do here cannot change an entrenched culture unless we want it to. When you pass a mirror, look into that mirror. In your mirror you see the activist of the 21st century—"Making Democracy Work" is truly up to us—each of us—because we are the League of Women Voters. Who benefits from our activism? You know, they are our daughters and their daughters and our sons and their sons, and the friend of our sons and daughters, black, white, brown, yellow, red.

Today's leadership must be as bold in its vision and action as our founders were in theirs. That is the only way the League can continue to be strong. Before we can hold the nation accountable, we must make sure that our own house is in order. Are we moving in the right direction? I joined the league because I wanted to make a difference. Working together I know we can make a difference. None of us in this hall underestimates the enormity of the challenges that lie ahead. Fortunately, we have tremendous leadership, tremendous state and local leagues, and a dynamic membership with which to work.

Now it is time for the next generation. Resistance, resilience, renewal. The future will be magnificent. None of us can do it alone! BUT together, no one can stop us. I like to think of League history, indeed the history of any organization as a ride on a roller coaster. You stand in line, you get strapped in, you go up, you go down, you go fast, you go slow, and in the end you are exhilarated and say to yourself "what a ride."

Let's imagine for a moment that we are there at the celebration of the league's 100th anniversary in the year 2020. And I hope most of us will be there, right? What will this organization be like then? If we do the right thing today, I can tell you with great confidence that it will be a much stronger league with an unmistakable presence at the local, state and national levels. I firmly believe that it is well within our grasp to substantially strengthen our position as the leading grassroots organization in the United States.

And, if we do the right thing today, at the League's 100th anniversary celebration they will toast those members and leaders who way back in the beginning of this new century had the courage and the vision to set a new course for the League—a course that set it up for growth, success and yes, viability in a new and exciting century.

The suffrage movement was not just about gaining the right to vote for women—it was about making our democratic system serve all citizens. As we know, there is a price to be paid for breaking barriers. Dr. Martin Luther King Jr. paid the ultimate price. In so doing he left this world a better place.

We must use time creatively, in the knowledge that the time is always ripe to do right. Now is the time to make real the promise of democracy and transform our pending national elegy into a creative psalm of brotherhood. Now is the time to lift our national policy from the quicksand of racial injustice to the solid rock of dignity.

These are not ordinary times, but we are not ordinary people. We will rise to the occasion. At a time when our nation is challenged, this is no time for the league to retreat, or allow internal politics to neutralize its impact. Together, let's reaffirm and commit ourselves to the challenge before us. History has shown that—as goes the League—so goes the United States. "Making Democracy Work," it's up to us! Let's change the league so that we can change the world.

Thank you very much.[19]

Conclusion

> We are anxious for you to know that we want to be and insist upon being considered a part of our American Democracy, not something apart from it. We know from experience that our interests are too often neglected, ignored, or scuttled unless we have effective representation in formative stages . . . We are not blind to what is happening. We are not humiliated. We are incensed.[20]

We are the architects of our own narratives as individuals and as organizations. We must proclaim the importance of history and use it as a blueprint for the future. Organizations such as the League of Women Voters cannot stem the tide of history through their policies, processes, and traditions. The forces of history converged for my election in 1998 and reelection in 2000. While more than half of my adult life has been spent in service to this organization, the very principles the league stood for needed to be challenged. As Barbara Stuhler, former national board member and author of one of the league's most referenced histories, pointed out in her preface, my election should have signaled a pivot for the league. What it showed, however, was that the pivot of such an entrenched culture would take more. In *Sustaining the League of Women Voters in America*, the author asks,

> Can a single civic association foster productive interpersonal dialogue among pluralistic cultures when its own environment is by degree a safe

haven of commonality? . . . Can a utilization of internal democratic structure widen personal member effectiveness in a way that also empowers
collective association voice?[21]

Through passion, a sense of purpose, and perseverance, as well as by
fielding the enormous expectations of navigating race and gender, women
of color have changed the history of the league. My determination to
honor the legacy of these women through my leadership was a weight I
was willing to carry. In many instances it required dissent, the type of
dissent embedded in the league's democratic ideology. Dissent is the
essence of what the league has stood for. Dissent in the form of change is
never easy. Dissent is often necessary.

Although the league has evolved and improved, it still does not reflect
the demographics of the nation in which we live. As a result, the good
work that is done and the impact it can have are not being fully realized.
The contradictions and paradoxes of an "everywoman's" organization that
did not address in any effective, sustainable way its most critical issue of
inclusion of all women calls into question whether this should be attributed to the institution or the ideology.

My place in league history, my story, is one of collective versus individual effort. This was a life-defining moment for me and the league. While
in some instances it was little noticed and much minimized, it exists as a
part of any story of the league that is to be told. The fact that I have a
unique perspective is why it was important for me to write this book. The
voices of leaguers of color have not been accurately reflected in what has
been published to date. Being first was a point of pride; being the only, a
point of disappointment.

My dream for this organization that has such promise is that in its next
one hundred years, it will recognize the value of all people in reality and
not just in rhetoric, in value not just voice (using visuals and symbols), in
beliefs not just benefits, with no quotas, no stereotypes, no double standards and without the residue of race! My hope is that it will be an organization that is true to its principles and ideals. As Dr. Condoleezza Rice,
former secretary of state, wrote in her contribution to the league publication *A Voice of Our Own: Leading American Women Celebrate the Right
to Vote*:

And those of us who are women and minorities owe a special debt to those
who pushed and shoved at closed doors so that opportunity would be
ours. To ignore the hard work still to be done in that regard would be fool-
hardy. But to pretend that little has been achieved, to assume that insur-
mountable barriers still stand in the way is, is to diminish what those great

pioneers achieved. That would be a great tragedy, for while our democratic journey as Americans is not complete, we are still very much farther down the road than those in many places who now look to us for confirmation that it is a road worth taking.[22]

Notes

1. Gordon et al., 1997.
2. League of Women Voters Papers filed in LWVUS office, Convention Folder, 1956, April 30, May 4, Chicago, Illinois.
3. League of Women Voters Papers LWV Connecticut, 1983, June 10, Remarks by Percy Maxim Lee.
4. League of Women Voters Papers, 1997, October.
5. Cooney, 2005, 420.
6. Cashin, 2012, 106.
7. hooks, 2015, xiii.
8. Maya Angelou.
9. League of Women Voters of the United States Bylaws, League Basics, 7.
10. League of Women Voters Papers, Convention Proceedings, 1992.
11. League of Women Voters Papers, Convention 2000.
12. This letter was placed on the chairs of all delegates in the plenary hall against League Fair Campaign Practices. It was signed by three members of the LWV of Bucks County, PA. The Cleveland *Plain Dealer* article referenced was "Panel Snubs League President in Bid for Re-election," Tom Brazaitis, 2000, June 13; personal papers of Carolyn Jefferson-Jenkins.
13. By league bylaws, the nominating committee consists of four members elected at convention and three appointed from the sitting board. This email was in response to a request for more information from a local league president about the nominating committee's decision (personal papers of Carolyn Jefferson-Jenkins).
14. These handwritten questions were provided by the then-president of the North Carolina league to the nominating committee (personal papers of Carolyn Jefferson-Jenkins).
15. League of Women Voters Papers filed in LWVUS office, Convention Folder, 2000.
16. Ibid.
17. League of Women Voters Papers filed in LWVUS office, Convention Folder, 2000.
18. Personal papers of Carolyn Jefferson-Jenkins, 2000, August.
19. Personal papers of Carolyn Jefferson-Jenkins.
20. Winbush Riley, 1993, 230–231. Mary McLeod Bethune speech given to the National Council of Negro Women, November 26, 1938.
21. Cashin, 2012, 105.
22. Neuman, 1996, 230–231.

Epilogue: Moving Forward— The Unfinished Fight

There is no greater agony than hearing an untold story inside you.
—Maya Angelou

A story is a detailed organization of narrative events and actions into a unified whole. All stories have settings, characters, plots, and endings. This is true of the league's story, and if the league accepts the challenge, it will have the chance to embrace a new beginning and get its story right. The history of any organization is told most poignantly through the stories of its members—*all* of its members. Everything that makes the league the league is what will continue to make the organization relevant as it adapts to a dynamic twenty-first century. *The Untold Story of Women of Color in the League of Women Voters*, our story, is a remarkable testament to the unrelenting tenacity and spirit of women who were in many instances marginalized in the organization and its recorded history.

The League of Women Voters, just like the United States, has a complicated history encircling its relationship with women of color. Often, these women's stories of passion, purpose, and perseverance are overlooked or detailed only in the footnotes of the organization's mainstream narrative. By telling the story of these women of color who have not been fully represented in existing histories, this book serves to honor the history of *all* members and inspire the next generation of young women to continue the "fight."

The Untold Story discloses the organizational tensions between the league's principles and what it perceived as practicality in navigating both the internal and external challenges of prioritizing gender over race. It seeks to make sense of the complexity of the organization whose principles espoused rights for all but whose action or intentional inaction often excluded women of color from full participation and recognition. This story provides context for the decisions made by the national leadership regarding the league's relationships with its members of color and allows us to appreciate the great inheritance left to the league by women who chose to align themselves as members and supporters of the principles and ideals of this organization.

The League of Women Voters is a paradox in women's history. As the organization prepares to celebrate its centennial on February 14, 2020, it must acknowledge and honor its unabridged history. Many white women suffragists sought the vote only for themselves. Conversely, black women were universal suffragists in the sense that their voices called for the vote for all citizens, not just themselves.

Despite the increased research in women's history in recent years, documentation of the contributions of black women has been often neglected. The 1976 Schlesinger Library, with support from the Rockefeller Foundation, began its Black Women Oral History Project to provide new source material for scholars and researchers. Black women may perhaps have less frequently created written records, and what was preserved did not often find its way into libraries and archives. *This Untold Story* is just the beginning of the quest to learn more about the contributions of women of color in the league. There are volumes of work that can be assembled at the state and local levels, each adding a different dimension.

Lessons Learned

The League of Women Voters, when it is the best version of itself, as it has been throughout certain periods of its history, is an organization to be reckoned with. When it is anything less, it is less. The history of the league as the legacy organization of the suffrage movement is not linear, because the history of this country has never been linear. Completing the league's history by telling the story of women of color matters because it concedes the power of progress.

At the dawn of its next one hundred years, the league is pursuing its mission and values in ways that are both new and familiar, using the lessons learned. Those lessons are that themes in league history, if allowed, repeat themselves; that the league's reputation allows it to take the lead on issues to transform itself and society to reflect the nation we are and want to be; that if we stay true to the fundamental principles, the league will remain relevant; that recognizing mistakes of the past clear the path for the future; that evolution in an entrenched culture is hard work; and that each member has value and leadership is critical.

In *A Portrait of the League of Women Voters*, written by Marguerite Wells, former national president, published by the League of Women Voters in April 1938, and revised in April 1940, Wells offered insight into the league as an organization and mirrored the themes throughout the league history as to how the organization would remain relevant. Her treatise would serve as a precursor to the league's complex relationship with its members of color.

> The League is now "grown up" and it is appropriate that it should look at itself with an appraising eye . . . It would be unworthy of the League not to decide its destination and chart its course. If it finds itself off course, it must re-orient itself. It must travel with compass or drift. It must naturally expect to veer with the wind, avoid shoals and follow channels. It must only take care that it does not become the sport of every breeze that blows and scud from one channel to another regardless of the course it has set.[1]

Wells also expressed her view of the league in 1942:

> that institutions bore within themselves the seeds of their own decay. The structure of an organization should "facilitate constant and direct inter-pretation of its core purpose". . . . As the price of survival it had to refit itself to the time and occasion.[2]

This was a prelude to the sweeping revision of the bylaws that would bring league members directly within the embrace of the national leader-ship. The league nationally would become a close-knit, unitary organiza-tion of local leagues.

Since leagues represent the communities in which they are established, many formal and informal barriers were used to prevent women of color from joining the league. Leagues realistically recognized the importance of having access to women of color and worked closely throughout the organization's history with the National Council of Negro Women. This relationship was more transactional, however, than it was transforma-tional, and did not afford women of color the full rights of league mem-bership. The images, photos, and symbols of the league did not begin to reflect any type of diversity until the era of the civil rights movement. Because there was an acceptance that there were Negro women's organiz-ations that black women could belong to, there was no real outreach by many local leagues to "their" communities.

Throughout league history, formal data on race was not collected by the national leadership and not required to be collected at the state and local levels. So, the only data about race was anecdotal and came from observations of individual local leagues. Informally, however, there were constant inquiries made to the national president and local and state leagues asking for guidance about how to handle requests from women of color to join the organization. In the 1970s, an attempt was made to collect data on the racial composition of the membership initiated by the league's black caucus. That data collection lasted for two years and then did not appear to occur again. When I became a national board member in 1994, I asked about membership data and was told that to collect such data was anathema to the league philosophy of being open to all. This explanation while interesting at best, was proven to be consistent in league history.

Wells's message was echoed sixty-four years later in my final presidential remarks, presented to the League of Women Voters at the forty-sixth convention, urging leaguers to make the twenty-first century the most notable for the league. I emphasized that the story of the League of Women Voters is the story of a consistent cycle of resistance, resilience, and renewal. Over the hundred years of its existence, the league has undertaken many self-studies in various efforts to remain a vital organization. Some have led to reform, while others have been shelved and disregarded. Its enduring principles, however interpreted, have stood the test of time. What the league should have learned is that radical change has occurred before, and the knowledge obtained should give us courage to change again.

My legacy is to have the league live up to its ideals, just as women of color have done for the hundred years of the organization. The question for me was why an organization committed to social justice did not more aggressively tackle issues of discrimination and race. What I suspected has been proven by my research; for as much as leaguers were passionate about issues that had a direct impact on them, without voices of color in the conversation, issues of diversity and equity did not rise to the level of priority. There was a marked difference, however, during the civil rights era, because the nation was changing and the league had to change with it to remain relevant. Cashin's research confirms this:

> The League of Women Voters has occasionally been capable of being its own worst enemy while presenting itself above "narrow regard" and

championing the "less fortunate." From the organization's beginnings in 1920, members have purported to celebrate difference and reform the world. Often they live up to what could be judged their self-righteous trumpets. Convinced of its righteousness and excellent timing, with accompanying naïve faith in the American version of democracy can unintentionally exhibit condescension toward cultural, racial, class or activist difference on the basis of presumed expertise, rectitude and public applause.[3]

Such behavior, when it occurs, can undo the league's positive impact and impede its stated goal of being inclusive.

Moving Forward

The League of Women Voters of the United States is at a crossroads. At a time when the fundamental tenets of a democratic nation are being challenged, there is no time for the organization to retreat. Leaguers can be the architects of a vision that moves the organization forward, truly becoming an inclusive "everywoman's" organization by honoring all of its members and moving the accomplishments of women of color past, present, and future out of the footnotes and into the main narrative. The actions the league takes must not be by crisis but by design. This is our opportunity to get it right!

The league's strength is in its work to educate and inform voters in a factual and nonpartisan way. A vision of a diverse, equitable and inclusive league and an agenda to make it happen must materialize. Hard choices are required. Fiscal and ideological tensions must be resolved. The organization must accept that demographics will drive much of the national political debate in the coming decade. The league must position itself to embrace that premise or risk being left on the sidelines of history. Before the league can hold the nation accountable to its ideals, it must make sure that its own house is in order. Since an organization reacts to both its internal and external environments, it faces times of transition that can only be resolved by the way the leaders navigate those times.[4]

Existing league histories record impressive principled members volunteering their time from its founding, the league has struggled to remain true to its principles while adapting to an ever-changing society. In preparation for the twentieth anniversary of the league, Carrie Chapman Catt stated in a communication to league leaders that "a promise of lofty ideals bind a nation—yeah an organization—together."

WOMAN'S CENTENNIAL CONGRESS, NOVEMBER 25-26-27, 1940
CARRIE CHAPMAN CATT, Chairman
Delegates will come from all over the country to
LOOK BACKWARD at achievements won
LOOK OUTWARD at discriminations still existing
LOOK FORWARD to the emphases imperative for the advancement of
mankind.[5]

These enlightened comments by Catt are often overshadowed by her recorded statements denigrating blacks—statements that formed the basis of the protest of the women of color at Iowa State University upon the dedication or the naming of a building after Catt. The contradiction of her remarks and the subsequent struggle the league had in forging a true relationship with its members of color represents the enigma that is the league.

Marching against the status quo was not easy for white women, but it was even more difficult for women of color confronted with both the racist sentiment of the day and the resistance of white suffragists who did not favor suffrage for black women.

Throughout league history, the national league leadership has been keenly aware of this contradiction and responded to it in one of three ways; choosing action through the two-year study process, choosing intentional inaction, and sometimes choosing to remain silent on the issue.

In her address at the fiftieth anniversary convention banquet on May 7, 1970, Marian Wright Edelman, a thirty-one-year-old attorney and civil rights leader, challenged the league to define its future for all. While her focus was for the league to take a bold stand on school desegregation, her remarks about the organization itself reflected some historic universal themes.

> I want to have a very frank talk with you tonight. I haven't prepared a speech, but I want to talk about what is on my mind as a black person . . .
> I have never seen as much reliance on good will, and today we don't need more good will and good faith, we need good work and quickly. I have never seen so much reliance on rhetoric, so many people getting caught in rhetorical rationales, denying the real problems that are confronting us. I have never been so afraid of inactivity and the ineffectualness of liberals and liberal organizations who think they can rely on their histories and their past glories, but who are not maintaining their relevance with the very tough problems of today. . . .
> What can we do? I hope that members of the League will begin to deal more honestly with the facts around them.[6]

In spite of the increase in diversity, equity and inclusion initiatives beginning in the late 1990s, the league has remained predominantly a white women's organization. In 2002, 5 percent of league members were "of color," though the numbers would increase marginally in some state and local leagues in areas with greater geographic diversity. New activism in the league following Convention 2016 has led to a renewed commitment to become a more inclusive, vibrant organization for the future.

Much like the activism spurred by other periods of reform in league history, the league's new strategic focus, will stimulate another round of intense debate over what kind of organization the League of Women Voters should be. As the league has evolved and improved, it still does not represent the demographics of the nation. As a result, the good work that is done and the impact it can have is not being fully realized. The contradictions and paradoxes of an "everywoman's" organization that does not address in any effective, sustainable way its most critical issue of inclusion of all women will cease to endure.

To celebrate the league's fiftieth anniversary, Louise Young, in her historic account of the league, stated:

> The demonstrated solidity and resilience of the League in its first fifty years, however, give every reason for confidence in its ability to rise to the demands of the future. Its enduring principles have stood the test of time. If past is prologue, it may be said with confidence that the League of Women Voters in its second half-century will be as vital and constructive a force in service of the public interest as it has been in the years described in this volume.[7]

In celebrating one hundred years of existence at the 2020 convention, the league should take pride in its accomplishments and recognize the magnitude of the challenges that lie ahead. Many of the themes are familiar, many may prove to be unpredictable. The changing nature of big-city populations and the difficulties a number of urban leagues experienced in sustaining their organizational capacities revealed one set of challenges to the league's ability to adapt. The massive entry of women into the workforce, which accelerated in the sixties, raised some concerns as to whether the available pool of member talent and energies would constantly be replenished. Upon reflection, this is a struggle for meaning, for a sense of who we are as an organization into the future. An opportunity like this occurs every hundred years.

After decades of organizational realignment, the league must build on past achievements while learning from its missteps. The league must be in a constant state of continuous improvement in order to adapt, evolve, and remain relevant in an ever-changing society. The strength of this federated organization remains at the state and local levels and the national leadership must be sure to place emphasis on league members' work at those levels.

A New "Fight to Finish"

Despite the risk of great personal loss, women of color have had a long tradition of civil and human rights activism. Their legacy continues today in the experiences and examples of a new generation of women activists and leaders. That legacy must be affirmed and their profound influence on the League of Women Voters recognized. *The Untold Story of Women of Color in the League of Women Voters* is my contribution to ensuring that their efforts rise to the level of importance that they deserve. This is a story of the struggle for meaning, for a sense of who we are and who we aspire to be.

My dream for this organization that has such promise is that in its next one hundred years, it will recognize the value of all people in reality, not just rhetoric; in value, not just voice/visuals; and in beliefs, not just benefits. The legacy for the next one hundred years should be a legacy without labels, without quotas, stereotypes, double standards, or any residue of race so that our ideals don't house the ugliness of racism and that women of color are no longer invisible, but brought out of the footnotes and into the mainstream narrative.

Because I have been inspired by the women in my life who have persevered to make this world a better place and whose stories parallel those of the women mentioned in this book, I honor their legacy using the framework shared with me by my grandmother. She recognized that each generation had a part to play; she called it her *cycle of life*. As we move through the stages of life, we are at different phases in the cycle and eventually are touched by the beliefs of them all.

A LIFETIME OF INVOLVEMENT: THE DREAMS OF MY GRANDMOTHER
Hope—My grandmother, born in 1903 in the segregated South, the first generation out of slavery, who picked cotton in the morning, taught at the colored normal school in the afternoon and spent her evenings teaching others to write so that they could sign their names so that they could register to vote. She recognized the irony of the celebration of the ratification of the Nineteenth Amendment, since the privileges of suffrage did not realistically apply to her until the passage of the Voting Rights Act of 1965 and even then not without the continued struggle to overcome the Jim Crow laws of the South. Her activism, despite enormous challenges, paved the way for the next generation. Hers was the generation of hope.

Promise—My parents, both born in the segregated South, where they endured the Depression and blatant discrimination and then moved North in the second Great Migration to build on my grandmother's hope that the next generation would have a better life. My parents, who had only a fourth- and eighth-grade education but were able to carve out a middle-class lifestyle, ensured that each of their children at the very least completed high school. They continued the legacy of civic activism by ensuring that voting and community involvement were household expectations. Theirs was the generation of promise.

Commitment—My generation, the beneficiaries of the civil rights movement, who benefitted from the struggles, encouragement, hope and promise of the previous generation to pursue what were previously unimaginable goals and dreams, to exceed their educational achievement, to pass on the legacy to keep the promise of upward mobility for the next generation, to not just view accomplishments as individual achievements, but collective ones, to share wisdom, to mentor, and to support. Mine is the generation of commitment.

Possibilities—The next generation of children, nieces, and nephews who fortunately should not have to endure the same degree of legal and social limitations imposed by racism and sexism. They have the opportunity to dream bigger, to rewrite the narrative of society, and to create the world that my grandmother hoped for, that my parents promised, and that I made a commitment to help shape. This is the generation of possibilities.

Grandparents and parents are gone. Times have changed. Uncertainty generates energy. This is only the beginning! Through stories, we are educated, inspired, and called to action. As the League of Women Voters uses its centennial celebrations to acknowledge its past and charts its future there is an unyielding responsibility to uncover the untold stories all of the women who have shaped the league's organizational life. *The Untold Story of the Women of Color in the League of Women Voters* is a story of real people whose dreams and disappointments are not so different from your own.

How much the world has changed in the past one hundred years? How much hasn't changed in its struggles with race and gender. When the last page of the last chapter of league history is written, what will it say about the organization and its members?

Notes

1. Wells, 1962, 3.
2. Young, 1989, 137.
3. Cashin, 2012, 119–120.

4. Osborn, 1994, 162.

5. League of Women Voters Papers filed in LWVUS office, Convention Folder, 1940. Pamphlet *Women's Centennial Congress* November 25–27, 1940.

6. League of Women Voters Papers filed in LWVUS office, Convention Folder, 1970. Excerpts from Marian Wright Edelman's remarks at LWVUS fiftieth Anniversary Convention.

7. Young, 1989, 178–179.

Appendices

Appendix 1: Former National Presidents

**Carrie Chapman Catt (1920–1947)

Maud Wood Park (1920–1924)

Belle Sherwin (1924–1934)

Marguerite M. Wells (1934–1944)

Anna Lord Strauss (1944–1950)

Percy Maxim Lee (1950–1958)

Ruth S. Phillips (1958–1964)

Julia Stuart (1964–1968)

Lucy Wilson Benson (1968–1974)

Ruth C. Clusen (1974–1978)

Ruth J. Hinerfeld (1978–1982)

Dorothy S. Ridings (1982–1986)

Nancy Neuman (1986–1990)

Dr. Susan S. Lederman (1990–1992)

Becky Cain Ceperly (1992–1998)

Dr. Carolyn Jefferson-Jenkins (1998–2002)

Kay J. Maxwell (2002–2006)

Mary Wilson (2006–2010)

Elisabeth McNamara (2010–2016)

Chris Carson (2016–)

**Carrie Chapman Catt retained her title as National League President until her death, as a sign of respect. League records list her entire time even though there were other official presidents handling the operation of the organization.

Appendix 2: National Board Members of Color

Josie Johnson (1968–1972), Minnesota

Faye Williams (1970–1972), Indiana

Dorothy McKinney Wright (1974–1975), Arkansas

Edith Bornn (1980–1982), U.S. Virgin Islands

Julia A. Holmes (1982–1986), New York

Julia T. Richie (1982–1986), Michigan

JoAnn Price (1986–1988), Maryland

Adrienne Latham (1990–1992), Tennessee

Debbie Macon (1992–1996), Michigan

Carolyn Jefferson-Jenkins (1994–2002), Colorado

Barbara Foston (1996–2000), Georgia

**F. Marie Brown (1998–2000), New Mexico

Rosetta M. Davis (2000–2003), Tennessee

Sheila Martin (2000–2004), Massachusetts

Odetta MacLeish-White (2004–2008), Florida

Stephanie Johnson (2006–2010), Arkansas

**2010–2016 no one of color

Toni Zimmer (2016–), New Jersey

Dr. Deborah Turner (2016–), Iowa

**Native American

Appendix 3: National Nominating Committee Member of Color

Cheryl Imelda Smith (1986–1998), New York

Vanessa Abernathy (1998–2000), Pennsylvania

Audrey Redmond (1998–2000), California

Appendix 4: LWVUS Executive Directors (designated as Executive Secretary until the late 1960s)

2018–	Virginia Kase***
2015–2018	Dr. Wylecia Wiggs Harris**/***
2000–2015	Nancy Tate
1998–2000	Dr. Jane Gruenebaum
1994–1998	Judith Conover
1990–1994	Gracia Hillman**
1986–1990	Grant P. Thompson
1983–1986	Carol C. Parr
1978–1983	Harriet Hentges
1972–1978	Peggy Lampl
1970–1972	Teresa Harmstone
1958–1970	Dixie Drake
1950–1958	Muriel Ferris

1934–1950	No Executive Secretary
1930–1934	Beatrice H. Marsh
1924–1930	Gladys Harrison
1923	Minnie Fisher Cunningham

**Women of color
***Executive Director designation changed to CEO

Appendix 5: Black League Members Attending Convention, May 11, 1970[1]

Bessye Bennett	Hartford, CT
Juanita Handy	East Providence, RI
Theo Palmer	Sumter, SC
Mildred Chavores	Columbus, OH
Natalie Howard	District of Columbia
Thelma Cofer	District of Columbia
Bette Pinkney	Arlington, MA
Jacqueline Etchison	Proviso, IL
Nellie M. Douglas	Wickliffe, OH
Margaret B. Dockery	District of Columbia
Louise Perry	District of Columbia
Ruth Patterson	Detroit, MI
Lavonne Lewis	Las Vegas, NV
Barbara M. Owens	Philadelphia, PA
Thelma Jackson	District of Columbia
Phyllis R. Gibson	Canton, MA
Roberta Wilson	Chicago, IL
Ann Rowe	Chicago, IL
Eleanor Suggs	Phoenix, IL
Inez B. Brewer	Gary, IN
Ruthan E. Jones	District of Columbia
Juanita H. Scott	San Bernardino, CA
Delores Welborne	Baltimore, MD
Connie Fortune	District of Columbia
Elnora Jackson	Cleveland, OH
Alethia Banks	District of Columbia
Dorothy H. Thomas	Chester, PA
Verneice Hensey	Wilmington, MA
Faye Williams	Indianapolis, IN (National Board)

Joy Fleisher	District of Columbia
Josie Johnson	Minneapolis, MN (National Board)
Christina Smith	District of Columbia (National Staff)
Elizabeth Polk	Nashville, TN
Olda Johnson	Lawrence, KS
Myrtle Davis	Atlanta, GA
Irma Braden	New Orleans, LA
Laura Hunt	Bronx, NY
Liz Gomer	Duluth, MN[2]

Appendix 6: Women of Color Who Are Known to Have Participated in National League Activities[3]

These are just some of the names that appear in national league documents. [Note: Information is as complete as possible based on available records.]

Mary Baldwin	
Aletha Banks	District of Columbia
J. Estelle Barnett	Ohio
Delilah Beasley	Alameda County, California
Bessye Bennett	Connecticut
Joyce Benson	
Mary McLeod Bethune	
Mrs. A. W. Blackwell	
Willia J. Bouldin	Maryland
Mrs. B. F. (Carrie) Bowles	St. Louis
Irma Braden	Louisiana
Mrs. David Bradley	Durham, North Carolina
Inez B. Brewer	Gary, Indiana
Ann Brown	California
Charlotte Hawkins Brown	North Carolina
Hallie Quinn Brown	Ohio
Mrs. S. Joe Brown	
Sue M. Brown	Iowa
Nannie H. Burroughs	District of Columbia
Sybil R. Burton	
The Honorable Jean Murrell Capers	Cleveland

Elizabeth C. Carter

Mary Ann Shadd Cary   District of Columbia

Mildred Chavores   Ohio

The Honorable Shirley Chisholm   New York

Augusta T. Chissell

Thelma Cofer   District of Columbia

Dr. Rebecca Cole

Dr. Mattie E. Coleman   Tennessee

Fannie Conner   New York

Anna Julia Cooper

Dorothy Rutledge Crawford   Charlotte, North Carolina

Ellen Crum

Myrtle Davis   Georgia

Anna Johnson Diggs   Detroit, Michigan

Margaret Dockery   District of Columbia

Nellie Douglas   Ohio

Alice Dunbar

Addie Rose Dunlap   Seattle, Washington

Beverly Earle   North Carolina

Maxine Eaves   North Carolina

Jacqueline Etchison   Illinois

Grace Baxter Fenderson

Joy Fleisher   District of Columbia

Margaretta Forten

Connie Fortune   District of Columbia

Verlee Fowler   North Carolina

Mrs. Frankie Freeman   St. Louis, Missouri

Margaret Gainer   Illinois

Phyllis R. Gibson   Massachusetts

Elizabeth Gilmore   Charleston, West Virginia

Irene Goins   Chicago, Illinois

Liz Gomer   Minnesota

Mrs. E. C. (Beatrice) Grady   St. Louis

Charlotte Forten Grimke   District of Columbia

Helen Hamlett   New Jersey

Juanita Handy	Rhode Island
Frances E. W. Harper	
Gladys Harrison	
Dr. Dorothy Height	
Mary Hennessey	St. Croix, Virgin Islands
Verniece Hensey	Massachusetts
Lavonne Henter	Nevada
Carrie Horton	
Natalie Howard	District of Columbia
Laura Hunt	New York
Alice Callis Hunter	District of Columbia
Jane Edna Harris Hunter	Ohio
Addie Waites Hunton	Illinois
Gladys Hyman	New York
Elnora Jackson	Ohio
Juanita Jackson	Georgia
Thelma Jackson	District of Columbia
Olda Johnson	Kansas
Ruthan E. Jones	District of Columbia
Marguerite Kisseloff	New York
Adrienne Latham	Tennessee
Bette Lawrence	Michigan
S. Willie Layton	
Dora Needham Lee	New York
Helen Lemme	Iowa City, Iowa
E. Lavonne Lewis	Nevada
Elizabeth Little	Alabama
Adella Hunt Logan	Alabama
Corneida Lovell	Arkansas
Maritcha Lyons	
Mildred Madison	Cleveland
Geneva Maiden	Ohio
Gloria Marquez	Pound Ridge, New York
Anna Marsh	District of Columbia
Victoria Earle Matthews	

Deborah McCrea	Providence, Rhode Island
Mary McCurdy	Georgia
Dorothy McKinney	District of Columbia
Janice Meek	Pennsylvania
Hettie L. Mills	Jacksonville, Florida
Enid H. A. Montes	St. Thomas, U.S. Virgin Islands
Barbara Moore	Illinois
Gertrude Bustill Mossell	
Viola Ross Napier	Georgia
Gloria Nesbitt	Pennsylvania
Barbara Owens	Pennsylvania
Theo Palmer	South Carolina
Ruth Patterson	Michigan
Louise Perry	District of Columbia
J. Frankie Pierce	Tennessee
Bette Pinkney	Massachusetts
Elizabeth Polk	Tennessee
JoAnn Price	Maryland
Doris E. Pritchett	Camden, New Jersey
Harriet Forten Purvis	
Caroline Remond Putnam	Salem, Massachusetts
Florence Spearing Randolph	
Lulu Reese	Tennessee
Iris G. Reeves	Maryland
Mrs. Henry Reid	Oak Park, Illinois
Sarah Parker Remond	
Florida Ruffin Ridley	
Charlotte Rollin	South Carolina
Frances Rollin	
Katherine Rollin	
Louisa Rollin	
Ann Rowe	Illinois
Josephine St. Pierre Ruffin	
Anna Cheek Scott	Charleston, West Virginia
Juanita H. Scott	California

Phyllis Shearer	Greenburgh, New York
Sandra Shreve	Denver, Colorado
Cheryl I. Smith	New York
Christina Smith	District of Columbia
Mrs. Joseph Snowden	Illinois
Mrs. J. Merrill Spencer	Flint, Michigan
Abbie Stebbins	New Jersey
Dr. Susan McKinney Steward	
Ora Stokes	Virginia
Eleanor Suggs	Illinois
Mary Church Terrell	
Dorothy H. Thomas	Pennsylvania
Janice Thurmond	Georgia
Hettie Tilghman	San Francisco, California
Sojourner Truth	
Maggie Lena Walker	
Margaret Murray Washington	
Alice Webb	Chicago, Illinois
Delores Welbourne	Maryland
Ida B. Wells- Barnett	
Ida Perkins West	Missouri
Fannie Barrier Williams	
Faye Williams	Indianapolis, Indiana
Irene Williams	Maryland
Louise Williams	New Jersey
Roberta Wilson	Illinois
Eva Nichols Wright	
Josephine Silone Yates	

Notes

1. The spelling of the names of members who attended the Convention is presented as it appeared on the league documents.

2. League of Women Voters Papers.

3. The spelling of the names, cities, and states of members who participated in National League Activities is presented in the way it appeared on the league documents.

Bibliography

Black, Naomi. 1983. "The Politics of the League of Women Voters." *International Social Science Journal* 35, no. 4: 385–603.

Brazaitis, Tom. 2000, June 13. "Panel Snubs League President in Bid for Re-election." Cleveland, Ohio Plain Dealer Bureau. https://www.newspapers.com/title _3916/the_plain_dealer/?xid=540&gclid=EAIaIQobChMIov27hcLi5QI VKP_jBx3xfQrmEAAYASAAEgLoMfD_BwE

Bucy, Carole Stanford. 2002, March 26. "Exercising the Franchise, Building the Body Politic: The League of Women Voters and Public Policy, 1945–1964." PhD diss., Vanderbilt University, Nashville, TN.

"Campaign Policies for Candidates for LWVUS Office." 1994. League of Women Voters of the United States Papers, filed in LWVUS Office, Convention Folder, 1994.

Cashin, Maria Hoyt. 2011. *The Democratic Merit and Sustainability of Participatory Public Interest Associations: A Case Study of the League of Women Voters.* Washington, D.C.: Georgetown University.

Cashin, Maria Hoyt. 2012. *Sustaining the League of Women Voters in America.* Washington, D.C.: New Academia Publishing.

Coggshall, Jane G., Amber Ott, Ellen Behrstock, and Molly Lasagna. 2009. *Supporting Teacher Effectiveness: The View from Generation Y.* Naperville, IL, and New York: Learning Point Associates and Public Agenda.

Colored Committee of the League of Women Voters of St. Louis. 1929. *The First Nine Years.* League of Women Voters Papers, Library of Congress, Box II: 188.

"Concerns about the League of Women Voters by a Group of Black Delegates and Observers at the 50th Anniversary Convention." 1970. League of Women Voters Papers Convention Folder, 1970.

Cooney, Robert P. J., Jr. 2005. *Winning the Vote: The Triumph of the American Woman Suffrage Movement.* Santa Cruz, CA, and Half Moon Bay, CA: American Graphic Press.

Dietrich, Diana. 1981. "The League of Women Voters of Raleigh-Wake Co: Function and Flexibility." Masters thesis, Duke University, Durham, NC.

Dodson, Angela P. 2017. *Remember the Ladies: Celebrating Those Who Fought for Freedom at the Ballot Box.* New York: Center Street.

DuBois, Ellen Carol. 1978. *Feminism and Suffrage.* Ithaca, NY, and London: Cornell University Press.

Du Bois, W. E. B. 1912a. *Disfranchisement.* New York: National American Woman Suffrage Association.

Du Bois, W. E. B. 1912b. "Suffering Suffragettes." *The Crisis.* Accessed October 27, 2019. http://www.sojust.net/essays/dubois_suffering.html.

Du Bois, W. E. B. 1928, December. "National Interracial Conference for the Study and Discussion of Race Problems in the United States in Light of Social Research Program." Special Collections and University Archives. University of Massachusetts. Amherst Libraries. MS 312.

Du Bois, W. E. B. n.d. "Special Collections." Papers of W. E. B. Du Bois. University of Massachusetts Archives. http://credo.library.umass.edu.

Elkholy, Sharin N. 2012. *Internet Encyclopedia of Philosophy.* Accessed May 20, 2019. http://www.utm.edu/fem/race.

Excerpt from "Remarks by Marian Wright Edelman at LWVUS 50th Anniversary Convention, 1970." League of Women Voters Papers, Convention Folder, 1970.

Excerpt from "Verbatim Minutes Council." 1928. League of Women Voters Papers, Library of CongressBox II: 188.

Giddings, Paula. 1999. *When and Where I Enter: The Impact of Black Women on Race and Sex in America.* New York: Harper Collins ebooks.

Giddings, Paula. 2006. "When and Where I Enter: The Impact of Black Women on Race." https://caringlabor.files.wordpress.com/2010/12/when-and -where-i-enter-_-the-impact-of-b-paula-giddings.pdf.

Gordon, Ann D., ed., with Bettye Collier-Thomas, John H. Bracey, Arlene Voski Avakian, and Joyce Avrech Berkman. 1997. *African-American Women and the Vote, 1837–1965.* Amherst: University of Massachusetts Press.

Hampson, Whitney. 2004. *On Account of Color or Sex: A Historical Examination of the Split between Black Rights and Women's Rights in the American Equal Rights Association, 1866–1869.* Indiana University of Pennsylvania. https://www.iup.edu/admissions/honors/majors/humanities/whitney -hampson-streed,--06/

Higginbotham, Evelyn Brooks. 1997. "Clubwomen and Electoral Politics." In *African American Women and the Vote, 1837–1965*, edited by Ann D. Gordon with Bettye Collier-Thomas, John H. Bracey, Arlene Voski Avakian, and Joyce Avrech Berkman, 148–151. Amherst: University of Massachusetts Press.

Hodge, Ruth E. 2000. *George M. Leader Papers.* http://www.phmc.state.pa.us /bah/aaGuide/AA-MG-207.html.

hooks, bell. 2015. *Feminist Theory: From Margin to Center.* New York: Routledge.

Internet Encyclopedia of Philosophy. 2015. "Feminism and Race in the United States." Accessed April 21, 2019. http://www.iep.utm.edu/fem-race/#H3.

Jefferson-Jenkins, Carolyn. 1994–2019. Papers and Files from League of Women Voters of the United States National Board service and presidency. https://spec.lib.miamioh.edu/home/western/

Kraditor, Aileen S., ed. 1968. *Up from the Pedestal: Selected Writings in the History of American Feminism.* Chicago, IL: Quadrangle Books.

Kraditor, Aileen S. 1981. *The Ideas of the Woman Suffrage Movement, 1890–1920.* New York: W. W. Norton. League of Women Voters. *Fair Campaign Practice Principles.* Basic Document. http://lwv.org.

League of Women Voters. 1953, Spring. *The Big City: An Inquiry into Civic Participation.* New York: Carrie Chapman Catt Memorial Fund, no. 4.

League of Women Voters. 1954. "Meeting of Presidents of Southern States in Atlanta Georgia" Integration Folder. Box III: 691, Library of Congress.

League of Women Voters. 1974. *The Report of the Findings of the League Self-Study.* Washington, D.C.: LWV.

League of Women Voters. 2009, December. *League Basics.* Washington, D.C.: LWVEF.

League of Women Voters Atlanta. 1921, April 14. *Report to the Second Quarterly Meeting of the League.* LWV File. Washington, D.C.: LWV, Library of Congress Box X, Series 4, Folder 5.

League of Women Voters of the United States. 1953, Spring. *Report of the Metropolitan Project Committee.* Washington, D.C.: LWVUS.

League of Women Voters of the United States. 1954. "Freedom Agenda." Library of Congress Box III: 667.

League of Women Voters of the United States. 1965. President Stuart's Address to Council. Library of Congress Convention and Council Meetings 1921–1986, Box IV: 31–44.

League of Women Voters of the United States Strategic Focus. 2016. *Transformation Journey.* https://www.lwv.org/sites/default/files/2018-06/transformation_roadmap_exec_summary_april_2018.pdf

League of Women Voters Papers. 1920–2002, filed in LWVUS Office. "Convention Materials, Mission and Vision Statements, Miscellaneous Correspondence, Meeting Summaries, Meeting Minutes."

League of Women Voters Papers. 1927, April 29. "Western Union Telegraph to Belle Sherwin from Wisconsin League." Library of Congress Box II: 188.

League of Women Voters Papers. 1956, April. "The National Board and Prospective Boarders." Convention Folder, 1956.

League of Women Voters Papers. 1966, October. *Ebony Magazine* 21, no. 12: 107–114.

Letter from Adele Clark to Maud Wood Park. 1921, May 21. League of Women Voters Papers, Library of Congress Box II: 188.

Letter from Agnes Hilton to Gladys Harrison. 1928, August 9. "Black League Members." League of Women Voters Papers, Library of Congress Box III: 897.

Letter from Bessie McD. Bricken to Minnie Fisher Cunningham. 1922, October 5. League of Women Voters Papers, Library of Congress Box II: 188.

Letter from Bishop S. L. Greene to Mrs. John Lee. 1955, April 25. League of Women Voters Papers, Library of Congress Box II: 100.

Letter from Blanche Rogers to Minnie Fisher Cunningham. 1923, June 13. League of Women Voters Papers, Library of Congress Box II: 188.

Letter from Delilah L. Beasley to Mrs. Warren Wheaton, Press Secretary. 1926, March 23. League of Women Voters Papers, Library of Congress Box II: 188.

Letter from Dixie Drake, Executive Secretary to Thomas R. Miller. 1922, October 27. League of Women Voters Papers, Library of Congress Box III: 897.

Letter from Dixie Drake, Program Organization Secretary LWVUS to Mrs. D.W. Reynolds, President Raleigh, N.C. 1955, November 18. League of Women Voters Papers, Library of Congress Box III: 897.

Letter from Elizabeth J. Hauser to Blanche Rogers. 1923, June 26. League of Women Voters Papers, Library of Congress Box II: 188.

Letter from Executive Secretary National League of Women Voters to Julia Lathrop. 1922, August 14. Rockford, IL: League of Women Voters, Special Committee on Negro Problems, 1920–1927, Library of Congress Box I: 50.

Letter from Executive Secretary to Mrs. Charles Elliot. 1922, July 12. League of Women Voters Papers, Library of Congress Box II: 188.

Letter from Julia Lathrop to Blanche Rogers Albany, Mississippi. 1922, January 18. "Special Committee." League of Women Voters Papers, Library of Congress Box II: 188.

Letter from Lavinia Engle to Minnie Fisher Cunningham. 1922, July 14. League of Women Voters Papers, Library of Congress Box II: 188.

Letter from Lavinia Engle to National Office. 1922, December 4. League of Women Voters Papers, Library of Congress Box II: 188.

Letter from LWV Hampton to National Office. 1957, January 21. League of Women Voters Papers, Interracial Committee, Library of Congress Box III: 897.

Letter from LWV Kentucky President to Percy Maxim Lee. 1954, July 14. League of Women Voters, Membership: Negro, 1949–1964, Library of Congress Box III: 897.

Letter from Minnie Fisher Cunningham to Blanche Rogers. 1923, May 5. League of Women Voters Papers, Library of Congress Box II: 188.

Letter from Mrs. Anne Williams Wheaton to Mrs. Delilah L. Beasley. 1926, March 30. League of Women Voters Papers, Inter-Racial Problems, Library of Congress Box II: 188.

Letter from Mrs. Ben Hooper to Elizabeth J. Hauser. 1927, April 2. League of Women Voters Papers, Library of Congress Box II: 188.

Letter from Mrs. D. W. Reynolds, President League of Women Voters of Raleigh, N.C. to Mrs. John G. Lee, President LWVUS. 1955, November 11. League of Women Voters Papers, Library of Congress Box III: 897.

Letter from Mrs. Etta Wright, President LWV Liberia to Percy Maxim Lee. 1927, April 25. League of Women Voters Papers, Library of Congress Box II: 188.

Letter from Mrs. J. B. O'Hara, Florida League to Minnie Fisher Cunningham. 1922, December 9. League of Women Voters Papers, Library of Congress Box II: 188.

Letter from Mrs. John Lee to Bishop S. L. Greene. 1955, May 5. League of Women Voters Papers, Library of Congress Box II: 100.

Letter from Mrs. John Lee to Mrs. Winston Brooks about Eleanor Roosevelt. 1956, February 29 League of Women Voters Papers, Library of Congress Box II: 100.

Letter from Mrs. John Lee to Mrs. Winston Brooks Regarding Eleanor Roosevelt Column. 1956, February 29. League of Women Voters Papers, Library of Congress Box III: 897.

Letter from Mrs. Robert Newton, Tennessee to Minnie Fisher Cunningham. 1954, May 27. League of Women Voters Papers, Library of Congress Box III: 691.

Letter from Mrs. William C. Pauley, President LWV Georgia, to Mrs. John Lee. 1954, July 14. "Atlanta Conference." League of Women Voters Papers, Library of Congress Box III: 691.

Letter from Mrs. W. R. Pfeiffer President LWV Virginia to Mrs. George H. Babcock Hampton Virginia. 1957, January 21. League of Women Voters Papers, Library of Congress Box III: 893.

Letter from National Negro Congress to National Office. 1945, April 25. League of Women Voters Papers, Library of Congress Box III: 897.

Letter from National Office to State and Local Leagues. 1953. *How to Get and Keep New Members.* League of Women Voters Papers, filed in LWVUS Office.

Letter from Program Organization Staff to Black Caucus. 1970, May 14. League of Women Voters Papers Convention Folder, 1970.

Letter from S. P. Breckinridge to Belle Sherwin. 1922, October 31. League of Women Voters Papers, Library of Congress Box II: 188.

Letter from Virginia Roderick to Minnie Fisher Cunningham. 1922, October 21. League of Women Voters Papers, Library of Congress Box II: 188.

Letter Response from Anne Williams Wheaton to Agnes Hilton. 1928, August 17. League of Women Voters Papers, Library of Congress Box II: 188.

Letter to Maud Wood Park from the League of Women Voters of Virginia. 1921, May 21. League of Women Voters Papers, Library of Congress Box II: 188.

Letter to State Presidents about Special Committee representation from the National League Office. 1922, July 12. "Special Committee." League of Women Voters Papers, Library of Congress Box II: 188.

Library of Congress. 1922, October 21. "Special Committee on the Study of the Negro Problem." Letter from Virginia Roderick to Minnie Fisher Cunningham. Box I: 50.

Library of Congress. 1958. "Proceedings of A National Conference for Human Rights." Philadelphia, 6. Box IV: 376.

Library of Congress. n.d. "File Indian Affairs." League of Women Voters Box II: 181.

Library of Congress. n.d. "Special Committee Negro Problem 1921–1923." Correspondence.

Library of Congress Field Report October 19, 1956 Box II: 450.

Library of Congress Files. n.d. "League of Women Voters, Problems, Inter-Racial Committee 1928–1934."

Library of Congress Files Articles Interracial 1947–1973 Box IV: 376 New York Times Story.

Library of Congress Special Committee on Inter-Racial Relations Box II: 100.

Lipson, S. L. 1980. "Consensus Building in the League of Women in East State." Unpublished PhD diss., Columbia University, New York.

Manuscript Division, Library of Congress. n.d. League of Women Voters (U.S.) Records 1884–1986. Accessed March 22, 2016. https://lccn.loc.gov// mm82029660.

McArthur, Judith N., and Harold L. Smith. 2003. *Minnie Fisher Cunningham: A Suffragist's Life in Politics*. Oxford: Oxford University Press.

McDonald, Annie L., Myrtle Ousley, Cassie Smith, Theodore Butterworth, and M. E. Cossack. 1944. *The Negro in the South*. Chapel Hill: UNC Press.

McGoldrick, Neale. 1995, September. "Women's Suffrage and the Question of Color." *Social Education* 59, no. 5: 270–273.

McGoldrick, Neale. 2018, May 14. "Women's Suffrage and the Question of Color." *National Council for the Social Studies*. http://www.socialstudies .org/sites/default/files/publications/se/5905/590503.html.

Memorandum from Dorothy McKinney to National Board. 1974. League of Women Voters Papers Convention, 1974 Folder.

Memorandum "Negro Members." 1953, April 7. League of Women Voters Papers, Library of Congress Box III: 897.

Memorandum to Leagues from Ruth Phillips. 1963. "Civil Rights." League of Women Voters Papers, filed in LWVUS Office.

Memorandum to Miss Sherwin from Miss Rocca. 1926, October 9. League of Women Voters Papers, Library of Congress Box II: 181.

Memorandum to National Board and Staff, President Strauss. 1945, December 28. "Interpretation of Certain Sections of Proposed Bylaws." League of Women Voters Papers, filed in LWVUS Office.

Metropolitan Area Project Committee. 1953. *The Big City: An Inquiry into Civic Participation*." New York: Carrie Chapman Catt Memorial Fund, no. 4.

"Minutes and Related Documents." 1985. Part 1: Meetings of the Board of Directors and the Executive Committees. St. Frederick, MD: League of Women Voters U.S.

"Minutes" from May 9, 1974. "Luncheon with Black Caucus and Lucy Wilson Benson." League of Women Voters Papers. Convention Folder, 1974.

Minutes "Meeting of Presidents of Southern States" Held in Atlanta, Georgia. 1954, July 27–28. League of Women Voters Papers, Box III: 691, Library of Congress.

"Minutes of the Conference of the Department of Organization." 1927, December 14. League of Women Voters Papers, Library of Congress Box III: 122.

Morial, Sybil Haydel. 2015. *Witness to Change: From Jim Crow to Political Empowerment*. Winston-Salem, NC: John Blair.

Motion by Mrs. Salley to Change the Composition of the Special Committee on the Study of Negro Problems. 1921, October 13. League of Women Voters Papers, Library of Congress Box II: 188.

National American Woman Suffrage Association. 1903, March 11. "Position on the Race Question." Letter to the *New Orleans Times-Democrat*. League of Women Voters Files, Library of Congress Box III: 126. https://books .google.com/books?id=LOe6xLxsezkC&pg=PA350&lpg=PA350&dq- =Position+on+the+race+question++letter+to+New+Orleans+Times-Demo crat+1903&source=bl&ots=oIhJVWR2tM&sig=ACfU3U3RfNoXNuZmY ibEK5ppyVIFIag8AA&hl=en&sa=X&ved=2ahUKEwjQltaDi7_lAhUFhO AKHb7aBJYQ6AEwAHoECAQQAQ#v=onepage&q=Position%20on%20 the%20race%20question%20%20letter%20to%20New%20Orleans%20

National Interracial Conference for the Study and Discussion of Race Problems in the United States in the Light of Social Research Program, December, 1928. League of Women Voters Papers, April 1, 1929. Library of Congress Box II: 188.

National Voter, The. 1963, September. League of Women Voters Papers, filed in LWVUS Office.

Neuman, Nancy M. 1994. *The League of Women Voters in Perspective: 1920–1995*. Washington, D.C.: League of Women Voters of the United States.

Neuman, Nancy M. 1996. *A Voice of Our Own: Leading American Women Celebrate the Right to Vote*. San Francisco, CA: Jossey-Bass Publishers.

Newman Ham, Debra. 2005. *A Colored Woman in a White World: Mary Church Terrell*. New York: Humanity Books.

Osborn, Eleanor R. 1994. *The Ladies Have Spoken: Recurring Tensions in the Discourse of the Presidents of the League of Women Voters*. San Jose, CA: San Jose State University.

Percy Maxim Lee Papers. 1942–1971. Schlesinger Library, Radcliffe Institute Harvard University Library. https://snaccooperative.org/ark:/99166 /w6m63b7w

Perry, Elisabeth Israels. 1995. *Women in Action: Rebels and Reformers 1920–1980*. Washington, D.C.: League of Women Voters Education Fund.

Philadelphia Female Anti-Slavery Society. 1833–1839. Historical Society of Pennsylvania. Accessed May 27, 2019. https://digitallibrary.hsp.org/index.php /Detail/objects/14653

"Problem of Work for the Special Committee." 1925. Adopted by the Executive Committee in 1924 and by General Council in 1925. Library of Congress Box II: 188.

"Questions Information Desired by Special Committee on Inter-Racial Problems." 1927. National League of Women Voters, Library of Congress Box II: 188.

Report Adele Clark, The Special Committee. July 29, 1927. Library of Congress Box II: 188.

Report "Candidates Meetings Continue: Segregation of Audience Required." 1956, November. Arlington, VA. League of Women Voters Papers, Library of Congress Box 3: 893.

Report I. The League Member Talks about the League. 1956. "A Study of the League of Women Voters of the United States." University of Michigan Survey, University Research Center Filed in LWVUS Office. https://babel .hathitrust.org/cgi/pt?id=mdp.39015009058135&view=1up&seq=7

"Report of the Special Committee." 1922, April 19. League of Women Voters Papers, Library of Congress Box II: 188.

"Report of the Special Committee on the Study of the Negro Problems" to the National Board. 1922, December 3. League of Women Voters Papers, Library of Congress Box II: 188.

"Report on Activity for the Organization of the Special Committee on Negro Problems." 1922, December 8. League of Women Voters Papers, Cunningham, Library of Congress Box II: 188.

"Report on the Status of the Special Committee," Lathrop. 1923, April 14. League of Women Voters Papers, Library of Congress Box II: 188.

Resolution Regarding the Woman Suffrage Statue. 1997, October 30. League of Women Voters Papers, filed in LWVUS Office.

Ruebhausen, Zelia. 1956, January. "Education by Exposure." *The National Voter*. League of Women Voters, Library of Congress Box III: 227.

Sayre, Linda D. 2002. *Volunteer Leaders: Learning and Development in the League of Women Voters*. New Jersey: Rutgers University.

Schuyler, Lorraine Gates. 2006. *The Weight of Their Votes—Southern Women and Political Leverage in the 1920s*. Chapel Hill: UNC Press.

Scott, Anne Firor, and William H. Chafe. n.d. "Papers of the League of Women Voters 1918–1974." Research Collection in Women's Studies. Durham, NC: Duke University.

Stanton, Elizabeth Cady, Susan B. Anthony, Matilda Gage, et al. 2018. *The Complete History of the Women's Suffrage Movement in the U.S.* ebooks.

Sterling, Dorothy. 1984. *We Are Your Sisters: Black Women in the Nineteenth Century*. New York: W.W. Norton & Company.

Stone, Kathryn. 1949. *A History of the League Program*. Washington, D.C.: League of Women Voters.

Structures and Procedures Committee 1968–1970. League of Women Voters Papers, filed in LWVUS Office. Convention Folder, 1968.

Stuhler, Barbara. 2000. *For the Public Record: A Documentary History of the League of Women Voters*. Westport: Greenwood Press.

Terborg-Penn, Rosalyn. 1998. *African-American Women in the Struggle for the Vote, 1850–1920*. Bloomington: Indiana University Press.

Terrell, Mary Church. 1898. "The Progress of Colored Women." NAWSA Fiftieth Anniversary Conference. Washington, D.C.: Smith Brothers printers.

Terrell, Mary Church. 1940. *A Colored Woman in a White World*. Washington, D.C.: Ransdell.

Terrell, Mary Church. n.d. Mary Church Terrell Papers. Library of Congress.

Tilly, Louise A., and Patricia Gurin, eds. 1990. *Women, Politics, and Change*. New York: Russell Sage Foundation.

Virginia Voter Service. 1956, October 19. "Field Report." League of Women Voters Papers, Library of Congress Box III: 897.

"Voters Unit Split Over Racial Issue." 1956, March 31. *New York Times*. League of Women Voters, Box IV: 376, Library of Congress.

Waisman, Charlotte S., and Jill S. Tietjen. 2008. *Her Story: A Timeline of the Women Who Changed America*. New York: HarperCollins.

Ware, Susan. 1985. *Papers of the League of Women Voters, 1918–1974*. Frederick, MD: University Publications of America.

Weiss, Elaine. 2018. *The Woman's Hour*. New York: Penguin Random House.

Wells, Marguerite. (1938) 1962. *A Portrait of the League of Women Voters*. Washington, D.C.: Overseas Education Fund, LWV.

Western Union Telegraph from Blanche Rogers to Cunningham. 1923, May 5. League of Women Voters Papers, Library of Congress Box II: 188.

Western Union Telegram Oshkosh, Wisconsin to Sherwin. 1927. League of Women Voters Papers, Library of Congress Box II: 188.

Winbush Riley, Dorothy, ed. (1991) 1993. *My Soul Looks Back, 'Less I Forget*. New York: Harper Perennial.

Young, Louise M. 1989. *In the Public Interest: The League of Women Voters, 1920–1970*. Westport, CT: Greenwood Press, Inc.

Index

Note: *Italic* page numbers reflect images in the book.

Madison, Mildred, *165*
Madison, WI league, 147
Maiden, Geneva, 177
Maine, 178
"Making Democracy Work," 1, 200, 204, 209, 210
"Many Voices, One Vision," 184
Marcy, Mrs. Carl, 133
Marquez, Gloria, 164
Maryland, 77, 93, 100, 101, 110, 177
Mason, Mrs. Vivian Carter, 199
Massachusetts, 66
McDonald, Mr. David J., 149
McDowell, Mrs. W. F., 100
McGinn, Thomas J., 146–147
McKinnell, Beverly, 192
McKinney, Dorothy, 173
Media, 193, 194, 206
Membership, league: continued to be operationally segregated, 30, 31, 38, 126, 134–135, 162; criteria, 8, 9, 41, 58, 127, 165; data, or the lack of, about the racial makeup of the, 30, 43, 80, 124, 126, 143, 144, 148, 216; is defined by the bylaws, 8, 44; men in the, 140; needed to include more working women and younger women, 169–170; a period of growth in, 119; reasons for choosing, 55, 174, 177; recruitment, 176; women of color in the, 2, 3, 10, 75, 105, 123, 134, 168–169; women typical of, 83–84, 160, 168
Membership and Organizational Development Committee, 177
Memphis, TN, 126, 134–135, 146
Men: abolitionists and the league disagreed over suffrage for black, 29, 56; of color, 16, 18, 19, 24, 66, 74, 84, 179; could become league members, 9, 83, 140, 172; equal political rights for women and, 28; the 19th amendment did not help colored women and, 68; white women could not empathize with

colored women and, 123; women of New York and political equals of, 71
Merriam, Mr. Lewis, 108
Michigan, 147, 163–164, 175
Miller, Mrs. Daniel, 97, 100
Miller, Mrs. Walter McNab, 101
Minneapolis, MN, 147, 156
Minnesota, 166
Minorities: difficultly for the league to recruit and elect, 84, 208; discrimination against, 121–122, 126; failed to share in the prosperity of whites, 48; growth rate compared to the rest of the U.S. population, 178; guaranteed equal rights for all, 157; how the U.S. treated, domestically vs. globally, 124; and limited opportunities in employment and education, 159, 161–162; no longer want to be treated as second-class citizens, 158; owe a debt to those who broke racial barriers, 211; voter registration for, 158
Mississippi: league, 101, 137, 141; represented at and reported to the Atlanta Conference of Southern Presidents, 42, 130, 133; represented at and reported to the Special Committee on Inter-Racial Problems, 77, 93, 100, 110
Missouri: *Ebony Magazine* article on women of color from, 163–164; league, 147; the Negro woman vote was a material factor in, 112; organized Negro leagues, 109; and the Special Committee on Inter-Racial Problems, 77, 91, 110, 111
Mobile, AL, 127
Montgomery County, MD, 147
Moon, Dr. R. R., 78
Morial, Sybil, 179

Morris, Miss, 91
Moten, Mrs. Lelia D., 161
Mott, Miss, 102
Mutual aid societies, 56

Nashville, TN league, 147
National American Woman Suffrage
Association (NAWSA): accepted
black members, 57; adopted a
states' rights policy, 58; continued
its racist policies, 68; conventions
and meetings of the, 18, 37, 57;
cosponsored a suffrage parade, 66;
and how it dealt with Southern
states, 57, 65; the internal
organizational struggle of the, 29;
and sacrificing black
enfranchisement for women's
suffrage, 54, 67; transitioned to the
(National) League of Women
Voters, 17, 36, 37; women's suffrage
associations were unified into the,
25. *See also* League of Women
Voters; National League of Women
Voters
National Association for the
Advancement of Colored People
(NAACP): cosponsored a
candidates' meeting in VA, 146;
published *The Crisis*, 27;
representatives of the, 6, 40, 168;
and the rights of black women
voters, 67–68, 79; sponsored the
National Interracial Conference,
78
National Association of Colored
Women (NACW), 18, 27, 57, 61,
103
National Association of Colored
Women's Clubs (NACW), 55,
61, 70
National Board YWCA, 78
National Catholic Welfare Conference,
78

National Conference for Human
Rights, 149
National Council for YMCA, 78
National Council of Negro Women
(NCNW): relationship between
league leaders, and the, 32–33, 156,
215; representatives from the, 44,
161, 162, 164, 168; started an
interracial coalition of women's
organizations, 69
National Federation of Settlements, 78
National League of Republican
Colored Women, 61, 62
National League of Women Voters:
colored women wanted an
opportunity to work with the, 74;
correspondence to and from the,
63–64, 72–73, 91–99, 103–105,
107; involvement of the, with the
committee on interracial problems,
111–112; and name change, 8, 40,
80, 203; the number of state and
local leagues in the, 79; reports to
the, 102–103, 106, 110–111; was
reconstituted from the NAWSA, 37.
See also League; League of Women
Voters; League of Women Voters of
the U.S.; National American
Woman Suffrage Association
National Negro Congress, 120
National Urban League, 78
National Voter, 46, 128, 158
National Woman Suffrage Association
(NWSA), 23, 24, 35 n.17, 54, 55
National Woman's Party, 63, 70–71
National Woman's Rights Convention,
23
Native American(s), 107, 163, 175. *See
also* Indian(s)
"Negro in the South, The," 120
Negro Industrial School for Wayward
Girls, 109
"Negro problem," 69, 90, 91, 104,
107, 111, 164. *See also* Special

About the Author

Carolyn Jefferson-Jenkins, PhD, served two terms as the fifteenth president of the League of Women Voters of the United States and chair of the League of Women Voters Education Fund (1998–2002). She is the only woman of color to have served as national president in the organization's first one hundred years. Since the early 1980s, she has served in a range of capacities at the local, state, and national levels of the league. Her career in public school and higher education spanned more than forty years. At the time of retirement, Dr. Jefferson-Jenkins continues to be an advocate and activist for civil rights, social justice, educational excellence, and stronger citizen participation in the electoral process for underrepresented populations. She actively serves on numerous boards and advises community-based organizations. She has received numerous awards for her contributions. Dr. Jefferson-Jenkins is currently an adjunct assistant professor in the School of Education at the University of North Carolina at Chapel Hill.